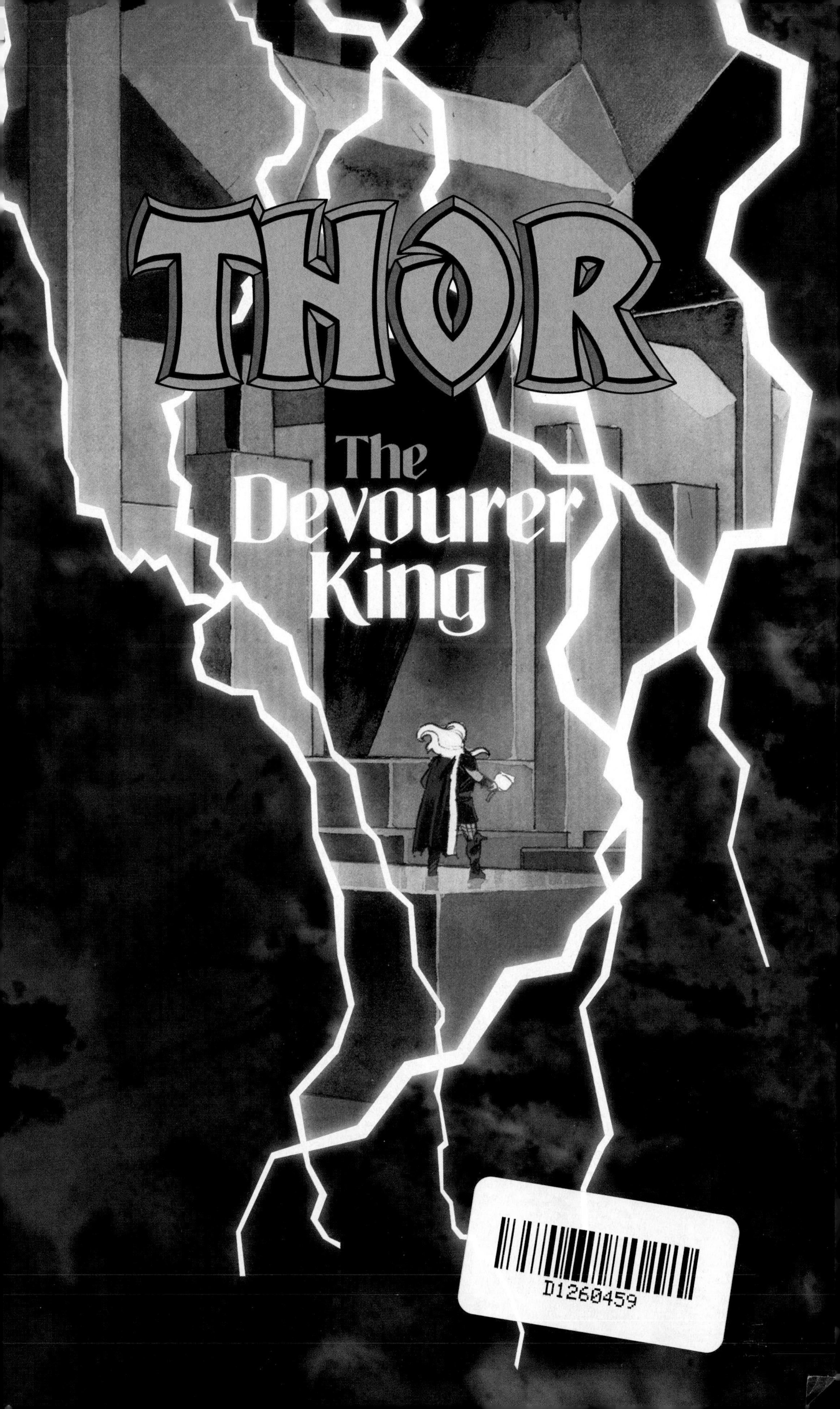
THOR
The Devourer King

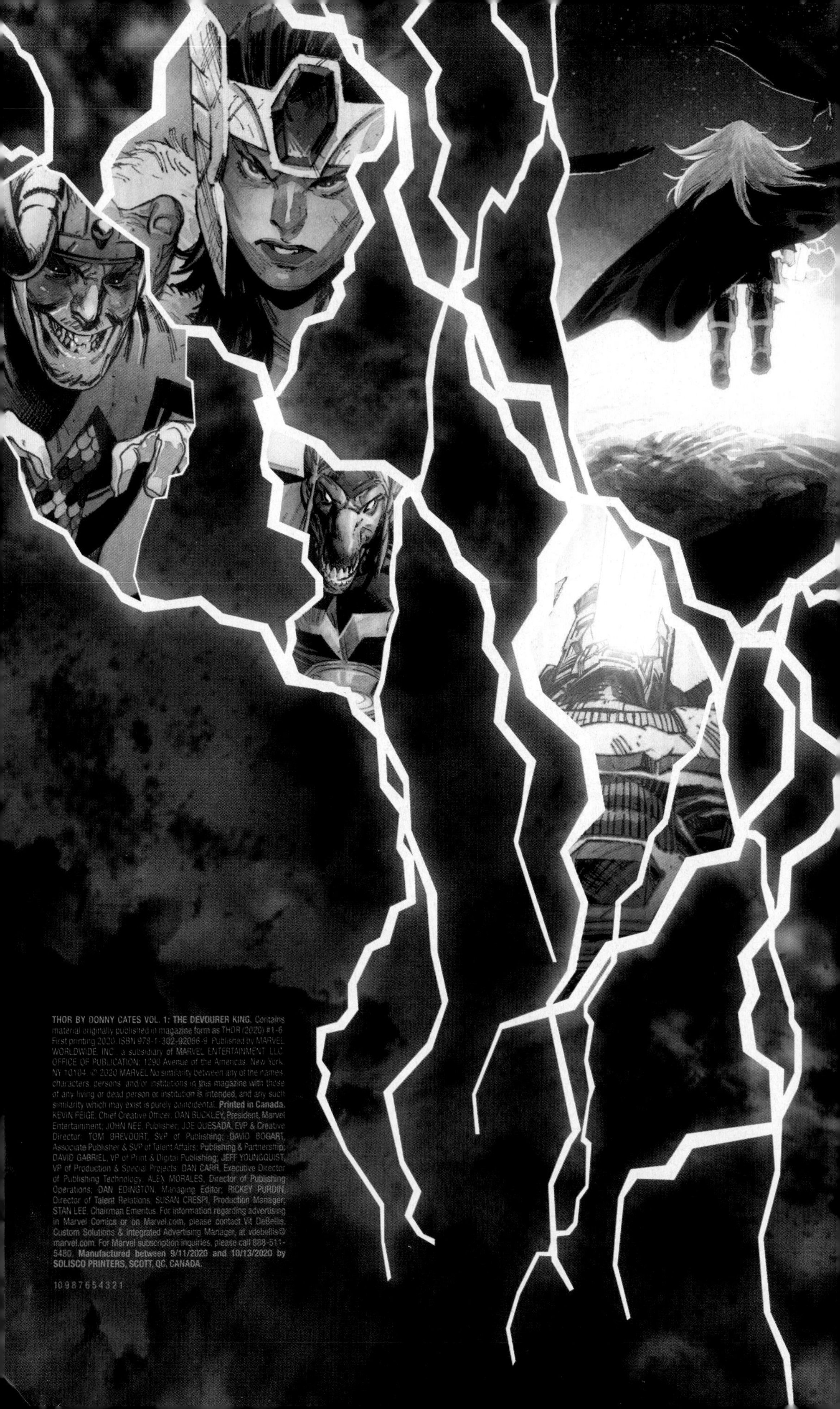

THOR BY DONNY CATES VOL. 1: THE DEVOURER KING. Contains material originally published in magazine form as THOR (2020) #1-6. First printing 2020. ISBN 978-1-302-92086-9. Published by MARVEL WORLDWIDE, INC., a subsidiary of MARVEL ENTERTAINMENT, LLC. OFFICE OF PUBLICATION: 1290 Avenue of the Americas, New York, NY 10104. **Printed in Canada.** KEVIN FEIGE, Chief Creative Officer; DAN BUCKLEY, President, Marvel Entertainment; JOHN NEE, Publisher; JOE QUESADA, EVP & Creative Director; TOM BREVOORT, SVP of Publishing; DAVID BOGART, Associate Publisher & SVP of Talent Affairs; Publishing & Partnership; DAVID GABRIEL, VP of Print & Digital Publishing; JEFF YOUNGQUIST, VP of Production & Special Projects; DAN CARR, Executive Director of Publishing Technology; ALEX MORALES, Director of Publishing Operations; DAN EDINGTON, Managing Editor; RICKEY PURDIN, Director of Talent Relations; SUSAN CRESPI, Production Manager; STAN LEE, Chairman Emeritus. For information regarding advertising in Marvel Comics or on Marvel.com, please contact Vit DeBellis, Custom Solutions & Integrated Advertising Manager, at vdebellis@marvel.com. For Marvel subscription inquiries, please call 888-511-5480. **Manufactured between 9/11/2020 and 10/13/2020 by SOLISCO PRINTERS, SCOTT, QC, CANADA.**

10 9 8 7 6 5 4 3 2 1

THOR

The Devourer King

WRITER	**Donny Cates**
ARTIST	**Nic Klein**
COLOR ARTIST	**Matthew Wilson**
LETTERER	**VC's Joe Sabino**
COVER ART	**Olivier Coipel & Laura Martin**
ASSOCIATE EDITOR	**Sarah Brunstad**
EDITOR	**Wil Moss**

THOR CREATED BY **Stan Lee, Larry Lieber** & **Jack Kirby**

COLLECTION EDITOR **JENNIFER GRÜNWALD**   ASSISTANT MANAGING EDITOR **MAIA LOY**
ASSISTANT MANAGING EDITOR **LISA MONTALBANO**   EDITOR, SPECIAL PROJECTS **MARK D. BEAZLEY**
VP PRODUCTION & SPECIAL PROJECTS **JEFF YOUNGQUIST**   BOOK DESIGNER **JAY BOWEN**
SVP PRINT SALES & MARKETING **DAVID GABRIEL**   EDITOR IN CHIEF **C.B. CEBULSKI**

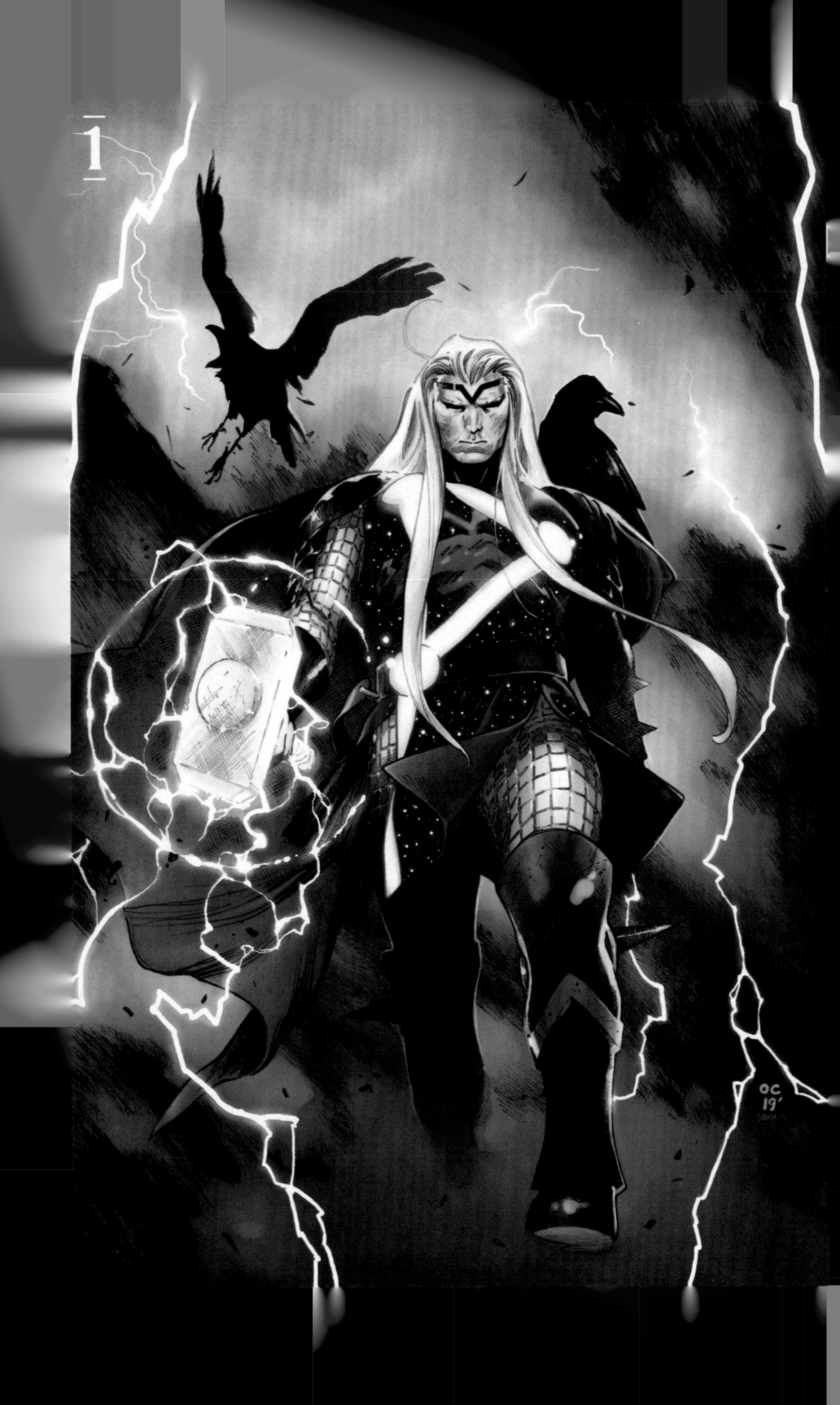
1

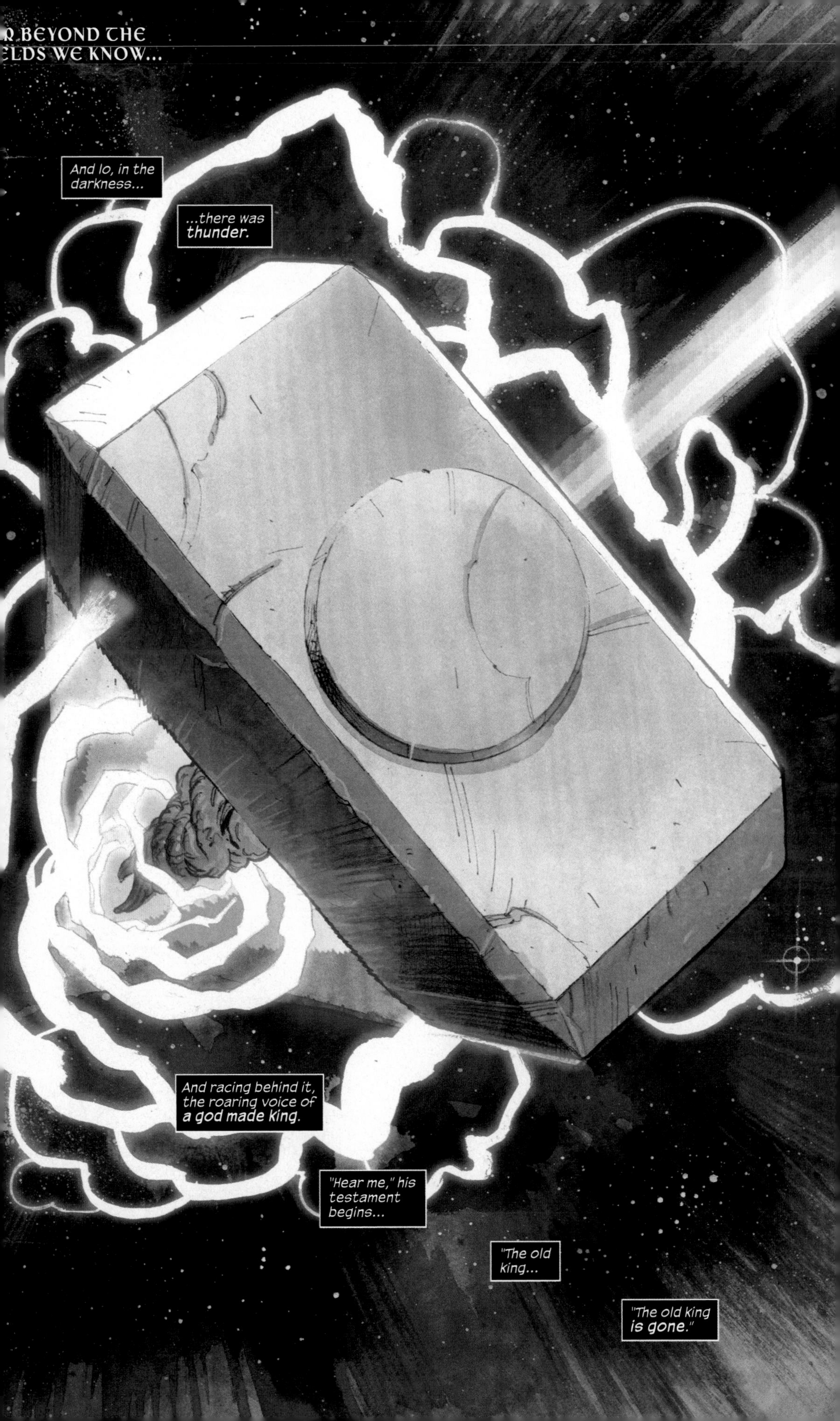
BEYOND THE
WE KNOW...
And lo, in the darkness...
...there was thunder.
And racing behind it, the roaring voice of a god made king.
"Hear me," his testament begins...
"The old king...
"The old king is gone."

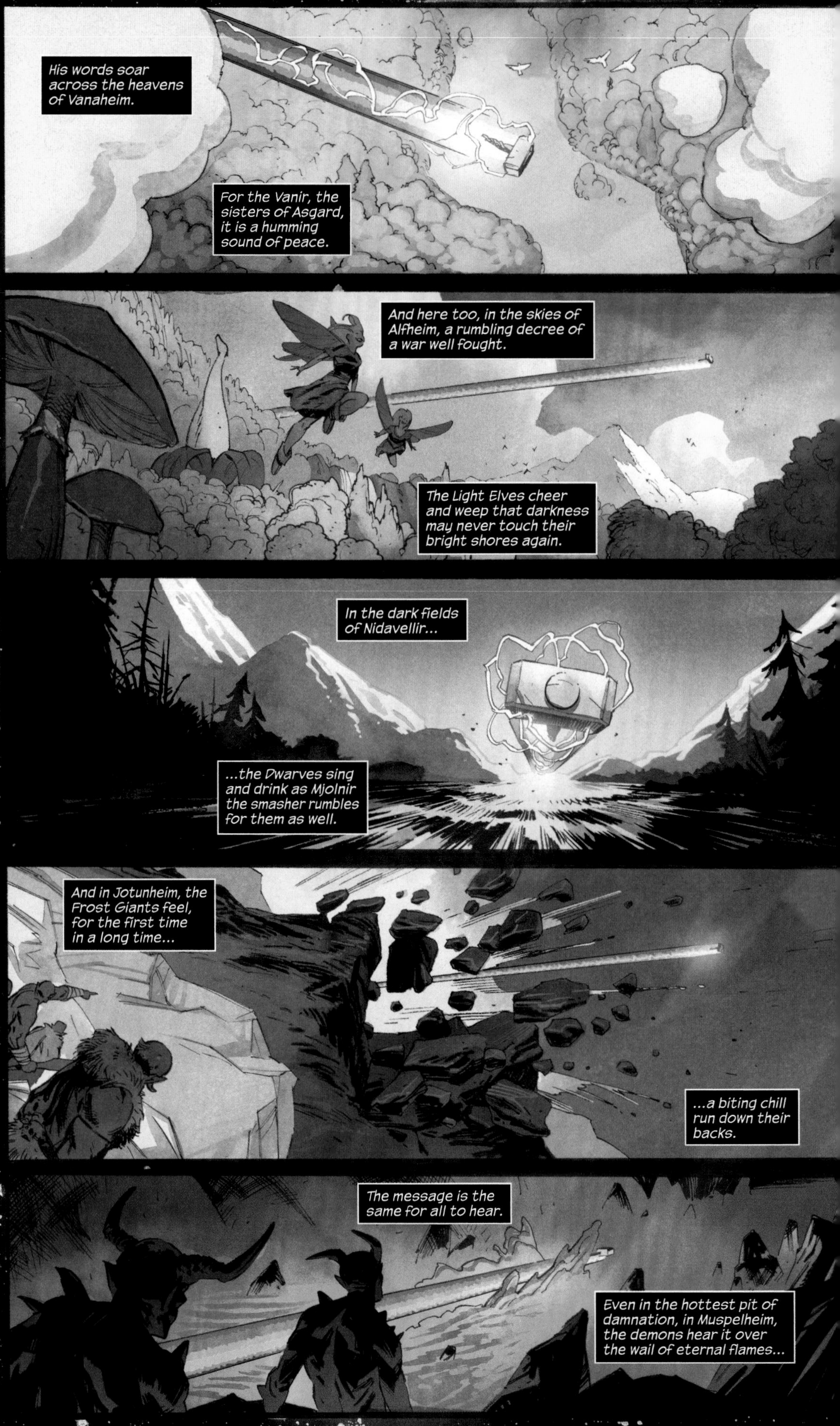
His words soar across the heavens of Vanaheim.
For the Vanir, the sisters of Asgard, it is a humming sound of peace.
And here too, in the skies of Alfheim, a rumbling decree of a war well fought.
The Light Elves cheer and weep that darkness may never touch their bright shores again.
In the dark fields of Nidavellir...
...the Dwarves sing and drink as Mjolnir the smasher rumbles for them as well.
And in Jotunheim, the Frost Giants feel, for the first time in a long time...
...a biting chill run down their backs.
The message is the same for all to hear.
Even in the hottest pit of damnation, in Muspelheim, the demons hear it over the wail of eternal flames...

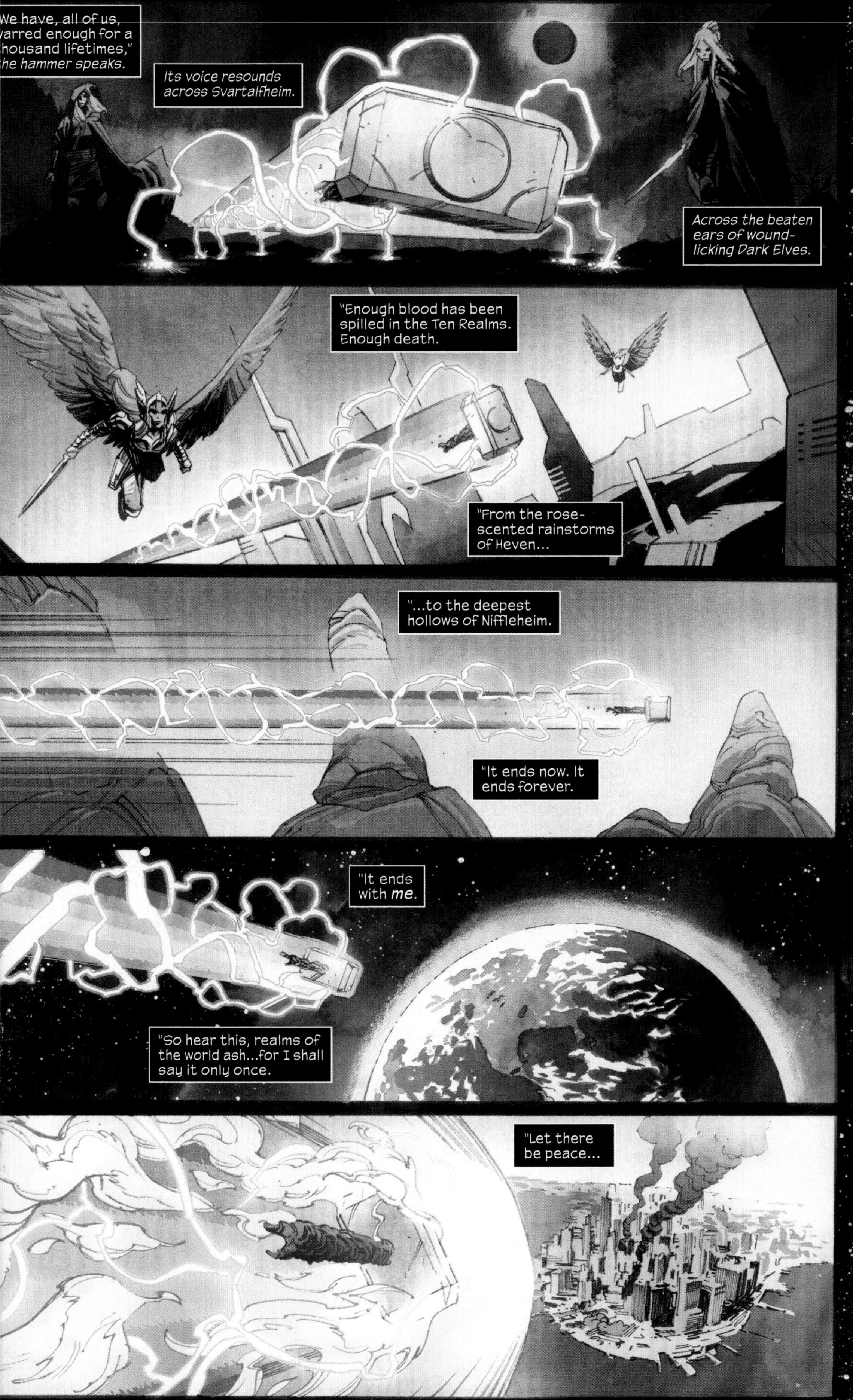

We have, all of us,
warred enough for a
housand lifetimes,"
he hammer speaks.
Its voice resounds
across Svartalfheim.
Across the beaten
ears of wound-
licking Dark Elves.
"Enough blood has been
spilled in the Ten Realms.
Enough death.
"From the rose-
scented rainstorms
of Heven...
"...to the deepest
hollows of Niffleheim.
"It ends now. It
ends forever.
"It ends
with *me*.
"So hear this, realms of
the world ash...for I shall
say it only once.
"Let there
be peace...

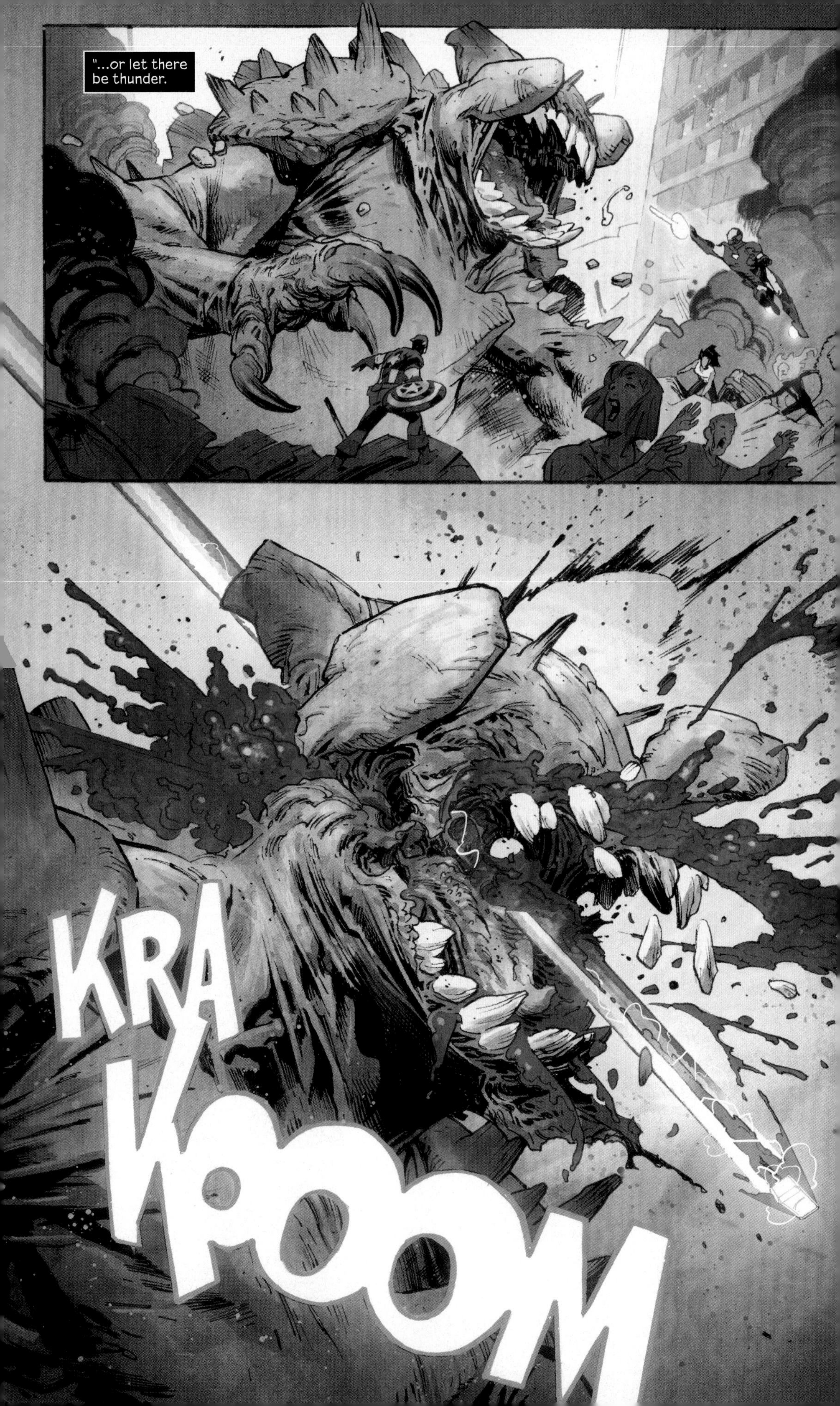
"...or let there be thunder.
KRA
KOOM

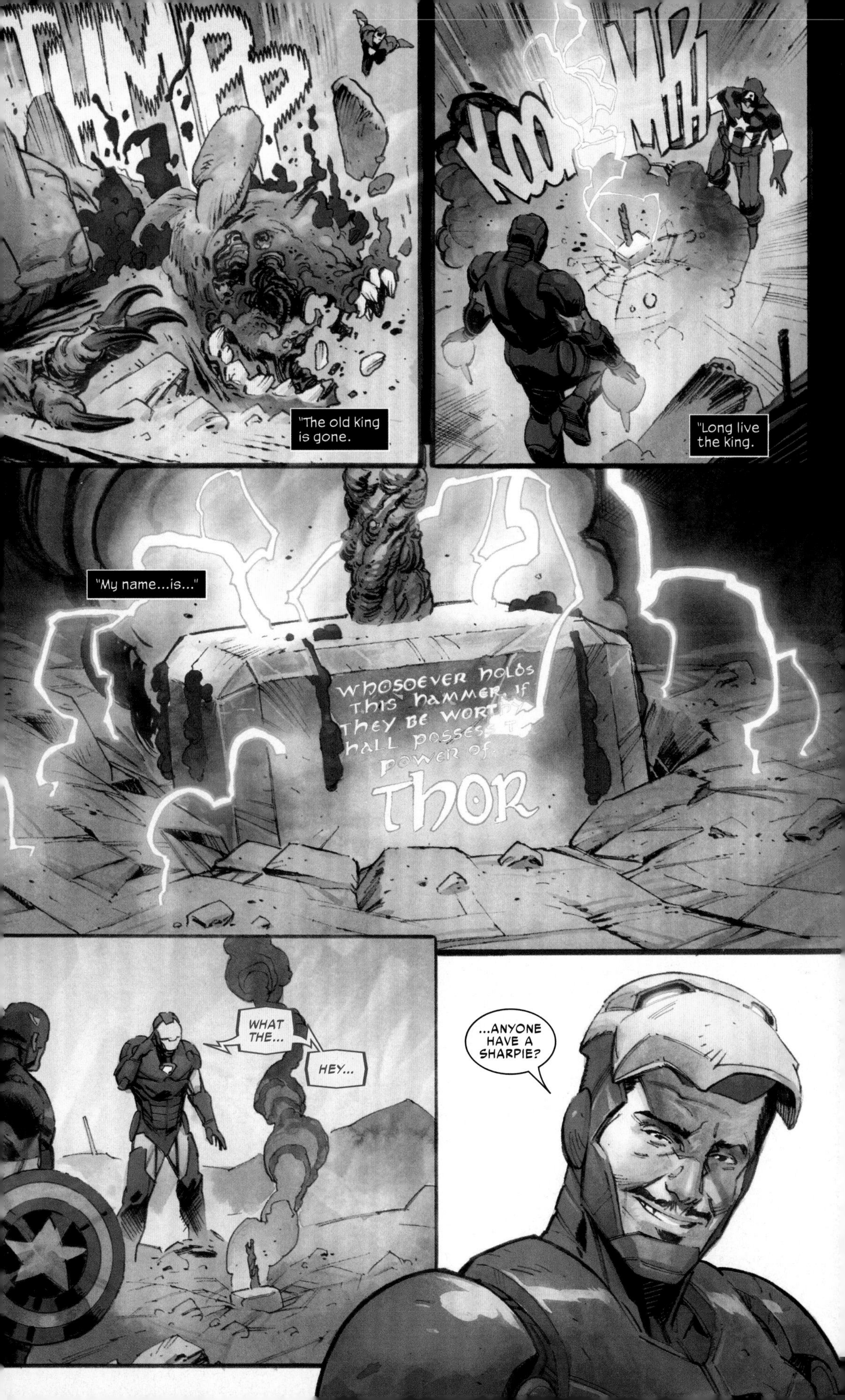
"The old king is gone.
"Long live the king.
"My name...is..."
WHOSOEVER HOLDS THIS HAMMER, IF THEY BE WORTH
HALL POSSESS
POWER OF
THOR
WHAT THE...
HEY...
...ANYONE HAVE A SHARPIE?

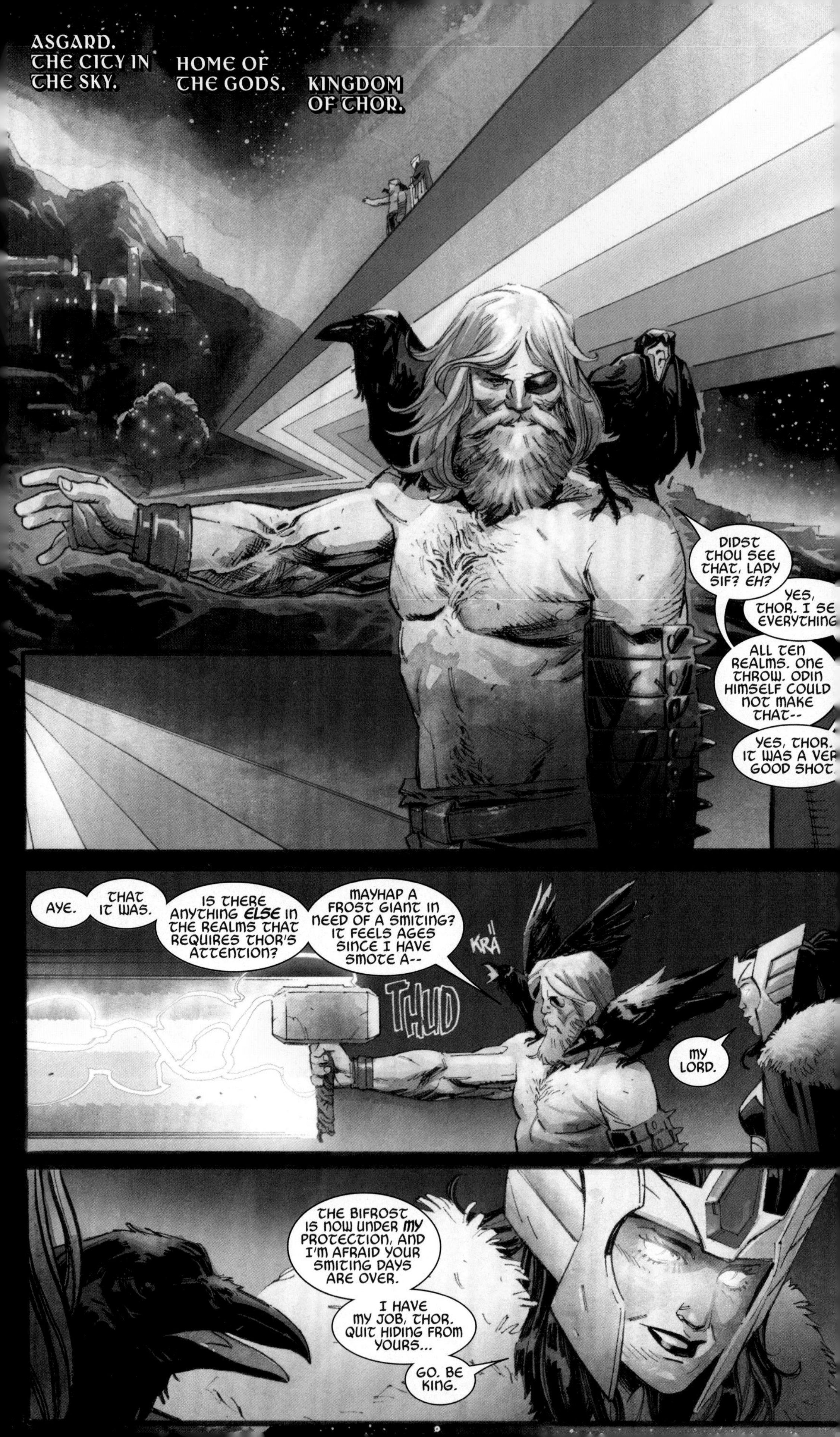
ASGARD. THE CITY IN THE SKY.
HOME OF THE GODS.
KINGDOM OF THOR.
DIDST THOU SEE THAT, LADY SIF? EH?
YES, THOR. I SE EVERYTHING
ALL TEN REALMS. ONE THROW. ODIN HIMSELF COULD NOT MAKE THAT--
YES, THOR. IT WAS A VER GOOD SHOT
AYE.
THAT IT WAS.
IS THERE ANYTHING ELSE IN THE REALMS THAT REQUIRES THOR'S ATTENTION?
MAYHAP A FROST GIANT IN NEED OF A SMITING? IT FEELS AGES SINCE I HAVE SMOTE A--
KRA
THUD
MY LORD.
THE BIFROST IS NOW UNDER MY PROTECTION, AND I'M AFRAID YOUR SMITING DAYS ARE OVER.
I HAVE MY JOB, THOR. QUIT HIDING FROM YOURS...
GO. BE KING.

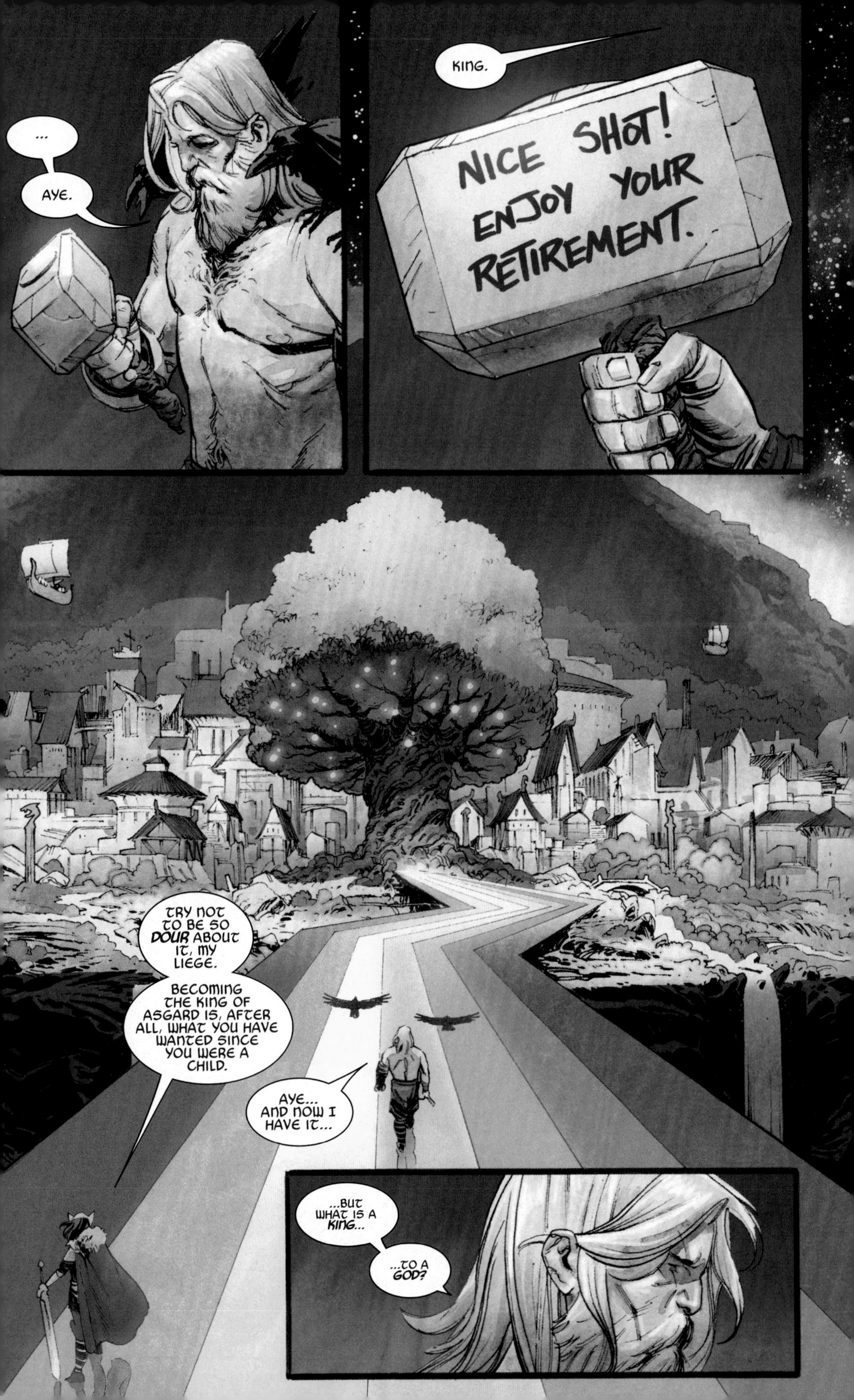
...
AYE.
KING.
NICE SHOT! ENJOY YOUR RETIREMENT.
TRY NOT TO BE SO DOUR ABOUT IT, MY LIEGE.
BECOMING THE KING OF ASGARD IS, AFTER ALL, WHAT YOU HAVE WANTED SINCE YOU WERE A CHILD.
AYE... AND NOW I HAVE IT...
...BUT WHAT IS A KING...
...TO A GOD?

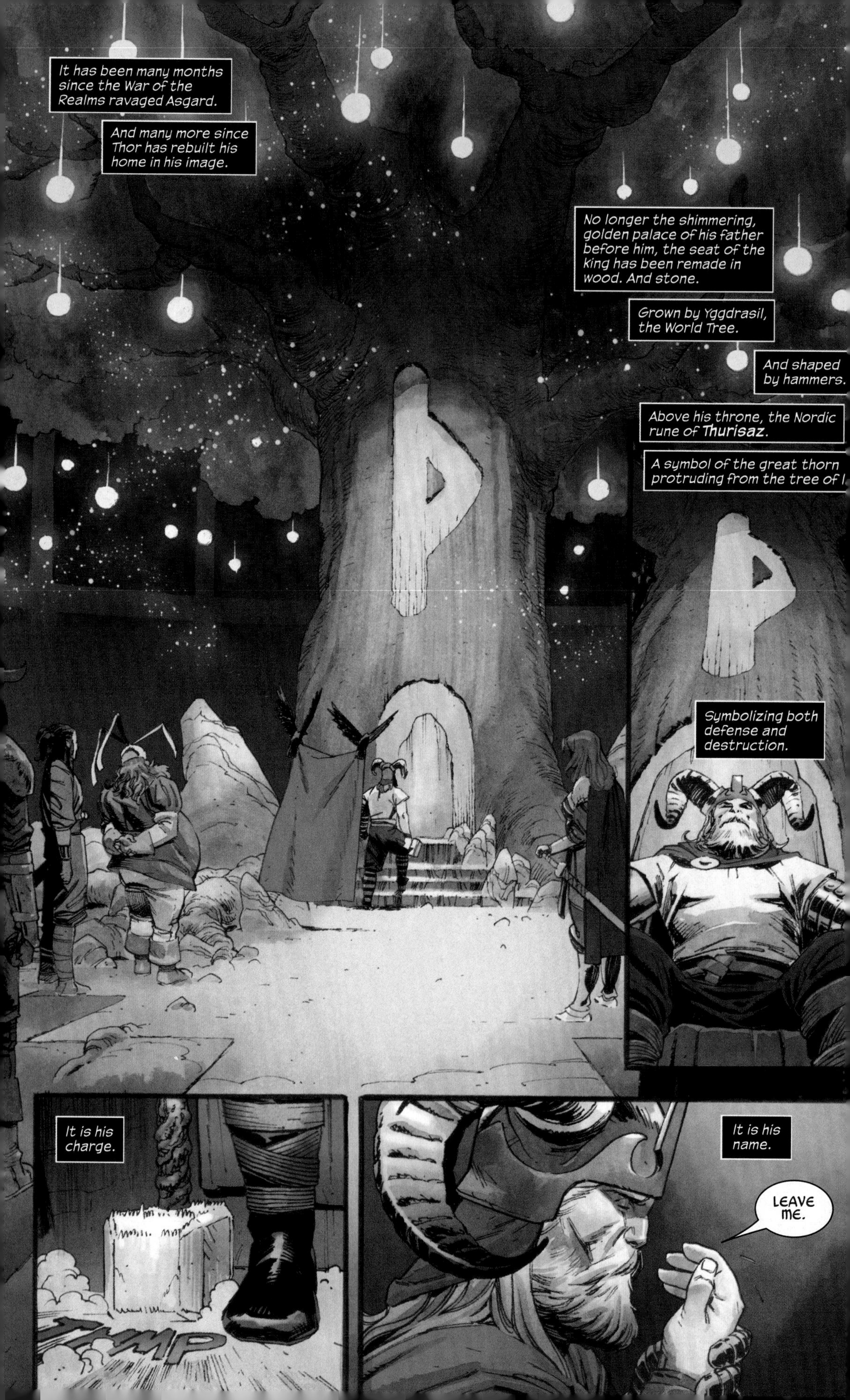
It has been many months since the War of the Realms ravaged Asgard.
And many more since Thor has rebuilt his home in his image.
No longer the shimmering, golden palace of his father before him, the seat of the king has been remade in wood. And stone.
Grown by Yggdrasil, the World Tree.
And shaped by hammers.
Above his throne, the Nordic rune of **Thurisaz**.
A symbol of the great thorn protruding from the tree of l
Symbolizing both defense and destruction.
It is his charge.
It is his name.
LEAVE ME.

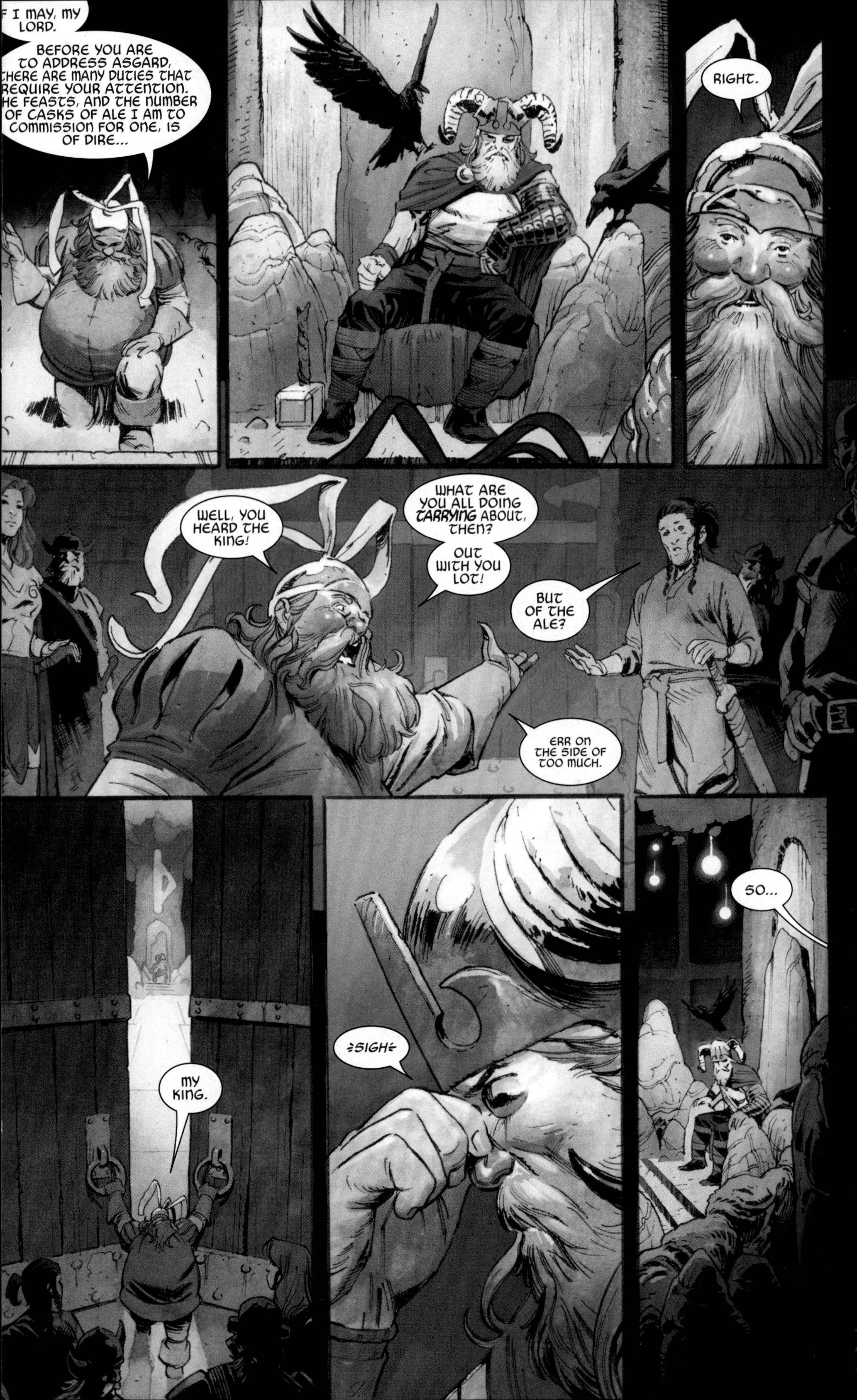

F I MAY, MY LORD.
BEFORE YOU ARE TO ADDRESS ASGARD, THERE ARE MANY DUTIES THAT REQUIRE YOUR ATTENTION. HE FEASTS, AND THE NUMBER OF CASKS OF ALE I AM TO COMMISSION FOR ONE, IS OF DIRE...
RIGHT.
WELL, YOU HEARD THE KING!
WHAT ARE YOU ALL DOING TARRYING ABOUT, THEN?
OUT WITH YOU LOT!
BUT OF THE ALE?
ERR ON THE SIDE OF TOO MUCH.
MY KING.
SIGH
SO...

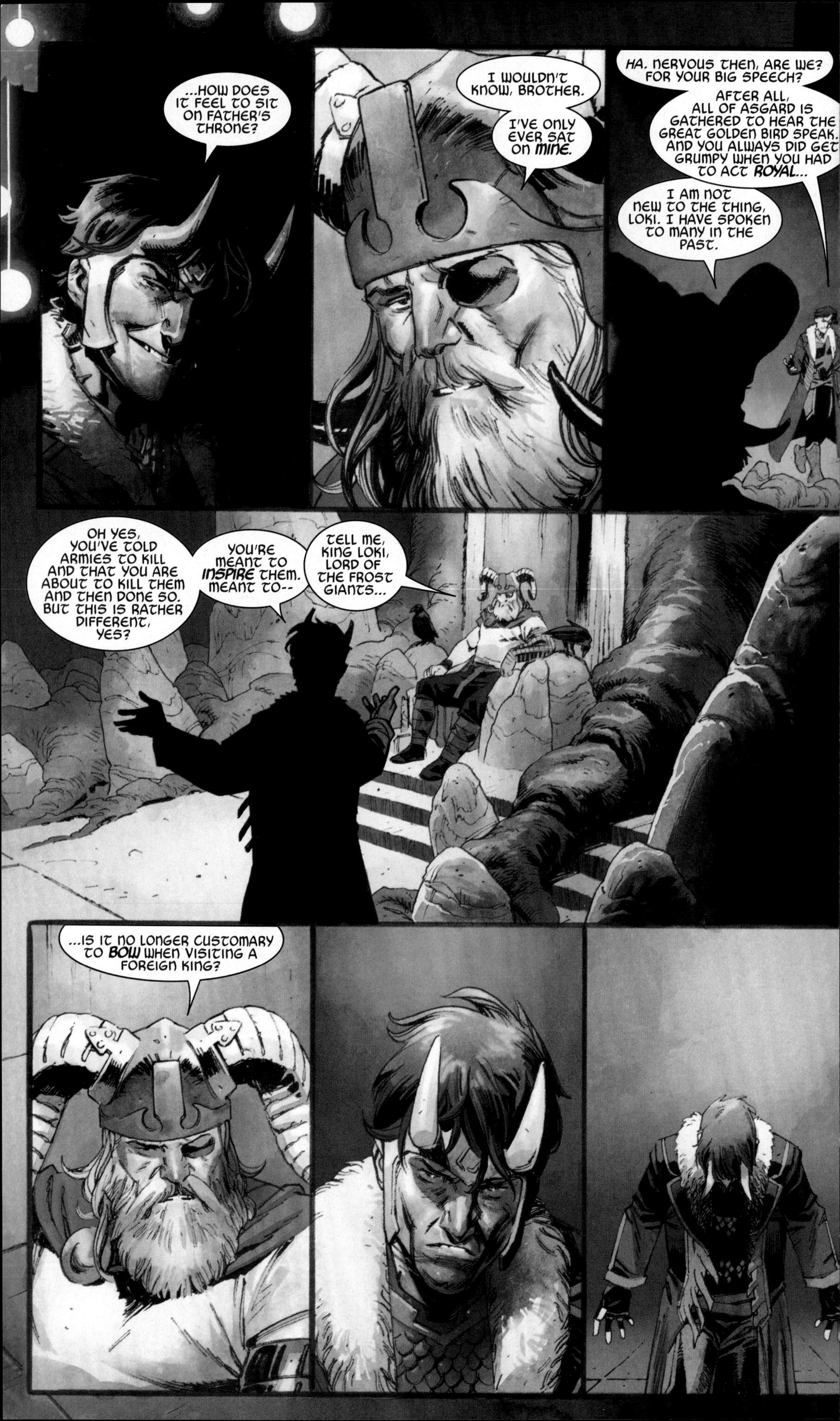
...HOW DOES IT FEEL TO SIT ON FATHER'S THRONE?
I WOULDN'T KNOW, BROTHER.
I'VE ONLY EVER SAT ON MINE.
HA. NERVOUS THEN, ARE WE? FOR YOUR BIG SPEECH?
AFTER ALL, ALL OF ASGARD IS GATHERED TO HEAR THE GREAT GOLDEN BIRD SPEAK. AND YOU ALWAYS DID GET GRUMPY WHEN YOU HAD TO ACT ROYAL...
I AM NOT NEW TO THE THING, LOKI. I HAVE SPOKEN TO MANY IN THE PAST.
OH YES, YOU'VE TOLD ARMIES TO KILL AND THAT YOU ARE ABOUT TO KILL THEM AND THEN DONE SO. BUT THIS IS RATHER DIFFERENT, YES?
YOU'RE MEANT TO INSPIRE THEM. MEANT TO--
TELL ME, KING LOKI, LORD OF THE FROST GIANTS...
...IS IT NO LONGER CUSTOMARY TO BOW WHEN VISITING A FOREIGN KING?

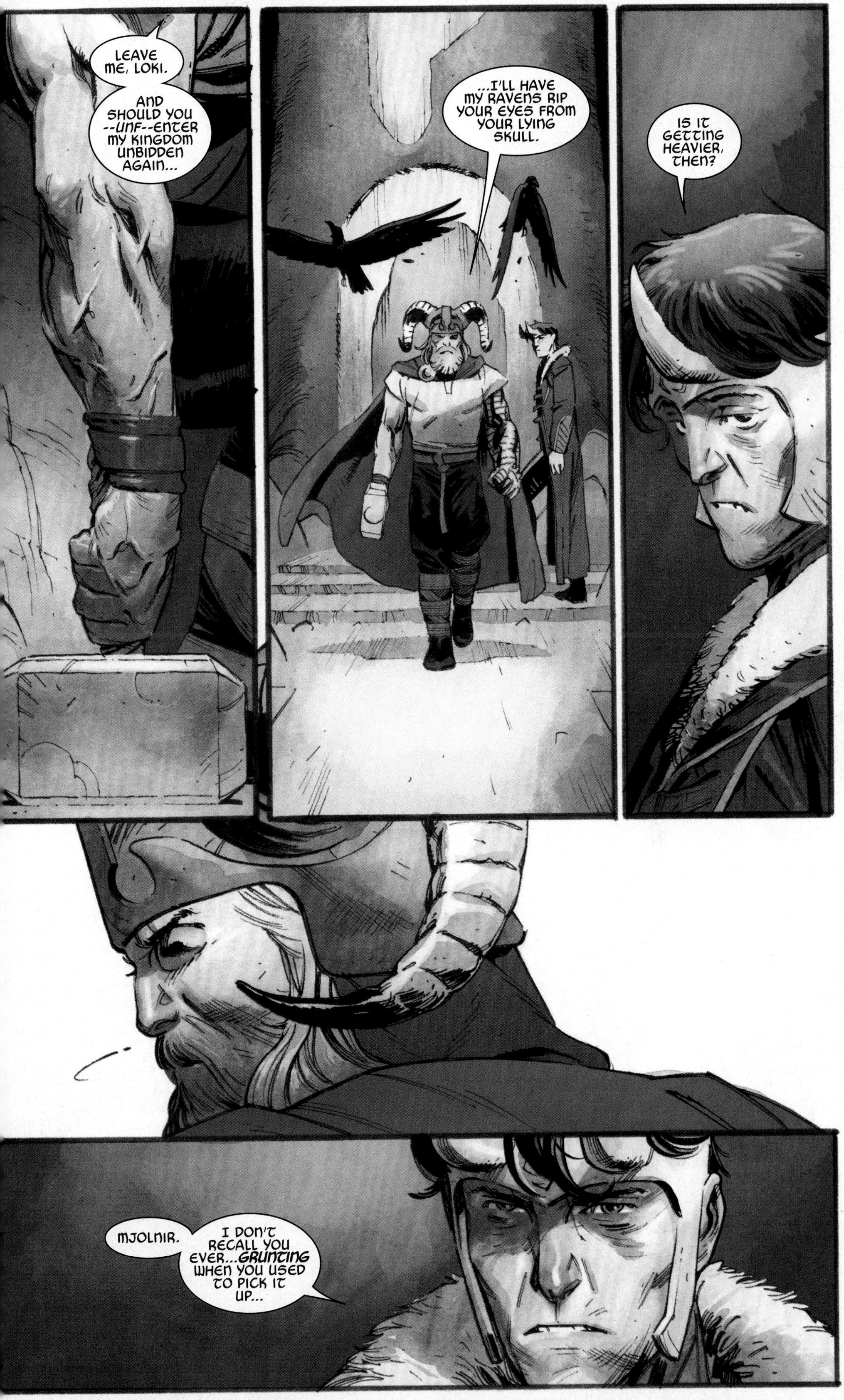

LEAVE ME, LOKI.
AND SHOULD YOU --UNF--ENTER MY KINGDOM UNBIDDEN AGAIN...
...I'LL HAVE MY RAVENS RIP YOUR EYES FROM YOUR LYING SKULL.
IS IT GETTING HEAVIER, THEN?
MJOLNIR.
I DON'T RECALL YOU EVER...GRUNTING WHEN YOU USED TO PICK IT UP...

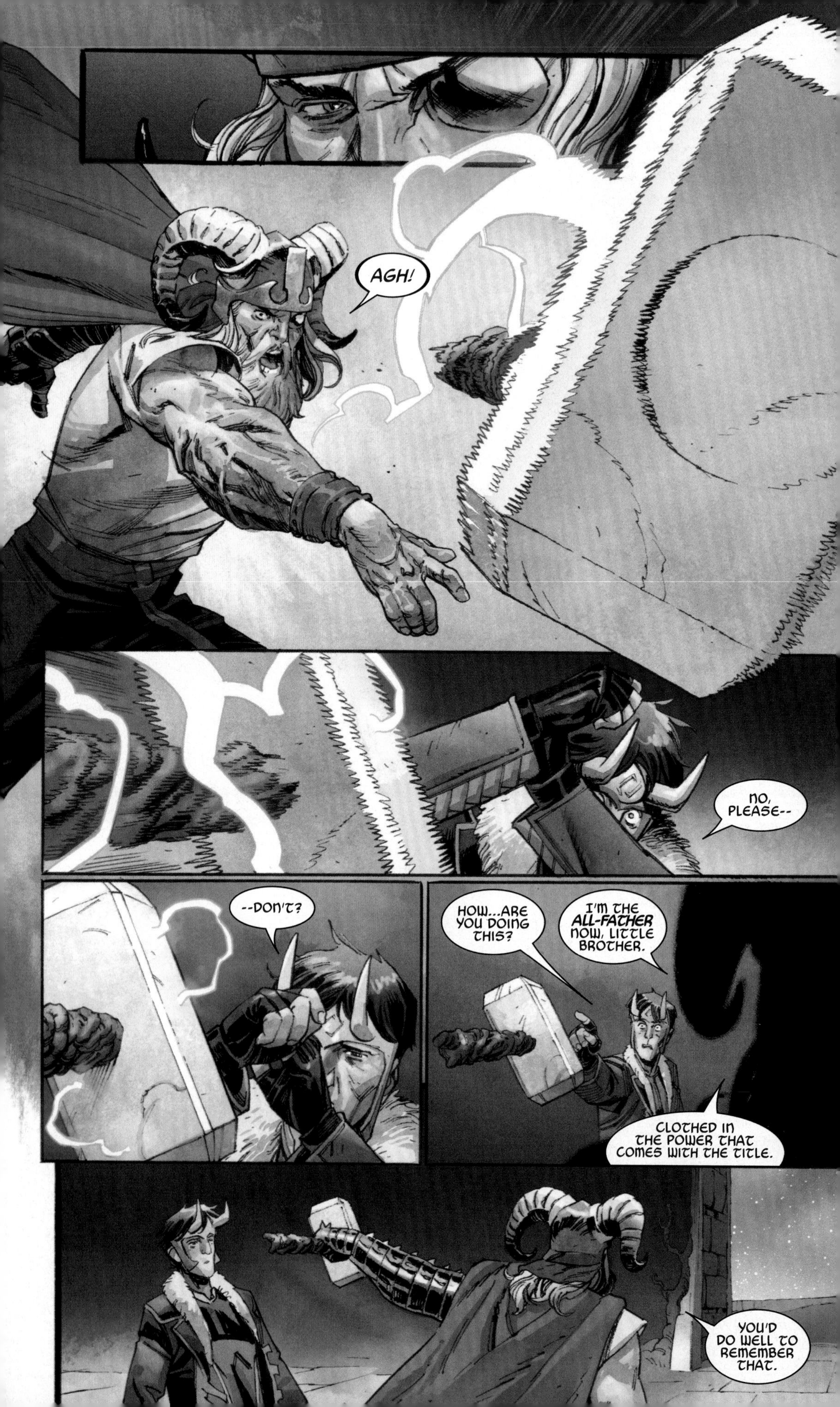
AGH!
NO, PLEASE--
--DON'T?
HOW...ARE YOU DOING THIS?
I'M THE ALL-FATHER NOW, LITTLE BROTHER.
CLOTHED IN THE POWER THAT COMES WITH THE TITLE.
YOU'D DO WELL TO REMEMBER THAT.

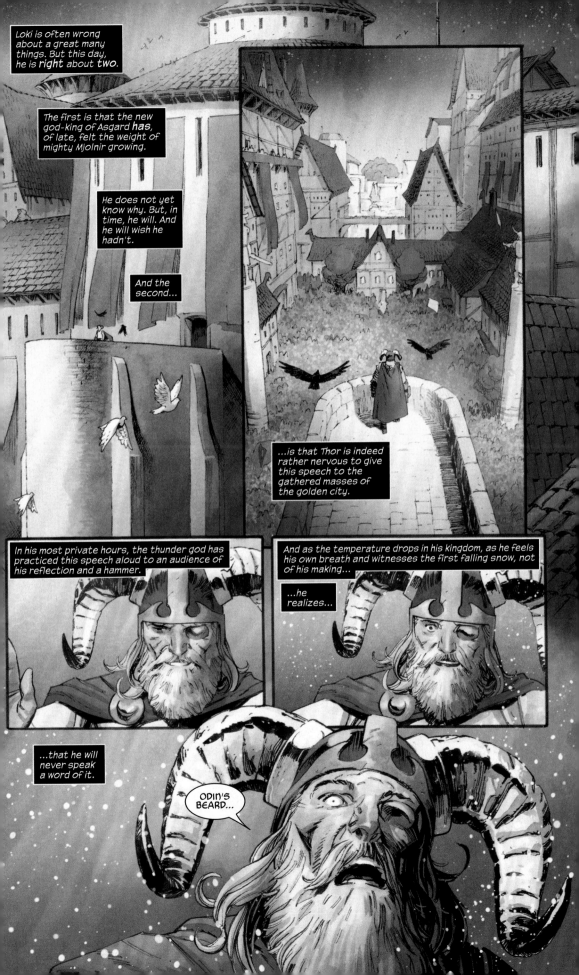

Loki is often wrong about a great many things. But this day, he is *right* about *two*.

The first is that the new god-king of Asgard *has*, of late, felt the weight of mighty Mjolnir growing.

He does not yet know why. But, in time, he will. And he will wish he hadn't.

And the second...

...is that Thor is indeed rather nervous to give this speech to the gathered masses of the golden city.

In his most private hours, the thunder god has practiced this speech aloud to an audience of his reflection and a hammer.

And as the temperature drops in his kingdom, as he feels his own breath and witnesses the first falling snow, not of his making...

...he realizes...

...that he will never speak a word of it.

ODIN'S BEARD...

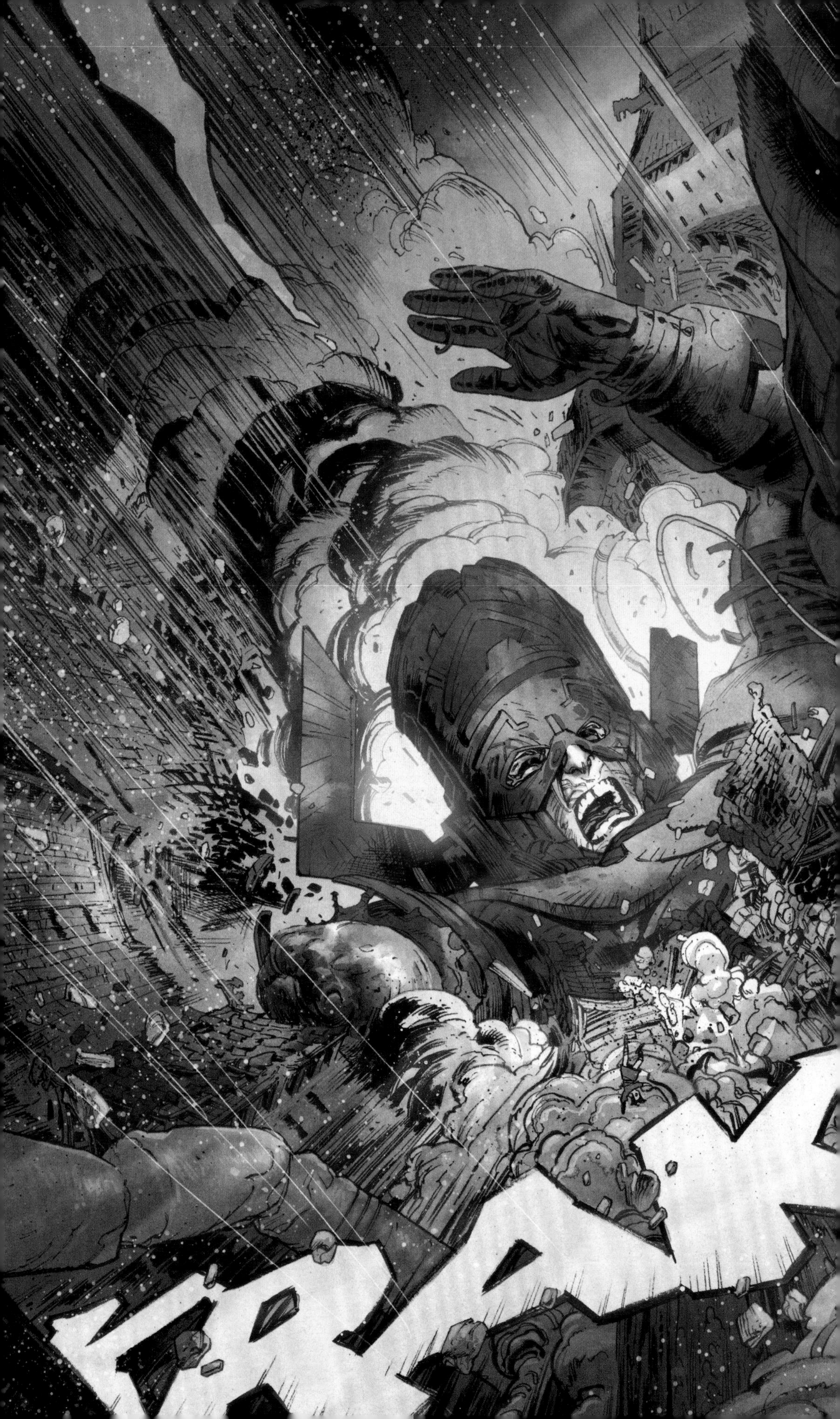

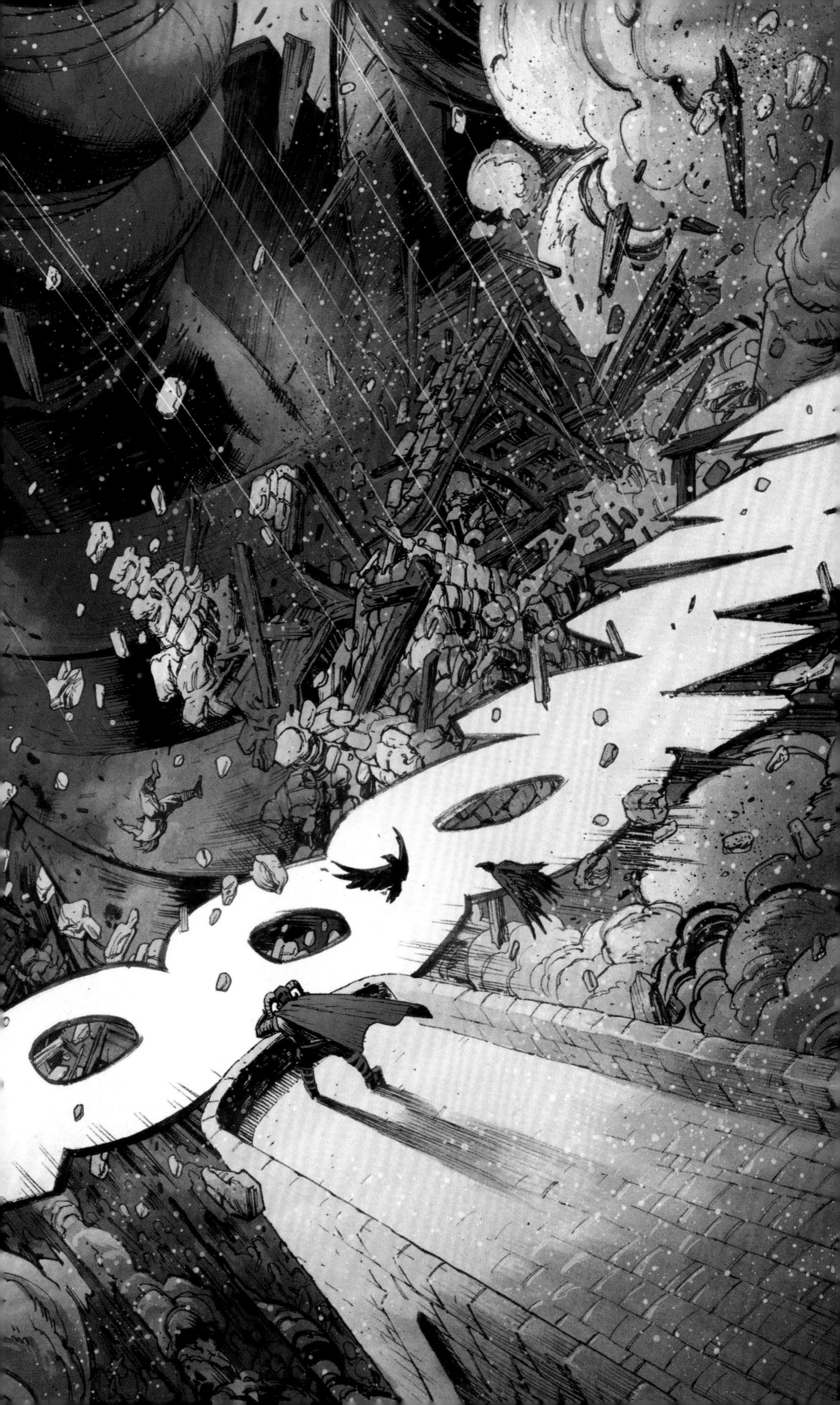

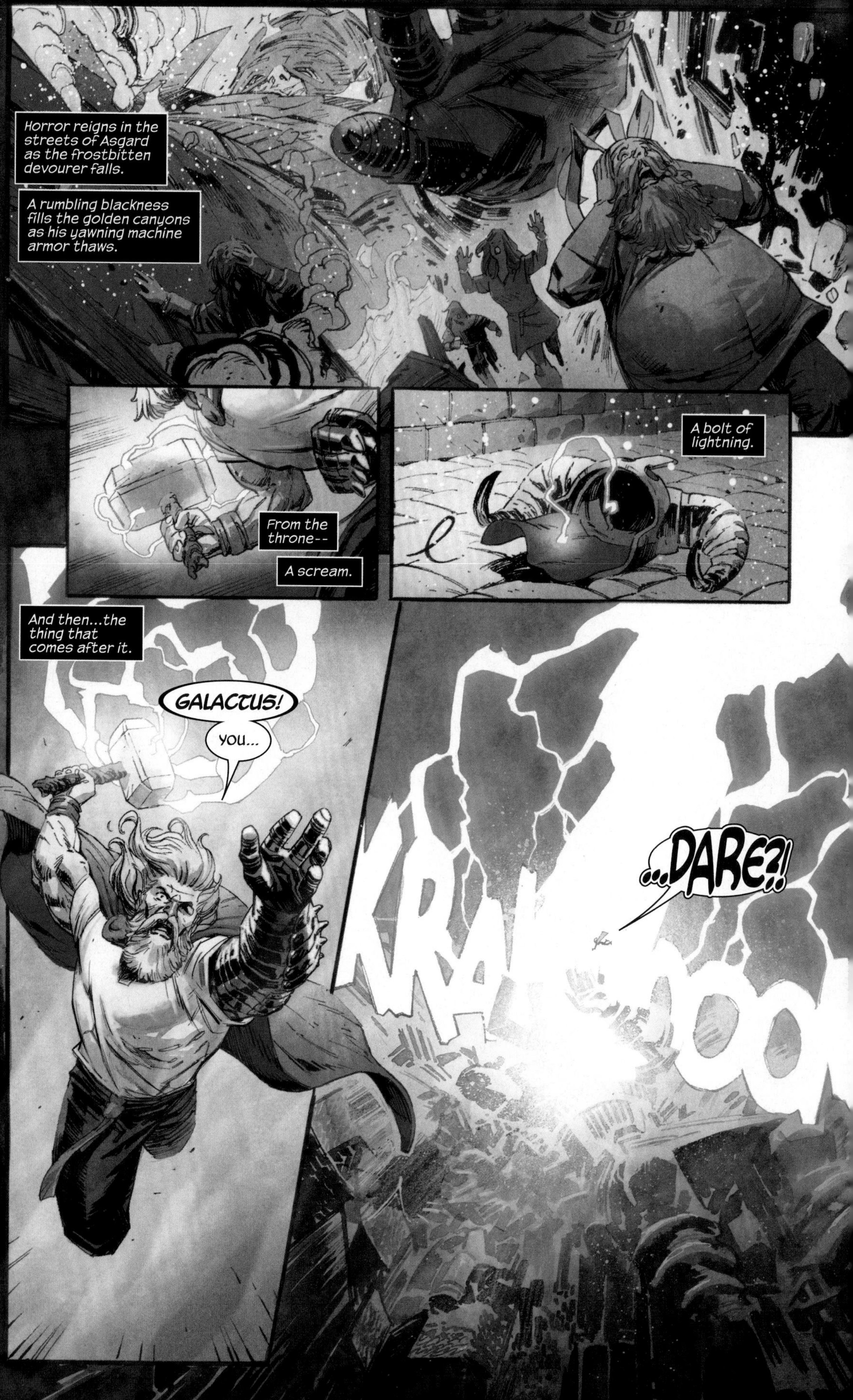

Horror reigns in the streets of Asgard as the frostbitten devourer falls.
A rumbling blackness fills the golden canyons as his yawning machine armor thaws.
From the throne--
A scream.
A bolt of lightning.
And then...the thing that comes after it.
GALACTUS!
YOU...
...DARE?!

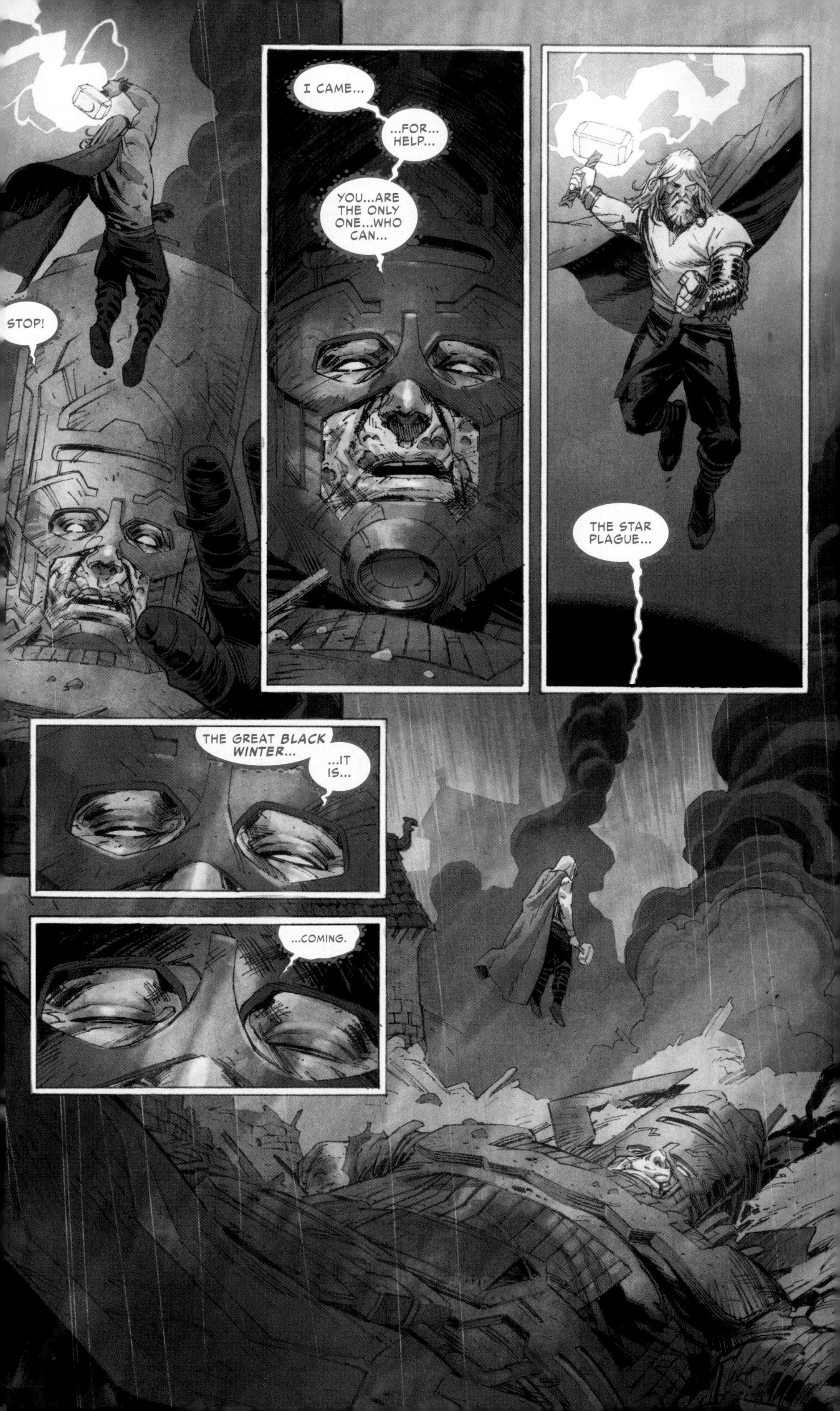
STOP!
I CAME...
...FOR... HELP...
YOU...ARE THE ONLY ONE...WHO CAN...
THE STAR PLAGUE...
THE GREAT BLACK WINTER...
...IT IS...
...COMING.

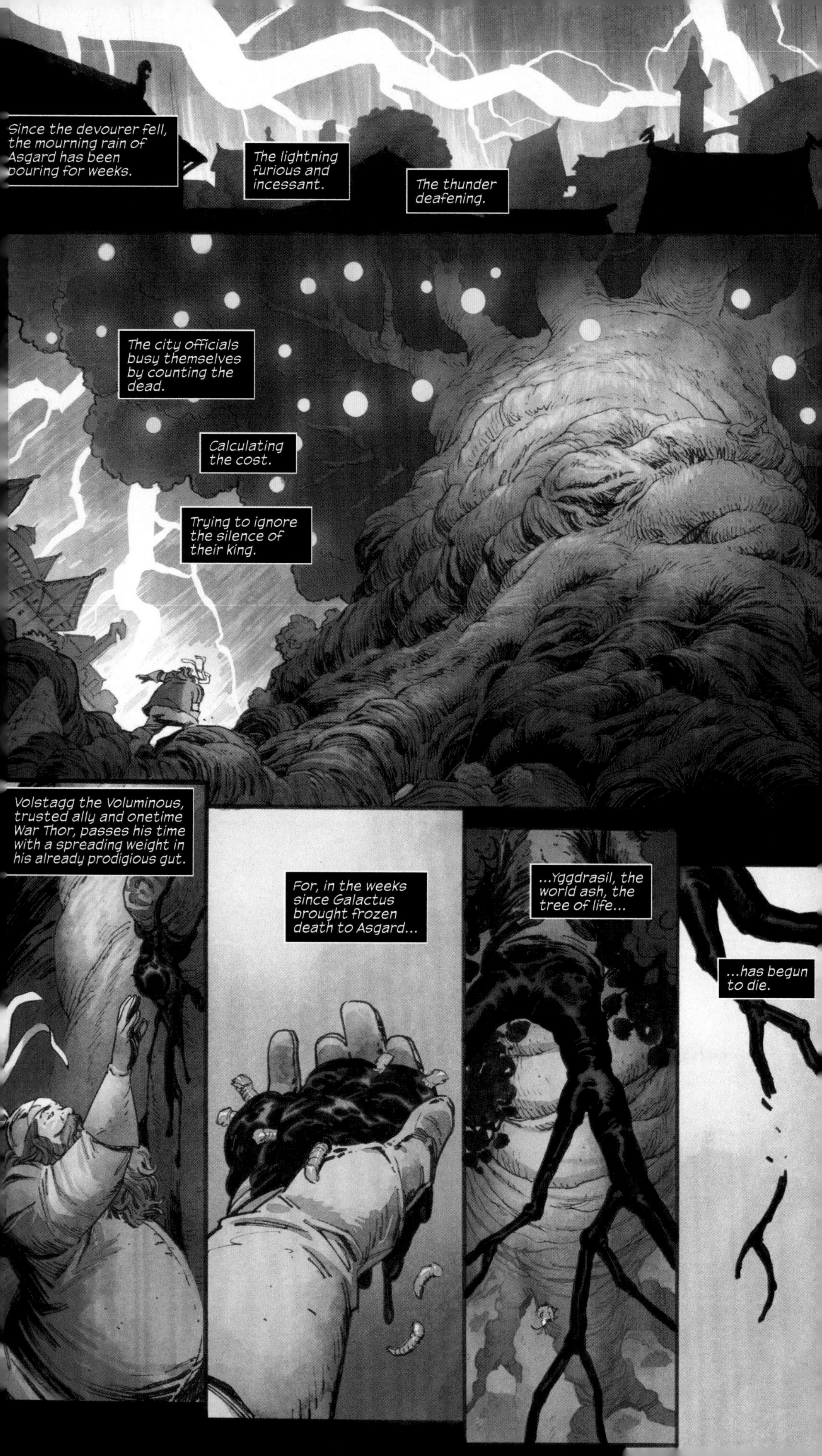
Since the devourer fell, the mourning rain of Asgard has been pouring for weeks.
The lightning furious and incessant.
The thunder deafening.
The city officials busy themselves by counting the dead.
Calculating the cost.
Trying to ignore the silence of their king.
Volstagg the Voluminous, trusted ally and onetime War Thor, passes his time with a spreading weight in his already prodigious gut.
For, in the weeks since Galactus brought frozen death to Asgard...
...Yggdrasil, the world ash, the tree of life...
...has begun to die.

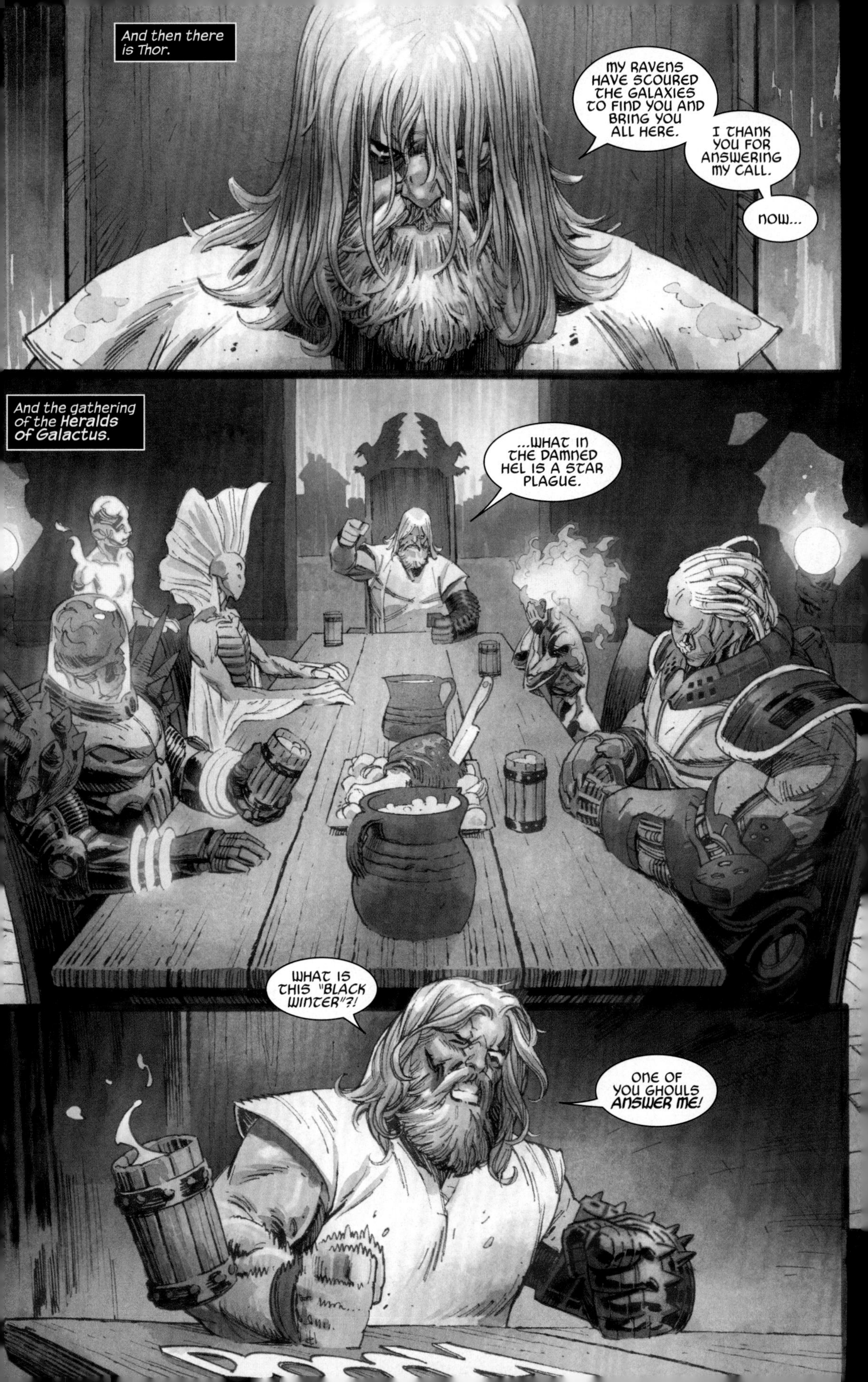
And then there is Thor.
MY RAVENS HAVE SCOURED THE GALAXIES TO FIND YOU AND BRING YOU ALL HERE.
I THANK YOU FOR ANSWERING MY CALL.
NOW...
And the gathering of the Heralds of Galactus.
...WHAT IN THE DAMNED HEL IS A STAR PLAGUE.
WHAT IS THIS "BLACK WINTER"?!
ONE OF YOU GHOULS ANSWER ME!

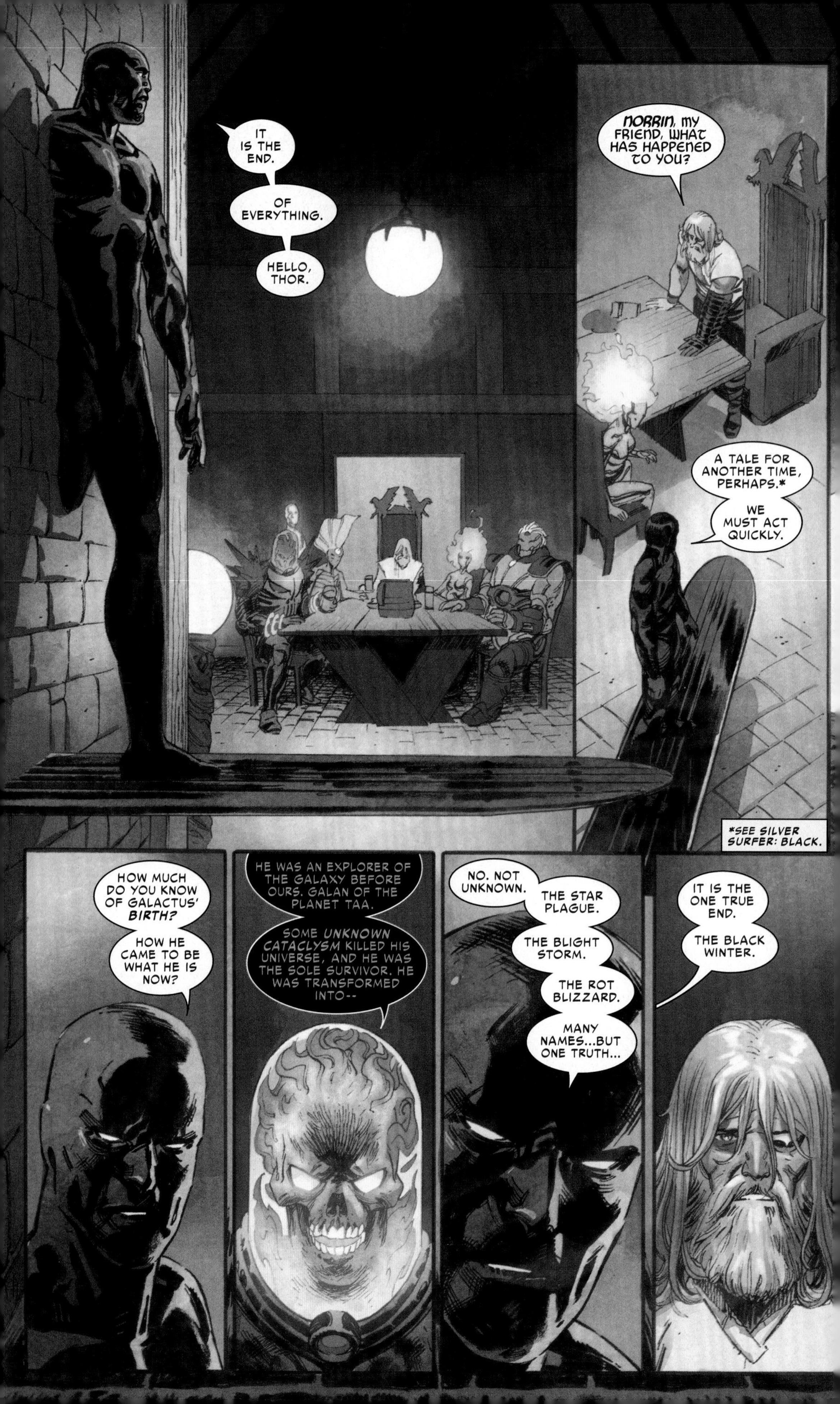

IT IS THE END.
OF EVERYTHING.
HELLO, THOR.
NORRIN, MY FRIEND, WHAT HAS HAPPENED TO YOU?
A TALE FOR ANOTHER TIME, PERHAPS.*
WE MUST ACT QUICKLY.
*SEE SILVER SURFER: BLACK.
HOW MUCH DO YOU KNOW OF GALACTUS' BIRTH?
HOW HE CAME TO BE WHAT HE IS NOW?
HE WAS AN EXPLORER OF THE GALAXY BEFORE OURS. GALAN OF THE PLANET TAA.
SOME UNKNOWN CATACLYSM KILLED HIS UNIVERSE, AND HE WAS THE SOLE SURVIVOR. HE WAS TRANSFORMED INTO--
NO. NOT UNKNOWN.
THE STAR PLAGUE.
THE BLIGHT STORM.
THE ROT BLIZZARD.
MANY NAMES...BUT ONE TRUTH...
IT IS THE ONE TRUE END.
THE BLACK WINTER.

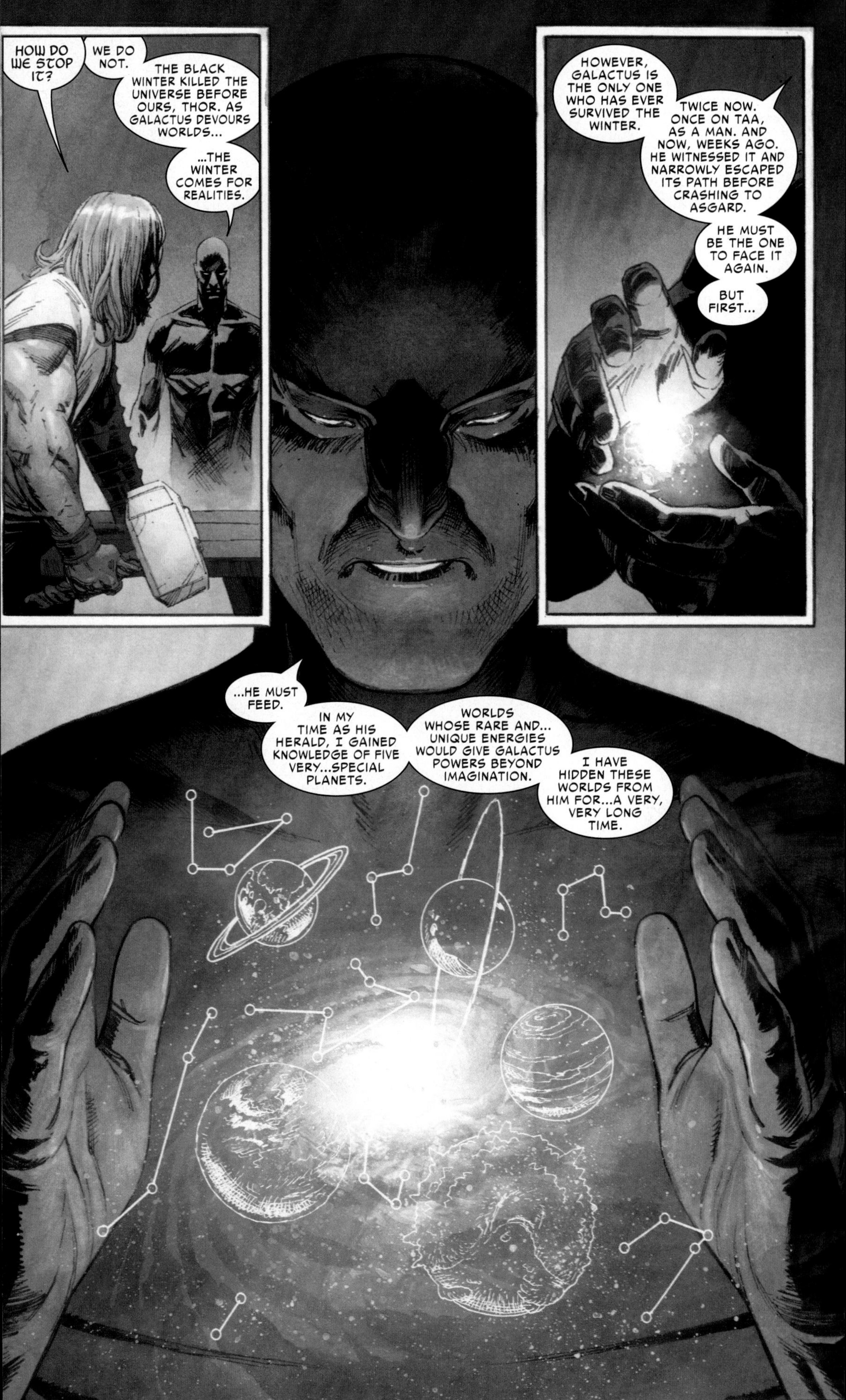
HOW DO WE STOP IT?
WE DO NOT.
THE BLACK WINTER KILLED THE UNIVERSE BEFORE OURS, THOR. AS GALACTUS DEVOURS WORLDS...
...THE WINTER COMES FOR REALITIES.
HOWEVER, GALACTUS IS THE ONLY ONE WHO HAS EVER SURVIVED THE WINTER.
TWICE NOW. ONCE ON TAA, AS A MAN. AND NOW, WEEKS AGO. HE WITNESSED IT AND NARROWLY ESCAPED ITS PATH BEFORE CRASHING TO ASGARD.
HE MUST BE THE ONE TO FACE IT AGAIN.
BUT FIRST...
...HE MUST FEED.
IN MY TIME AS HIS HERALD, I GAINED KNOWLEDGE OF FIVE VERY...SPECIAL PLANETS.
WORLDS WHOSE RARE AND... UNIQUE ENERGIES WOULD GIVE GALACTUS POWERS BEYOND IMAGINATION.
I HAVE HIDDEN THESE WORLDS FROM HIM FOR...A VERY, VERY LONG TIME.

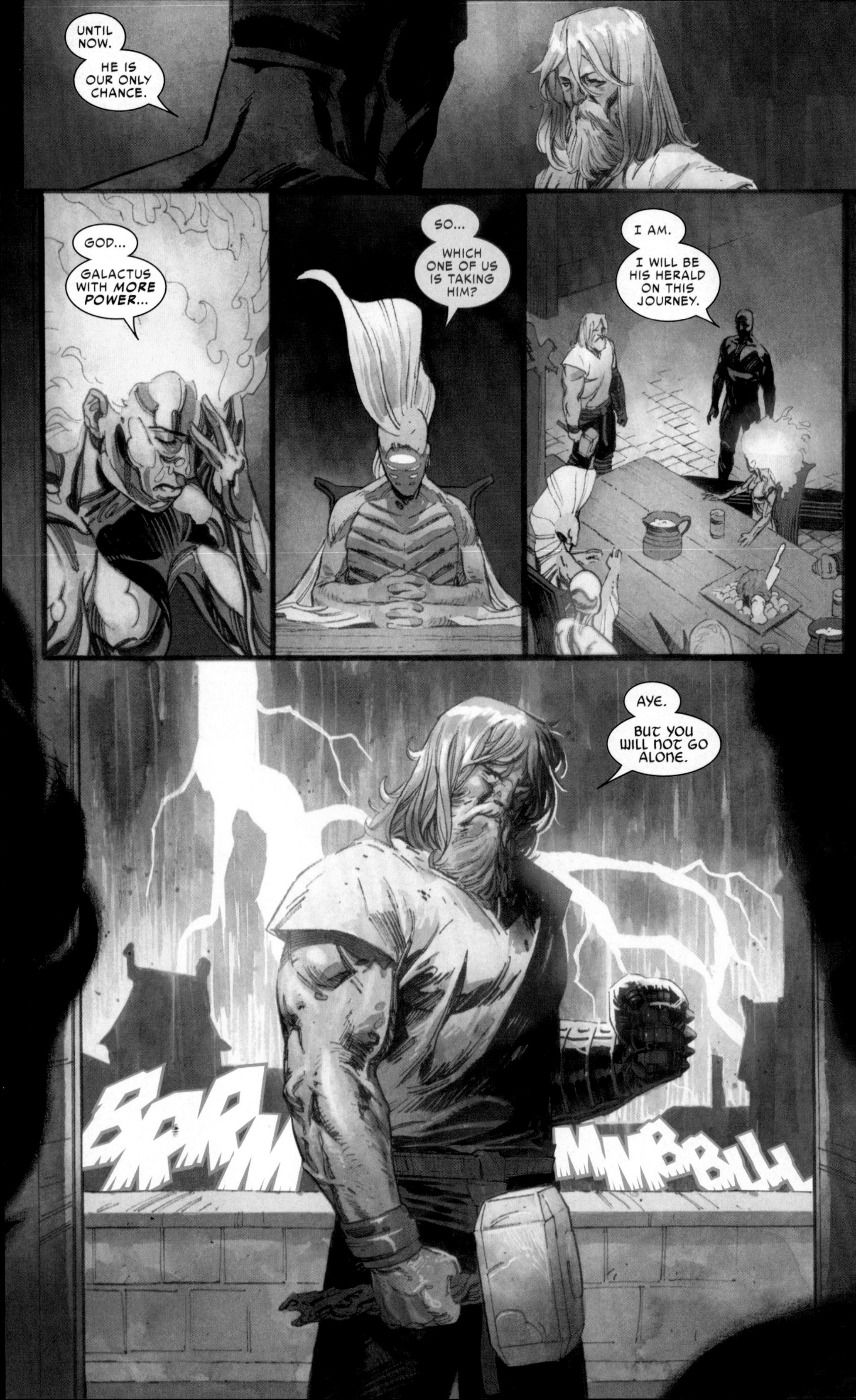

UNTIL NOW.
HE IS OUR ONLY CHANCE.
GOD...
GALACTUS WITH *MORE POWER*...
SO...
WHICH ONE OF US IS TAKING HIM?
I AM.
I WILL BE HIS HERALD ON THIS JOURNEY.
AYE.
BUT YOU WILL NOT GO ALONE.
BRRRMMMBBLLL

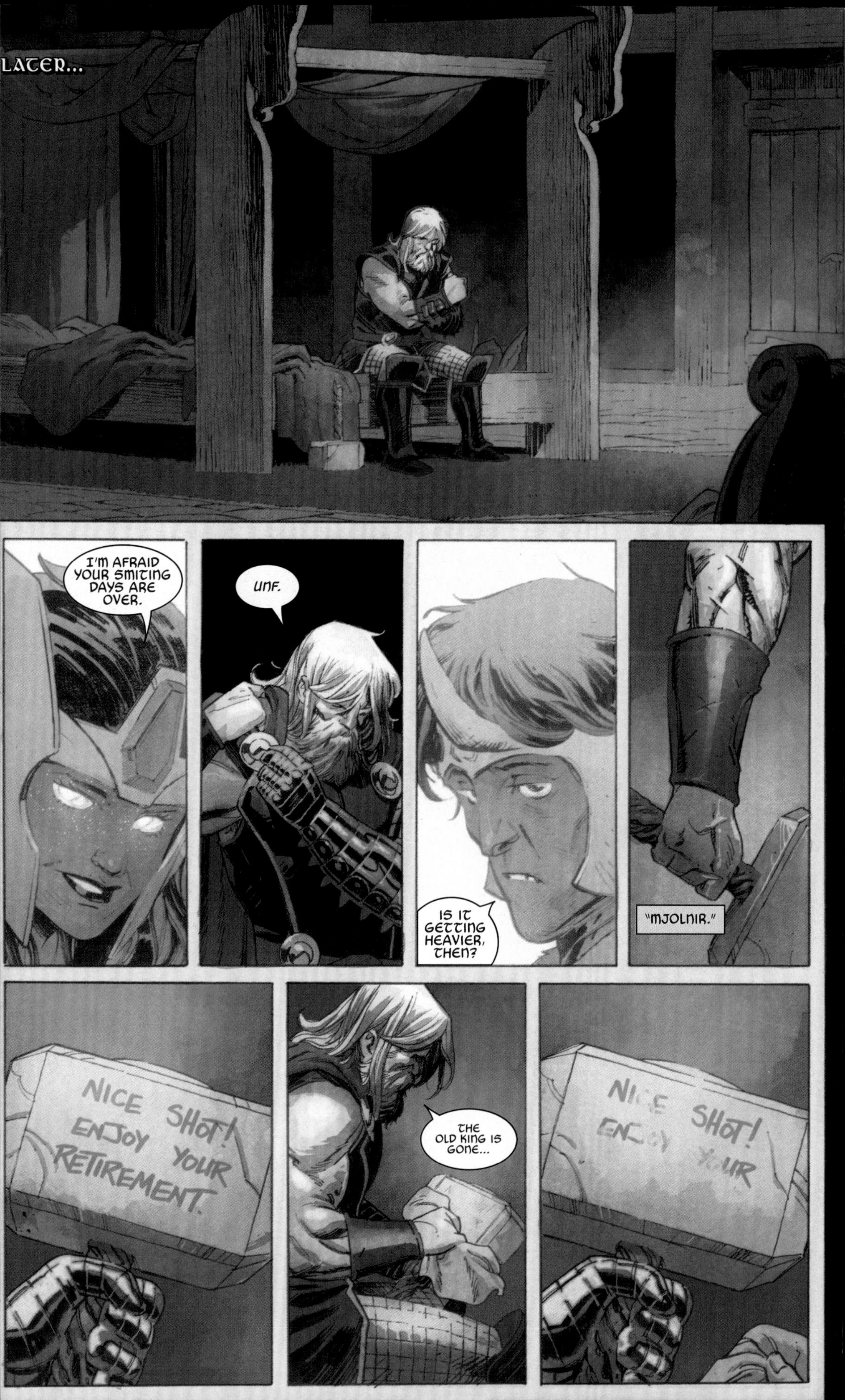
LATER...
I'M AFRAID YOUR SMITING DAYS ARE OVER.
UNF.
IS IT GETTING HEAVIER, THEN?
"MJOLNIR."
NICE SHOT! ENJOY YOUR RETIREMENT.
THE OLD KING IS GONE...
NICE SHOT! ENJOY YOUR

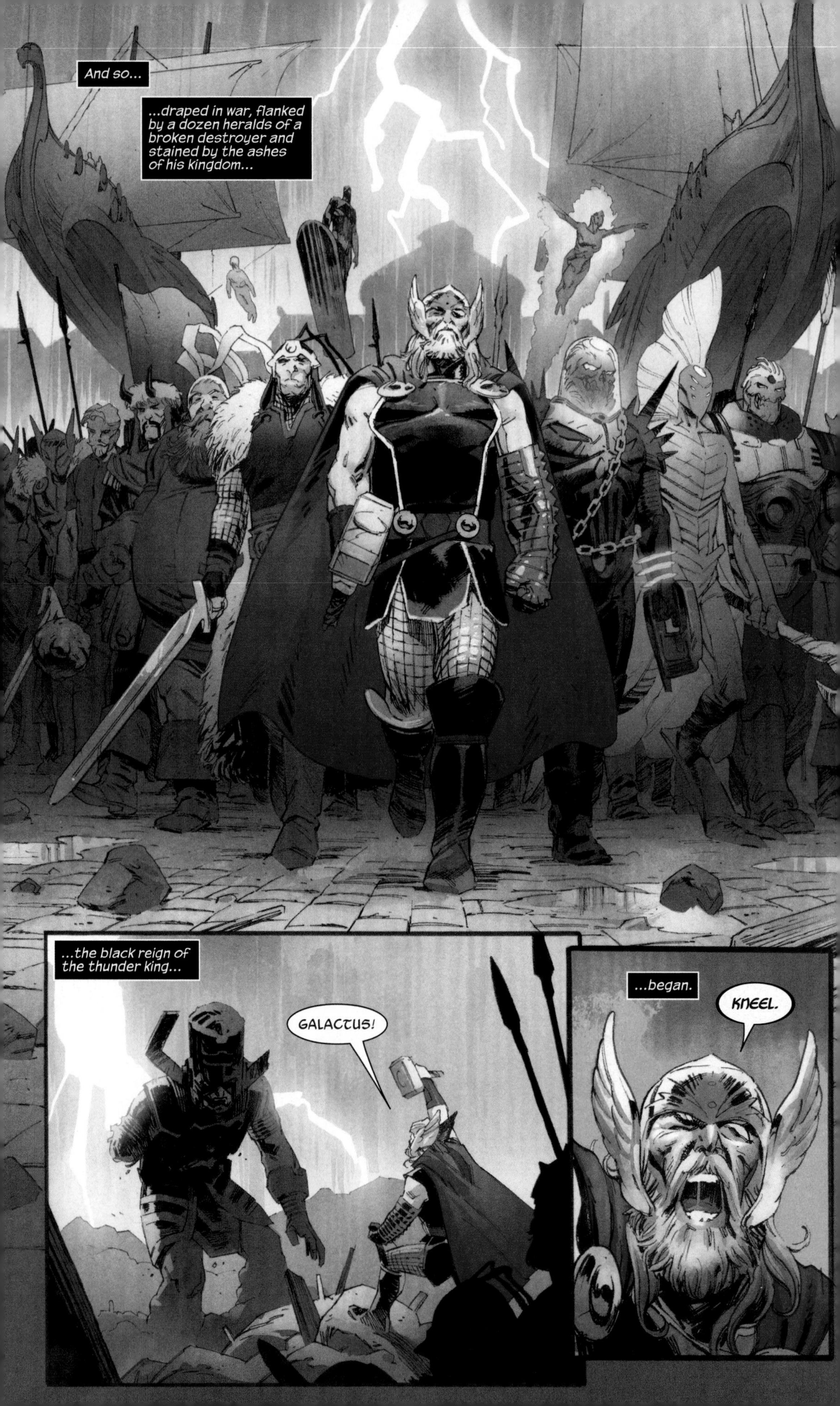
And so...
...draped in war, flanked by a dozen heralds of a broken destroyer and stained by the ashes of his kingdom...
...the black reign of the thunder king...
GALACTUS!
...began.
KNEEL.

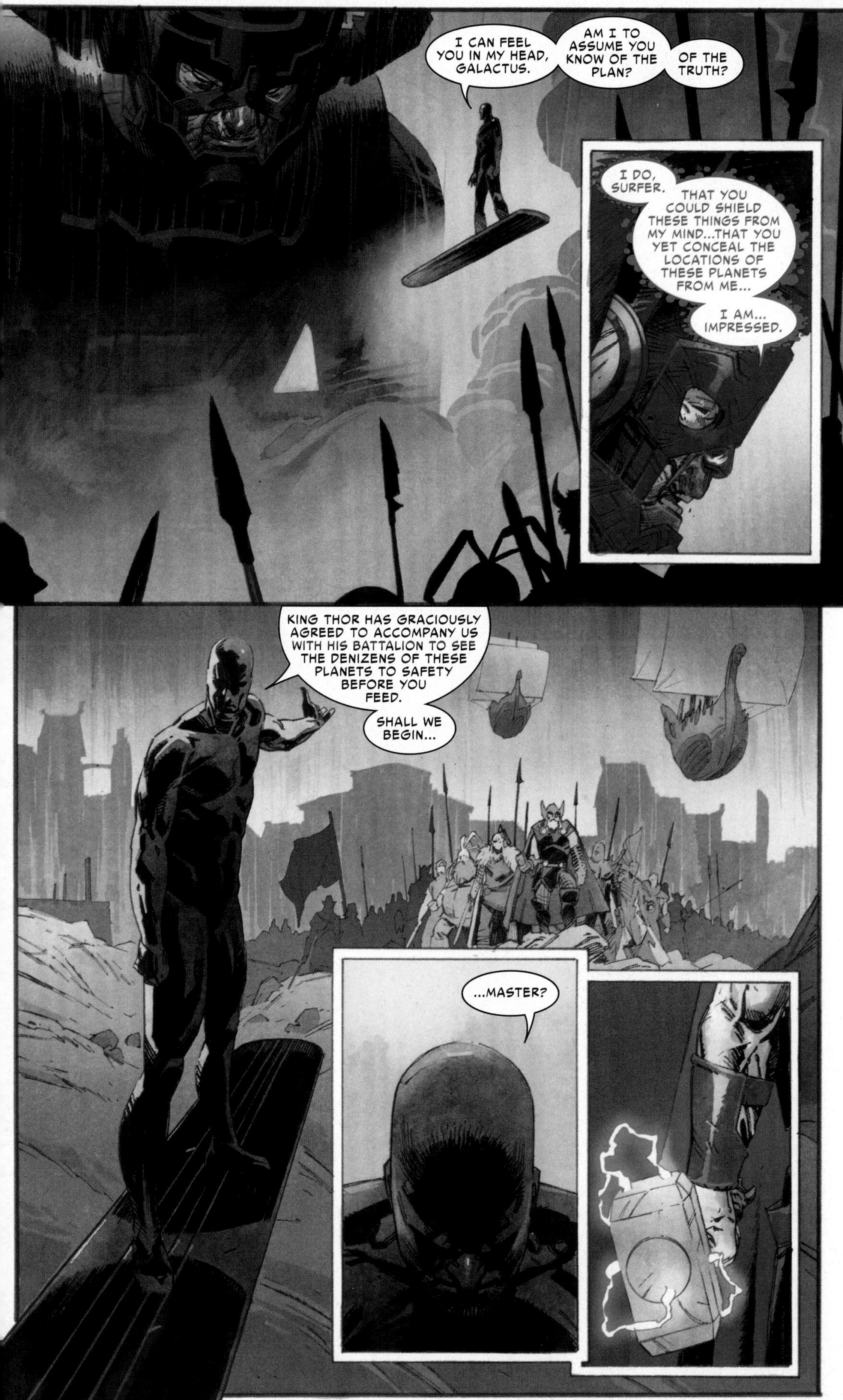
I CAN FEEL YOU IN MY HEAD, GALACTUS.
AM I TO ASSUME YOU KNOW OF THE PLAN?
OF THE TRUTH?
I DO, SURFER.
THAT YOU COULD SHIELD THESE THINGS FROM MY MIND...THAT YOU YET CONCEAL THE LOCATIONS OF THESE PLANETS FROM ME...
I AM... IMPRESSED.
KING THOR HAS GRACIOUSLY AGREED TO ACCOMPANY US WITH HIS BATTALION TO SEE THE DENIZENS OF THESE PLANETS TO SAFETY BEFORE YOU FEED.
SHALL WE BEGIN...
...MASTER?

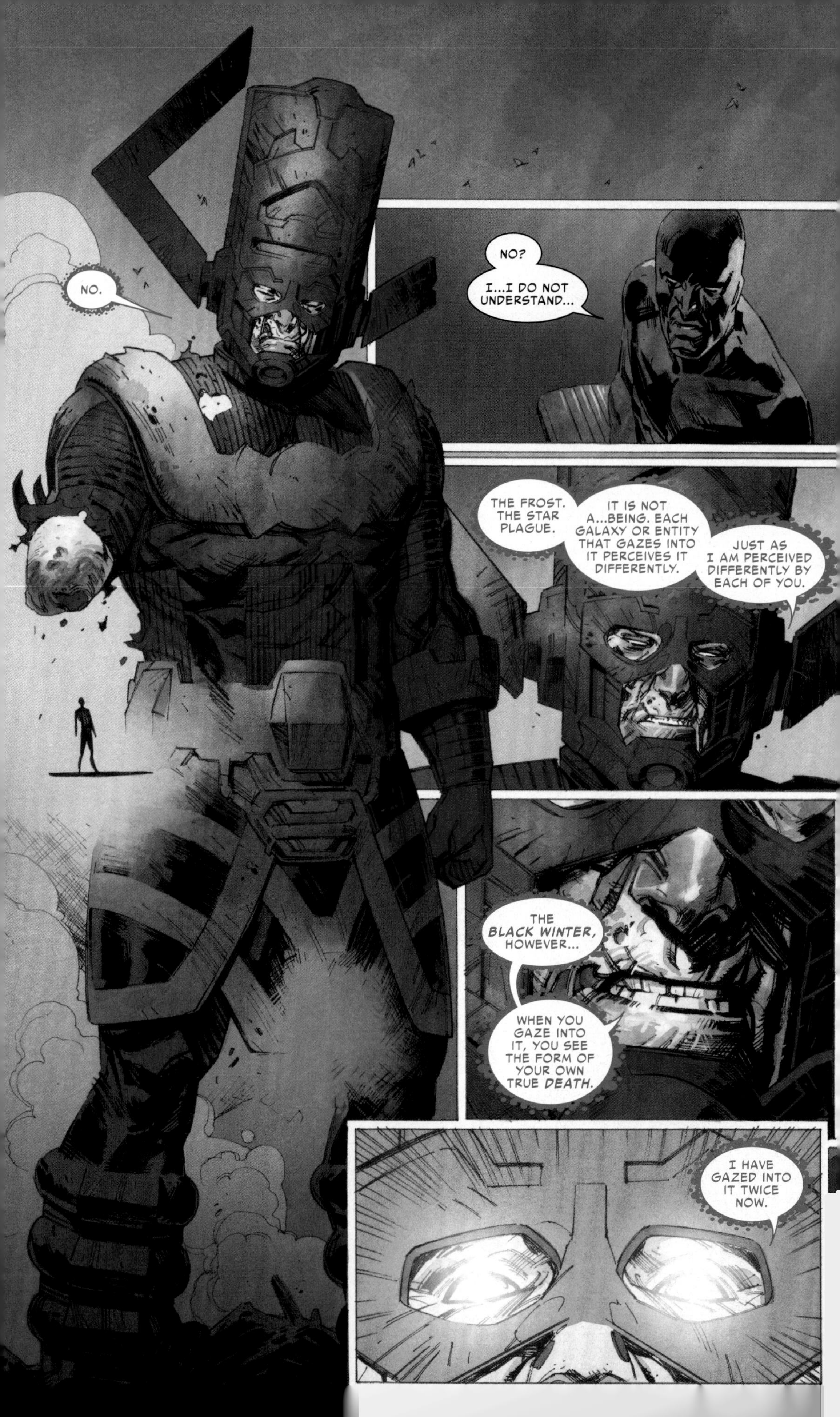
NO.
NO?
I...I DO NOT UNDERSTAND...
THE FROST. THE STAR PLAGUE.
IT IS NOT A...BEING. EACH GALAXY OR ENTITY THAT GAZES INTO IT PERCEIVES IT DIFFERENTLY.
JUST AS I AM PERCEIVED DIFFERENTLY BY EACH OF YOU.
THE *BLACK WINTER,* HOWEVER...
WHEN YOU GAZE INTO IT, YOU SEE THE FORM OF YOUR OWN TRUE *DEATH.*
I HAVE GAZED INTO IT TWICE NOW.

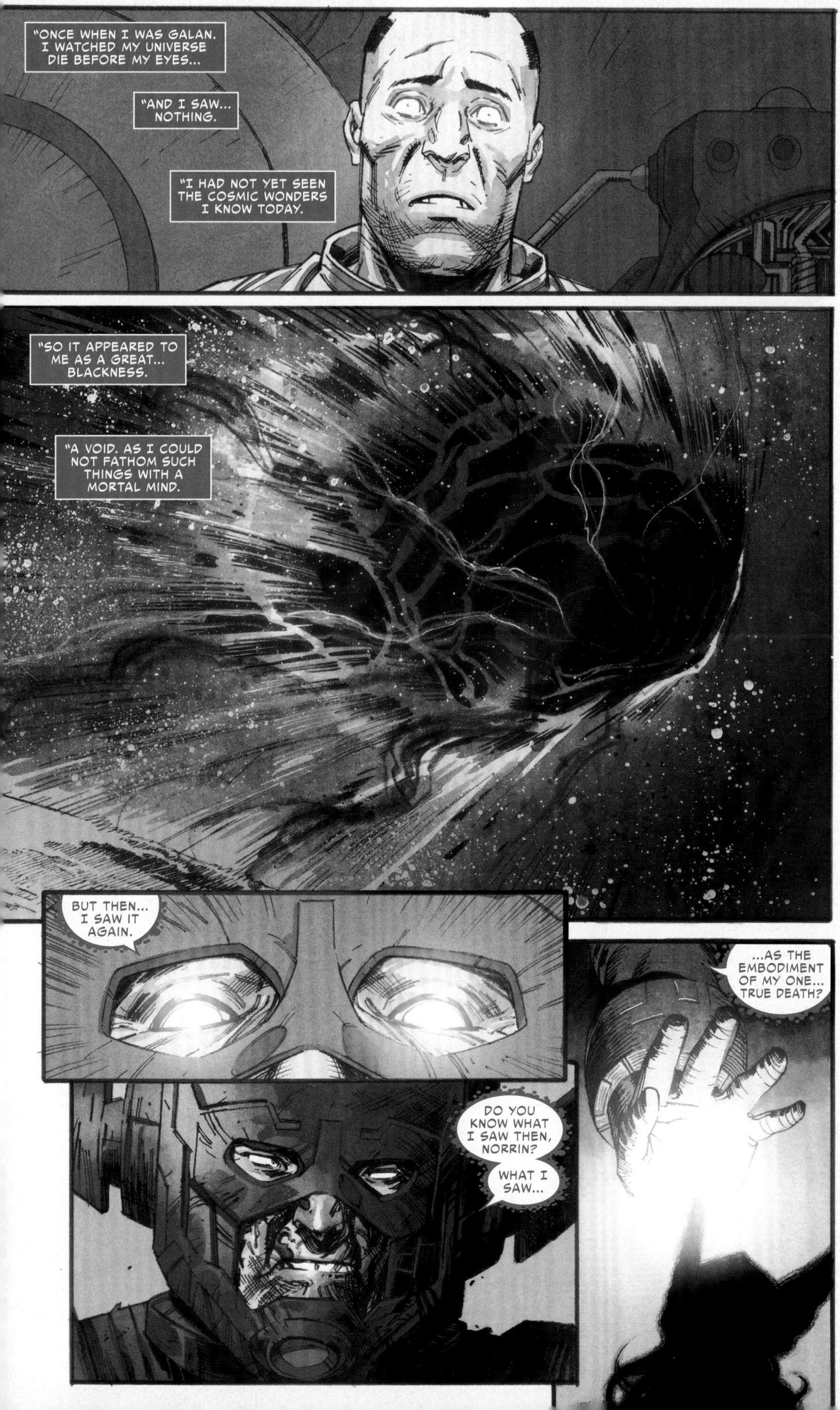
"ONCE WHEN I WAS GALAN. I WATCHED MY UNIVERSE DIE BEFORE MY EYES...
"AND I SAW... NOTHING.
"I HAD NOT YET SEEN THE COSMIC WONDERS I KNOW TODAY.
"SO IT APPEARED TO ME AS A GREAT... BLACKNESS.
"A VOID. AS I COULD NOT FATHOM SUCH THINGS WITH A MORTAL MIND.
BUT THEN... I SAW IT AGAIN.
...AS THE EMBODIMENT OF MY ONE... TRUE DEATH?
DO YOU KNOW WHAT I SAW THEN, NORRIN?
WHAT I SAW...

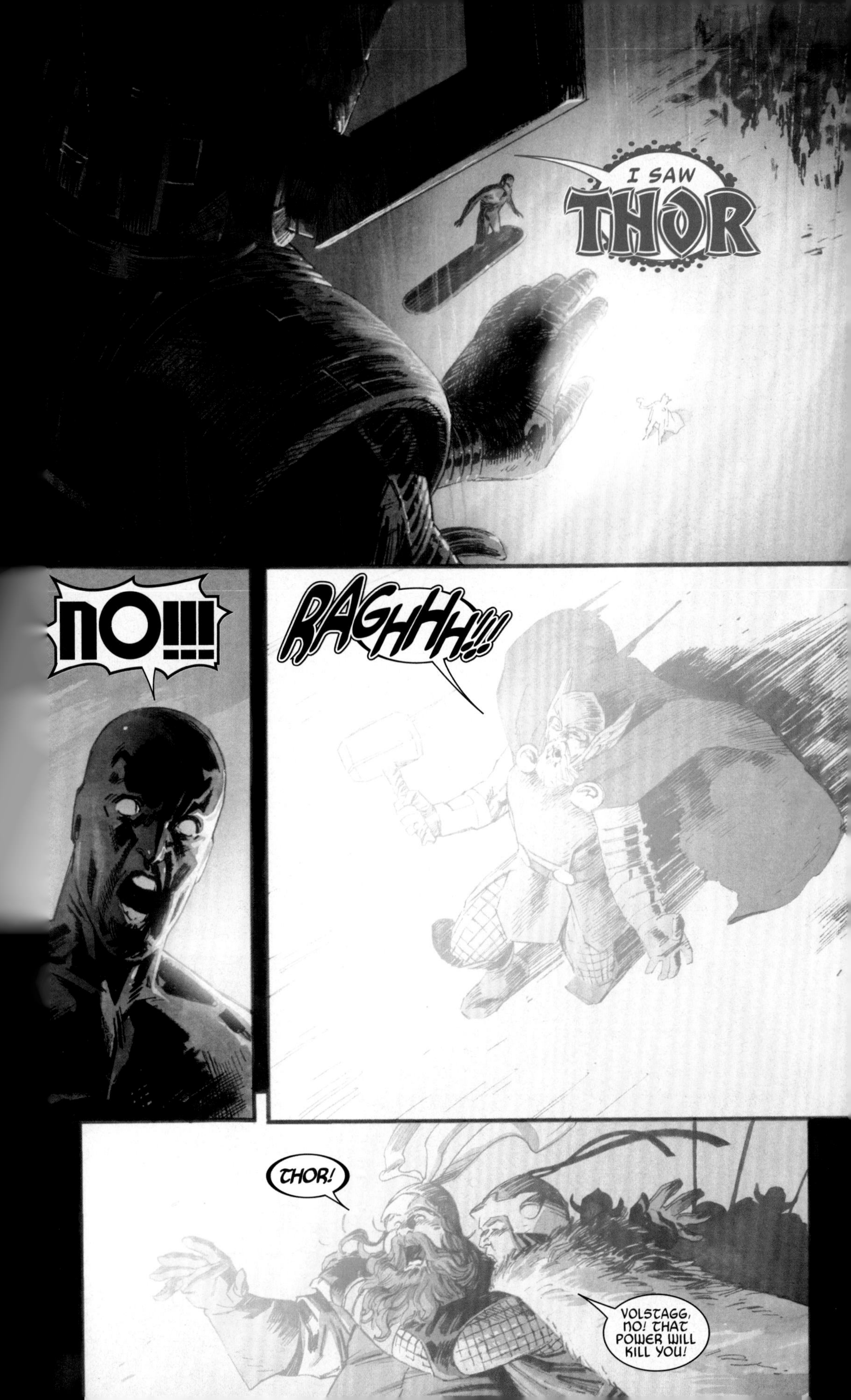
I SAW THOR
NO!!!
RAGHHH!!!
THOR!
VOLSTAGG, NO! THAT POWER WILL KILL YOU!

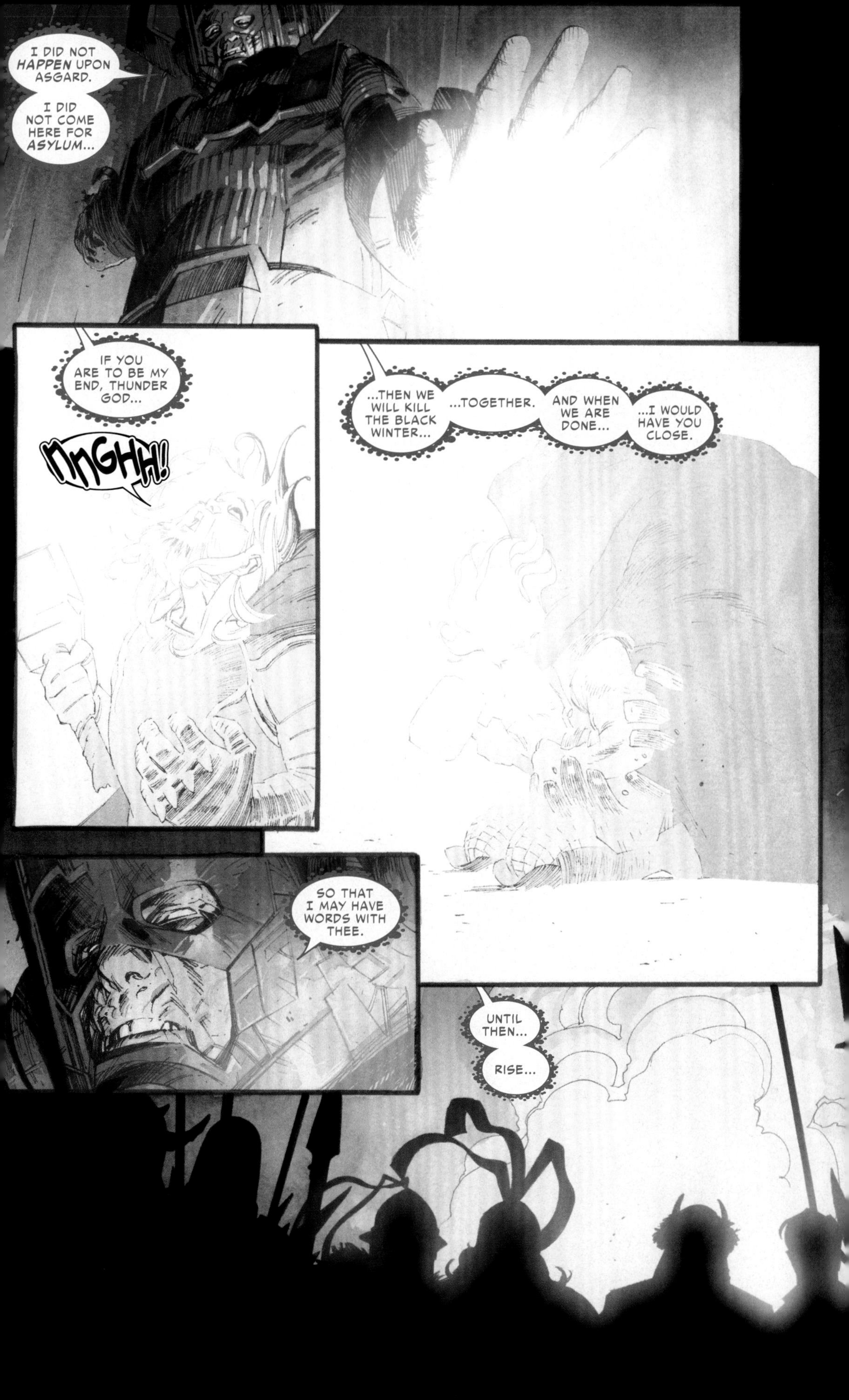
I DID NOT HAPPEN UPON ASGARD.
I DID NOT COME HERE FOR ASYLUM...
IF YOU ARE TO BE MY END, THUNDER GOD...
NNGHH!
...THEN WE WILL KILL THE BLACK WINTER...
...TOGETHER.
AND WHEN WE ARE DONE...
...I WOULD HAVE YOU CLOSE.
SO THAT I MAY HAVE WORDS WITH THEE.
UNTIL THEN...
RISE...

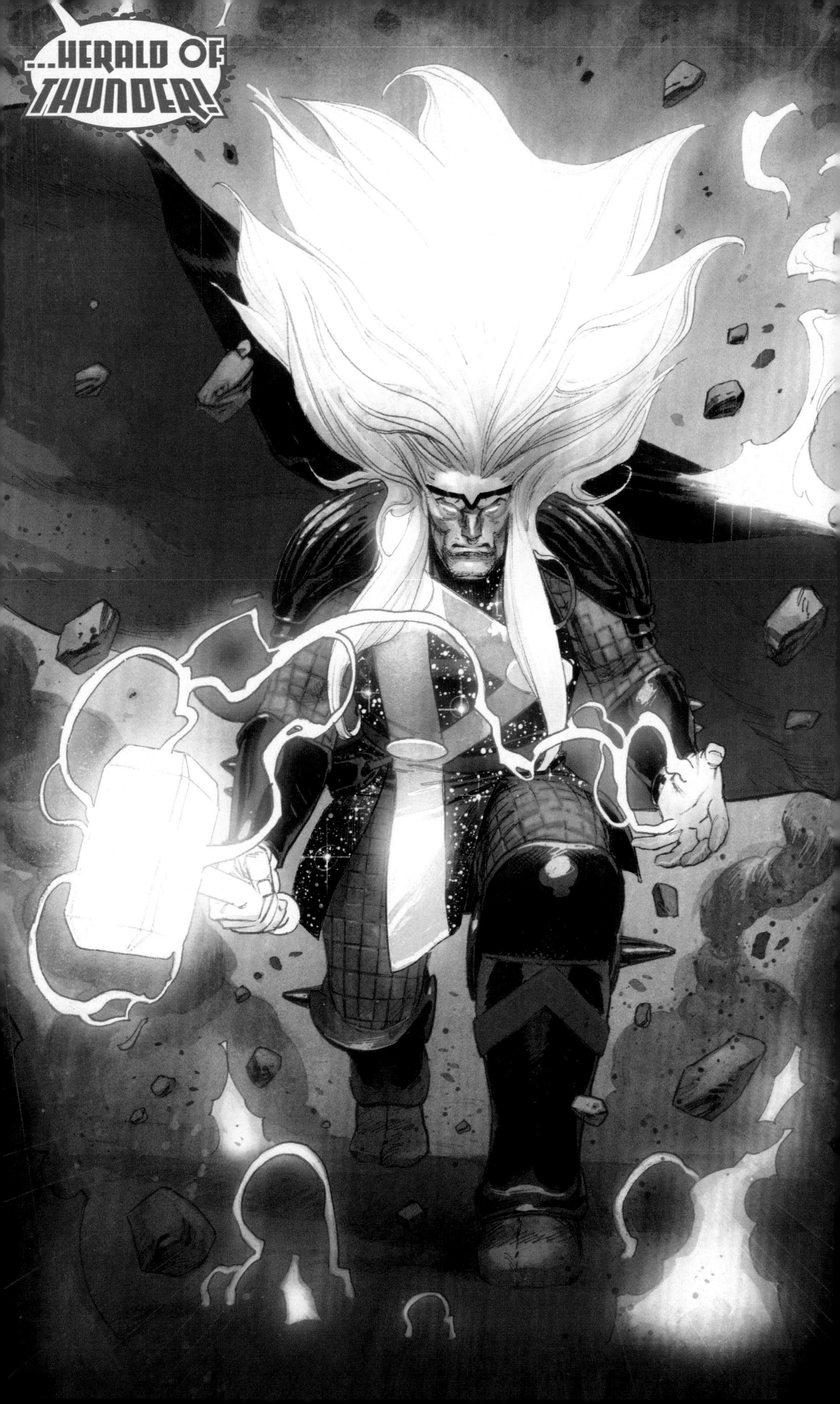
...HERALD OF THUNDER!

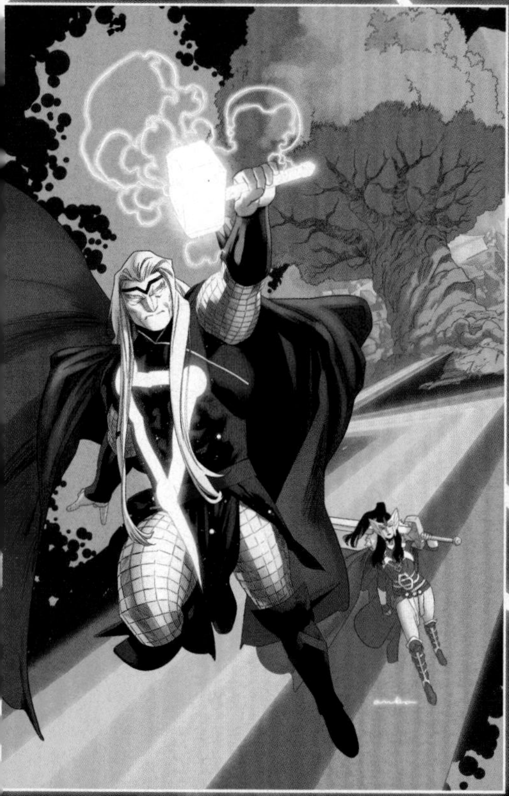

THOR 1 RAINBOW BRIDGE VARIANT BY
Kris Anka

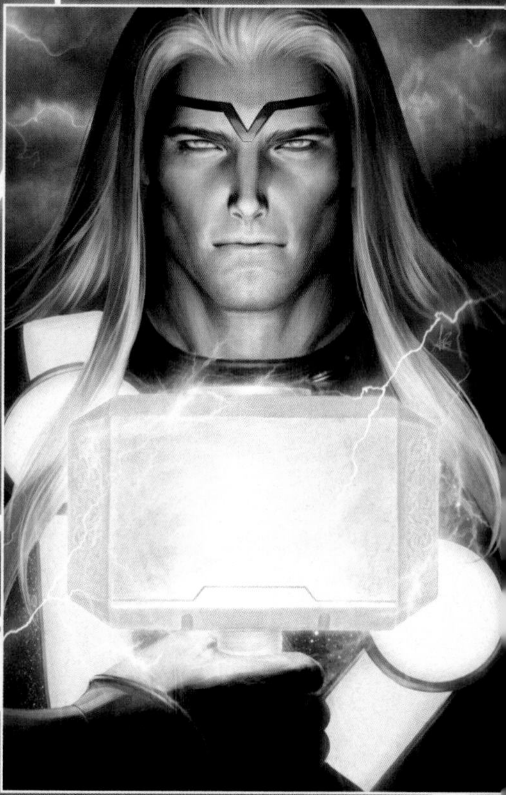

THOR 1 VARIANT BY
Stanley "Artgerm" Lau

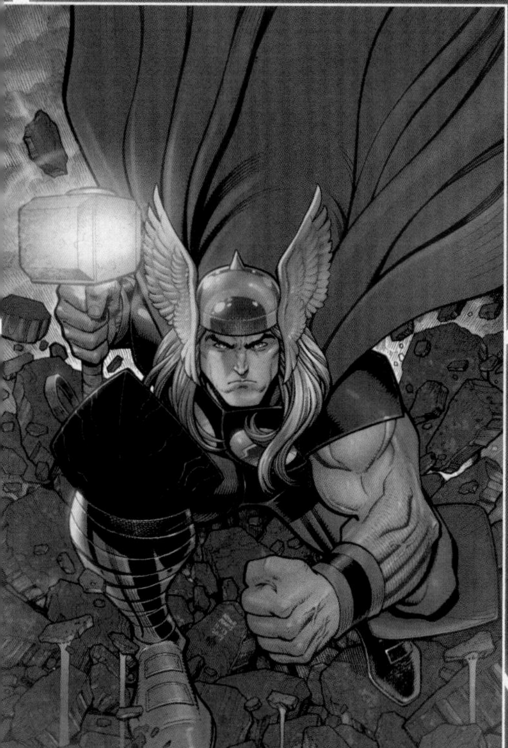

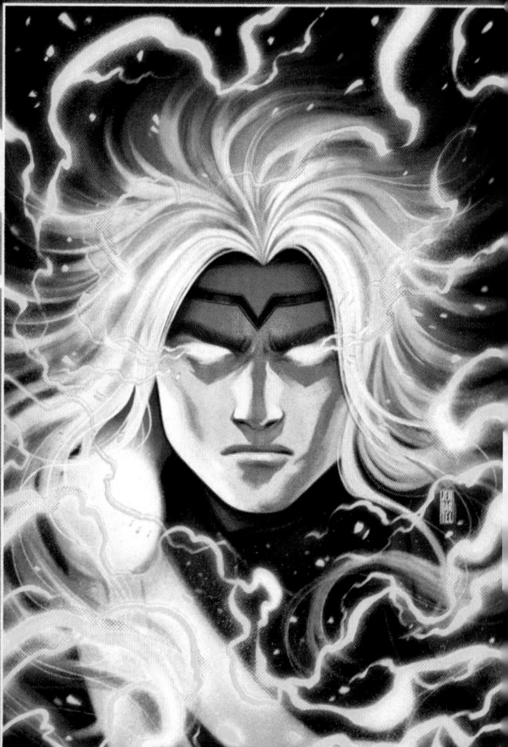

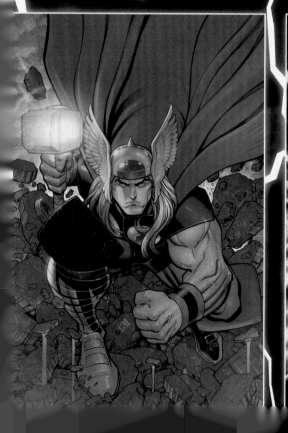

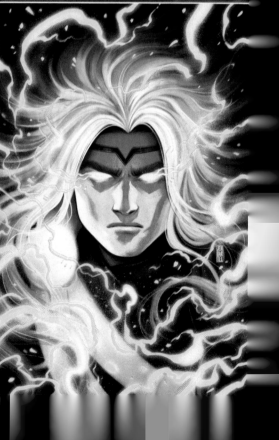

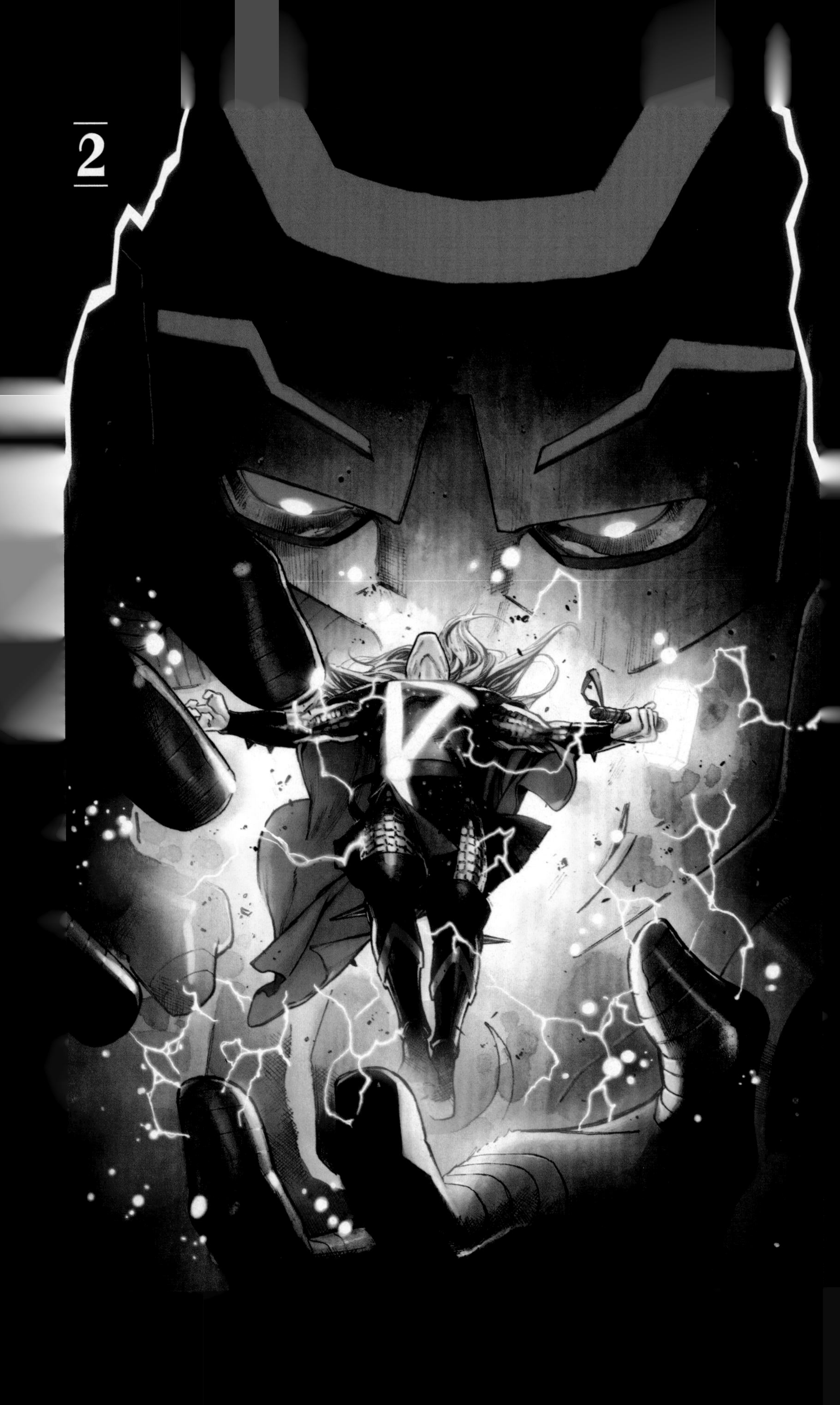
2

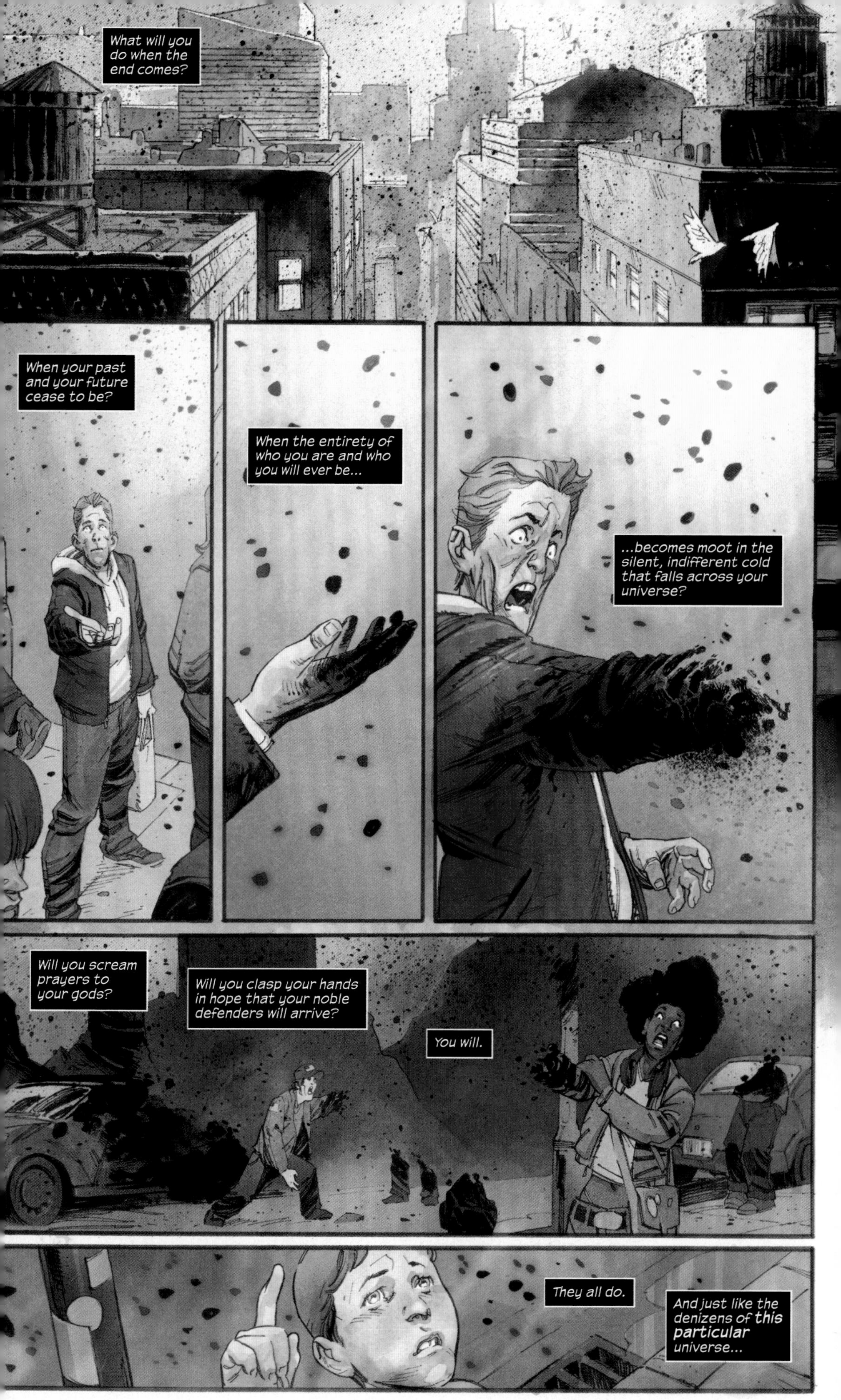
What will you do when the end comes?
When your past and your future cease to be?
When the entirety of who you are and who you will ever be...
...becomes moot in the silent, indifferent cold that falls across your universe?
Will you scream prayers to your gods?
Will you clasp your hands in hope that your noble defenders will arrive?
You will.
They all do.
And just like the denizens of this particular universe...

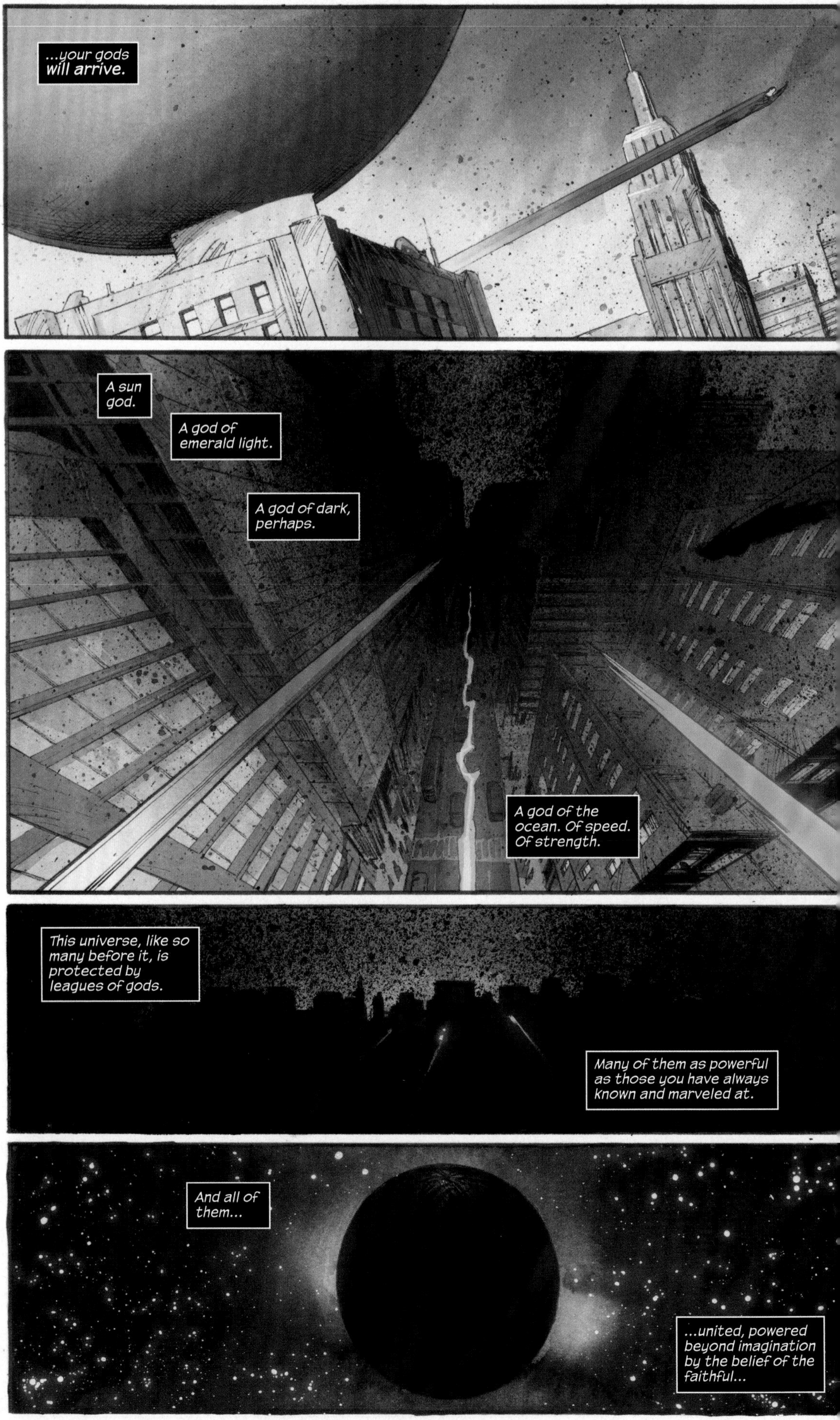
...your gods will arrive.
A sun god.
A god of emerald light.
A god of dark, perhaps.
A god of the ocean. Of speed. Of strength.
This universe, like so many before it, is protected by leagues of gods.
Many of them as powerful as those you have always known and marveled at.
And all of them...
...united, powered beyond imagination by the belief of the faithful...

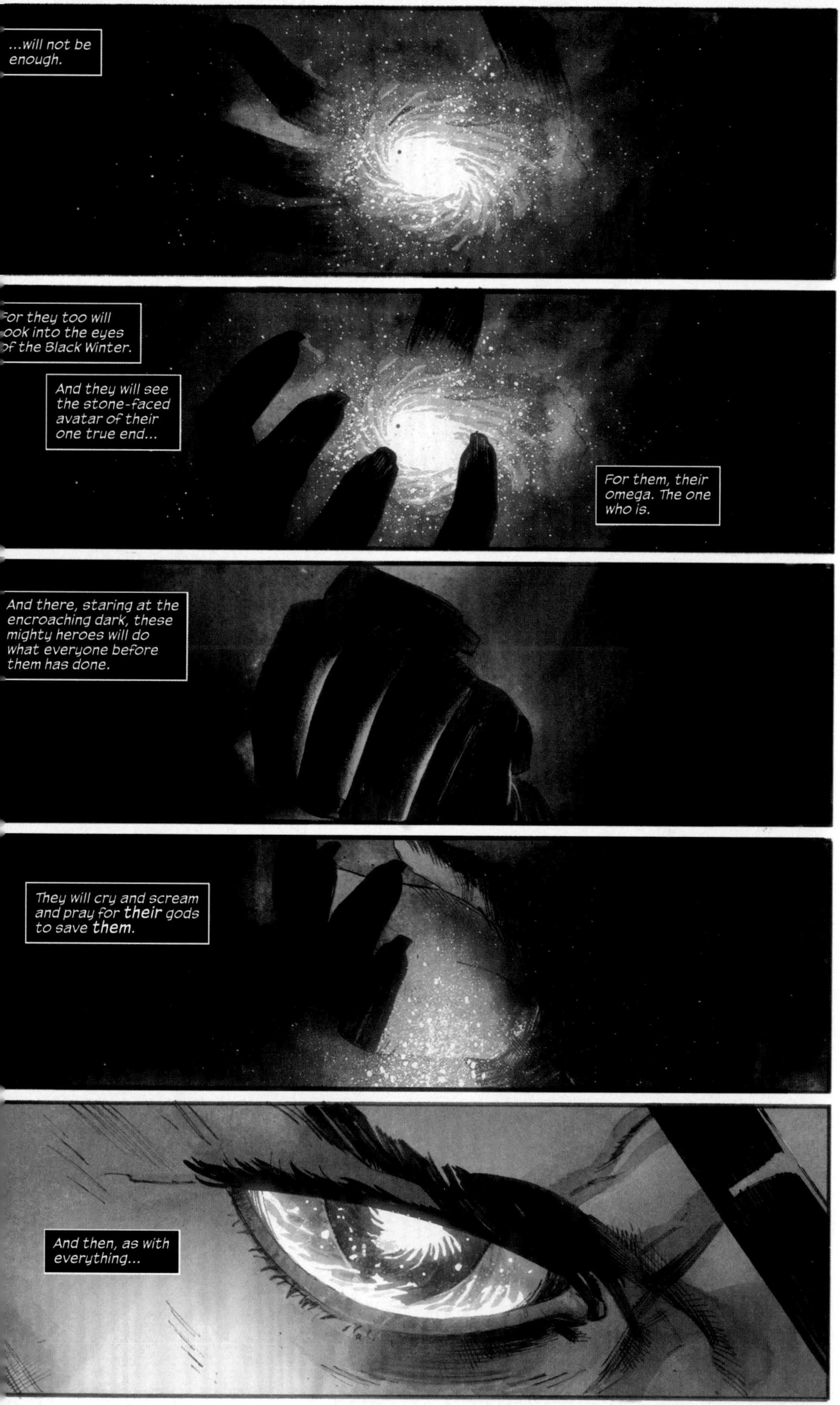
...will not be enough.
For they too will look into the eyes of the Black Winter.
And they will see the stone-faced avatar of their one true end...
For them, their omega. The one who is.
And there, staring at the encroaching dark, these mighty heroes will do what everyone before them has done.
They will cry and scream and pray for their gods to save them.
And then, as with everything...

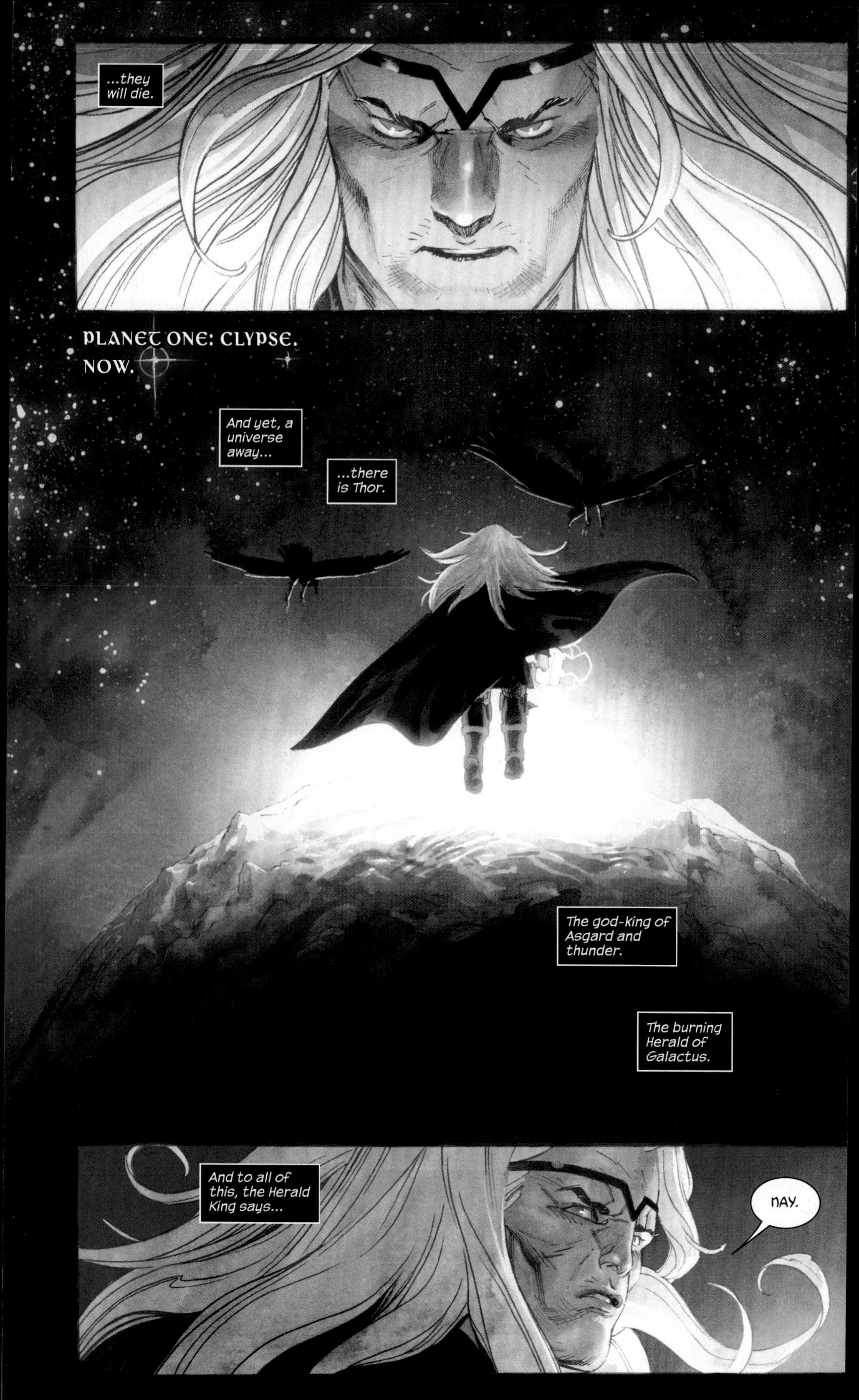
...they will die.
PLANET ONE: CLYPSE.
NOW.
And yet, a universe away...
...there is Thor.
The god-king of Asgard and thunder.
The burning Herald of Galactus.
And to all of this, the Herald King says...
NAY.

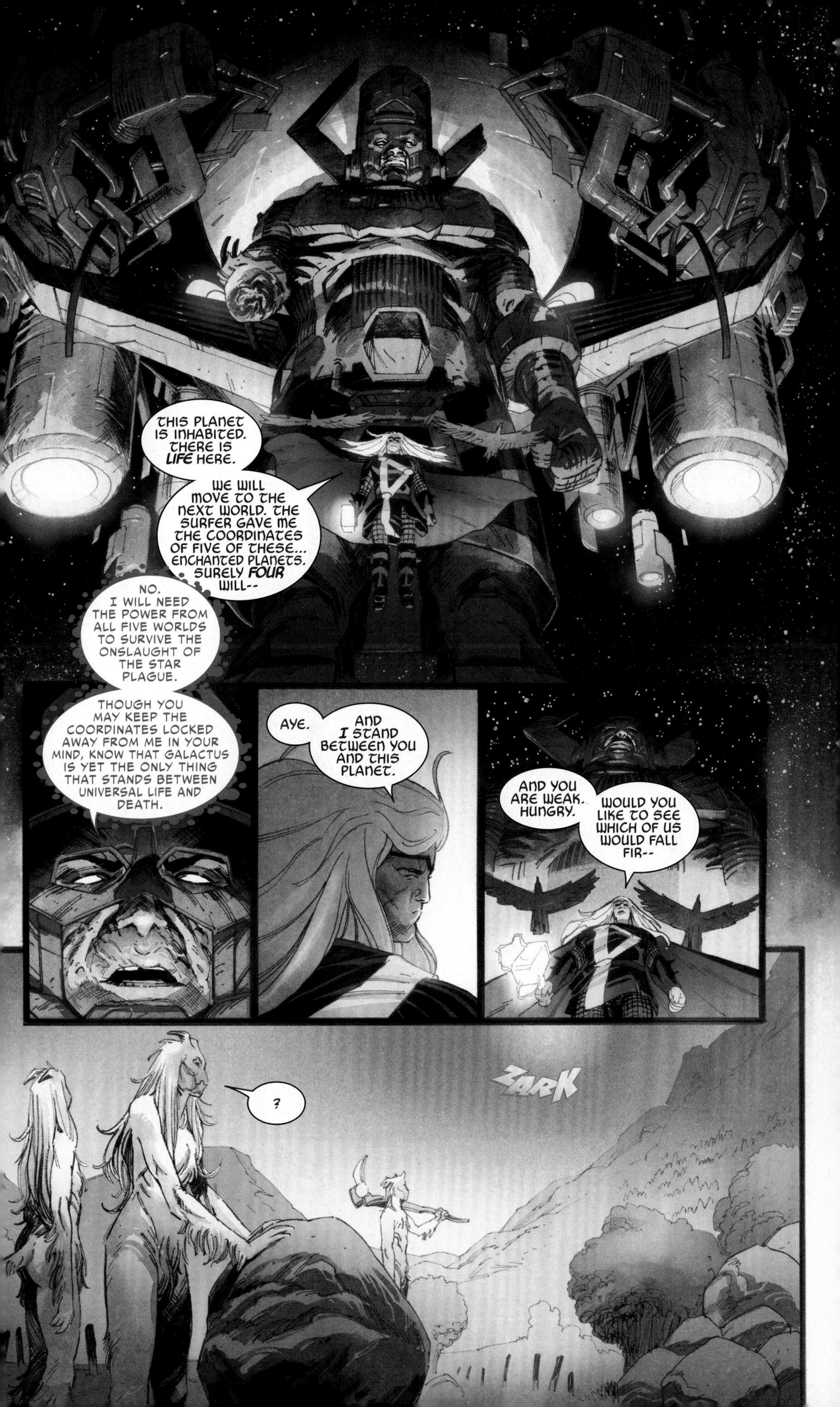

THIS PLANET IS INHABITED. THERE IS LIFE HERE.
WE WILL MOVE TO THE NEXT WORLD. THE SURFER GAVE ME THE COORDINATES OF FIVE OF THESE... ENCHANTED PLANETS. SURELY FOUR WILL--
NO. I WILL NEED THE POWER FROM ALL FIVE WORLDS TO SURVIVE THE ONSLAUGHT OF THE STAR PLAGUE.
THOUGH YOU MAY KEEP THE COORDINATES LOCKED AWAY FROM ME IN YOUR MIND, KNOW THAT GALACTUS IS YET THE ONLY THING THAT STANDS BETWEEN UNIVERSAL LIFE AND DEATH.
AYE.
AND I STAND BETWEEN YOU AND THIS PLANET.
AND YOU ARE WEAK. HUNGRY.
WOULD YOU LIKE TO SEE WHICH OF US WOULD FALL FIR--
ZARK
?

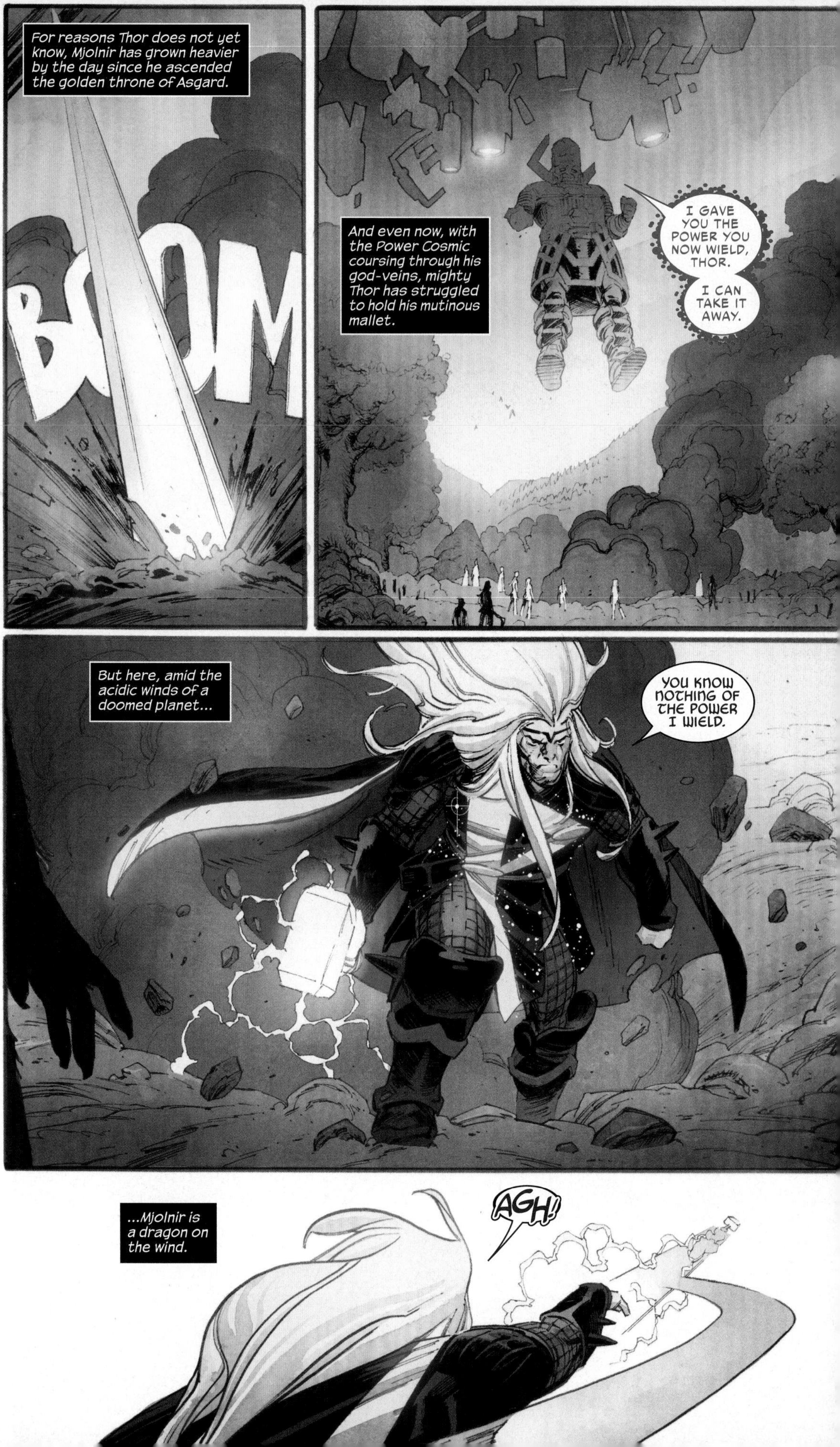
For reasons Thor does not yet know, Mjolnir has grown heavier by the day since he ascended the golden throne of Asgard.
BOOM
And even now, with the Power Cosmic coursing through his god-veins, mighty Thor has struggled to hold his mutinous mallet.
I GAVE YOU THE POWER YOU NOW WIELD, THOR.
I CAN TAKE IT AWAY.
But here, amid the acidic winds of a doomed planet...
YOU KNOW NOTHING OF THE POWER I WIELD.
...Mjolnir is a dragon on the wind.
AGH!

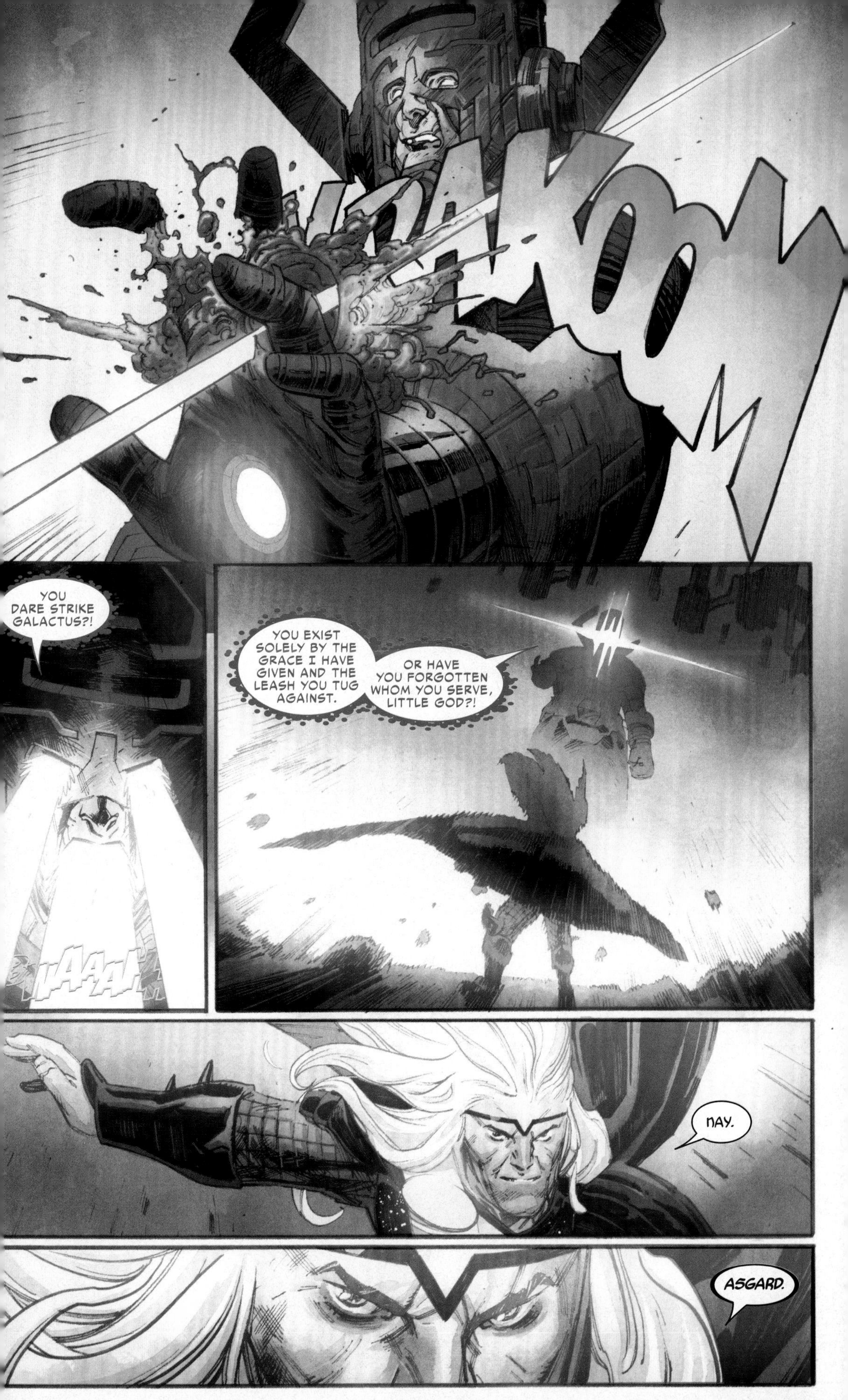

YOU DARE STRIKE GALACTUS?!
YOU EXIST SOLELY BY THE GRACE I HAVE GIVEN AND THE LEASH YOU TUG AGAINST.
OR HAVE YOU FORGOTTEN WHOM YOU SERVE, LITTLE GOD?!
NAY.
ASGARD.

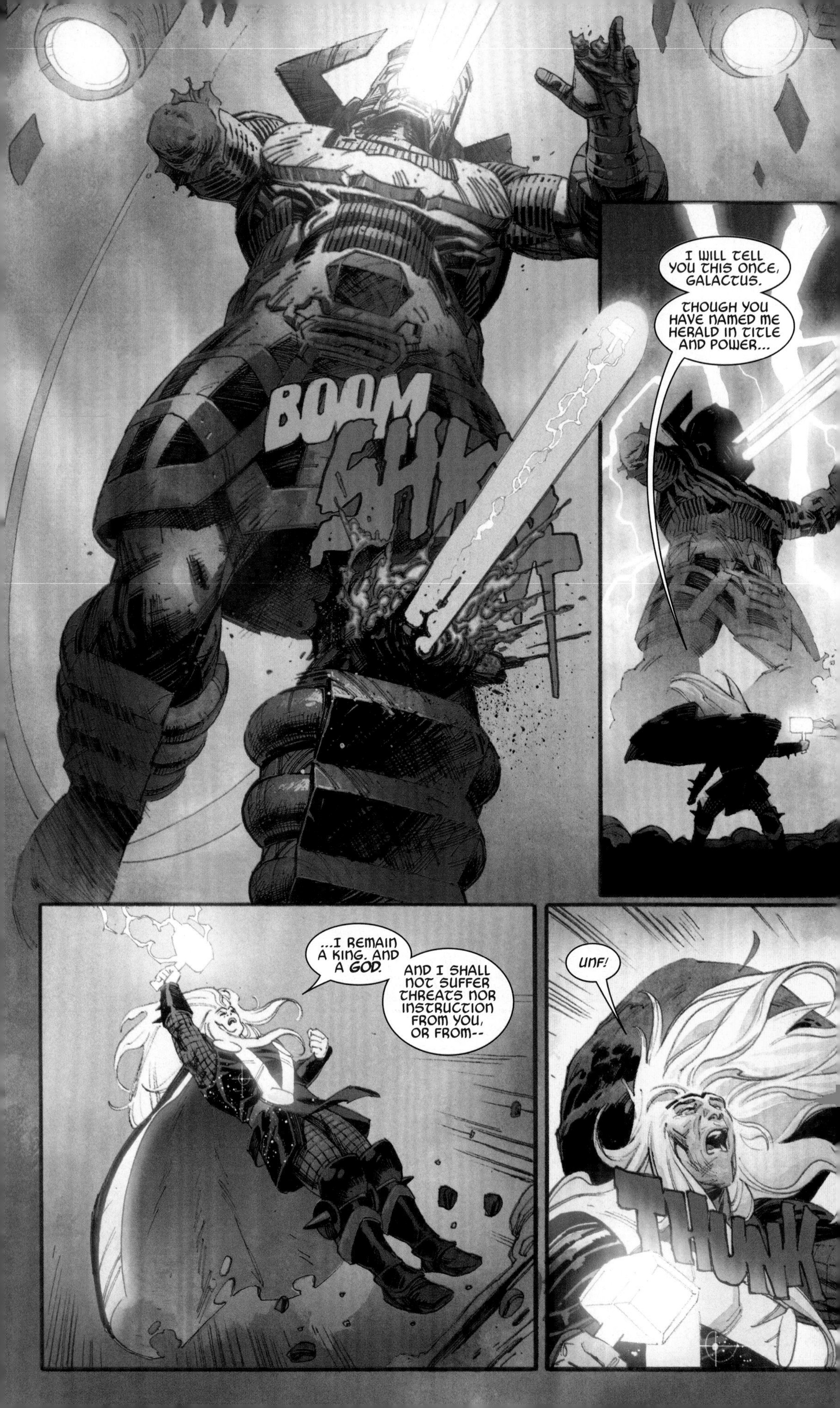

BOOM
I WILL TELL YOU THIS ONCE, GALACTUS.
THOUGH YOU HAVE NAMED ME HERALD IN TITLE AND POWER...
...I REMAIN A KING. AND A GOD.
AND I SHALL NOT SUFFER THREATS NOR INSTRUCTION FROM YOU, OR FROM--
UNF!
THUNK

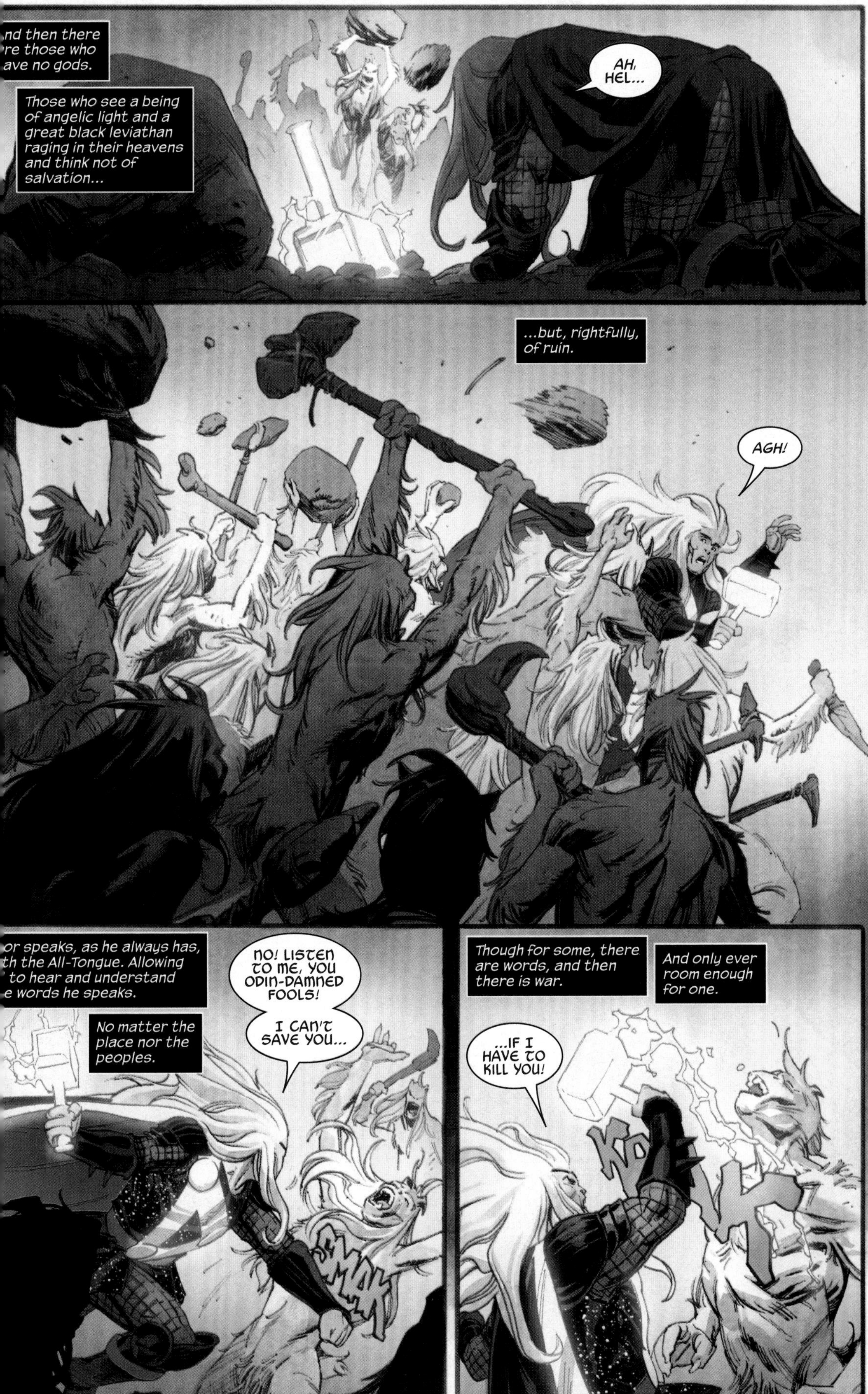

nd then there
re those who
ave no gods.
Those who see a being of angelic light and a great black leviathan raging in their heavens and think not of salvation...
AH, HEL...
...but, rightfully, of ruin.
AGH!
or speaks, as he always has, th the All-Tongue. Allowing to hear and understand e words he speaks.
No matter the place nor the peoples.
NO! LISTEN TO ME, YOU ODIN-DAMNED FOOLS!
I CAN'T SAVE YOU...
SMAK
Though for some, there are words, and then there is war.
And only ever room enough for one.
...IF I HAVE TO KILL YOU!

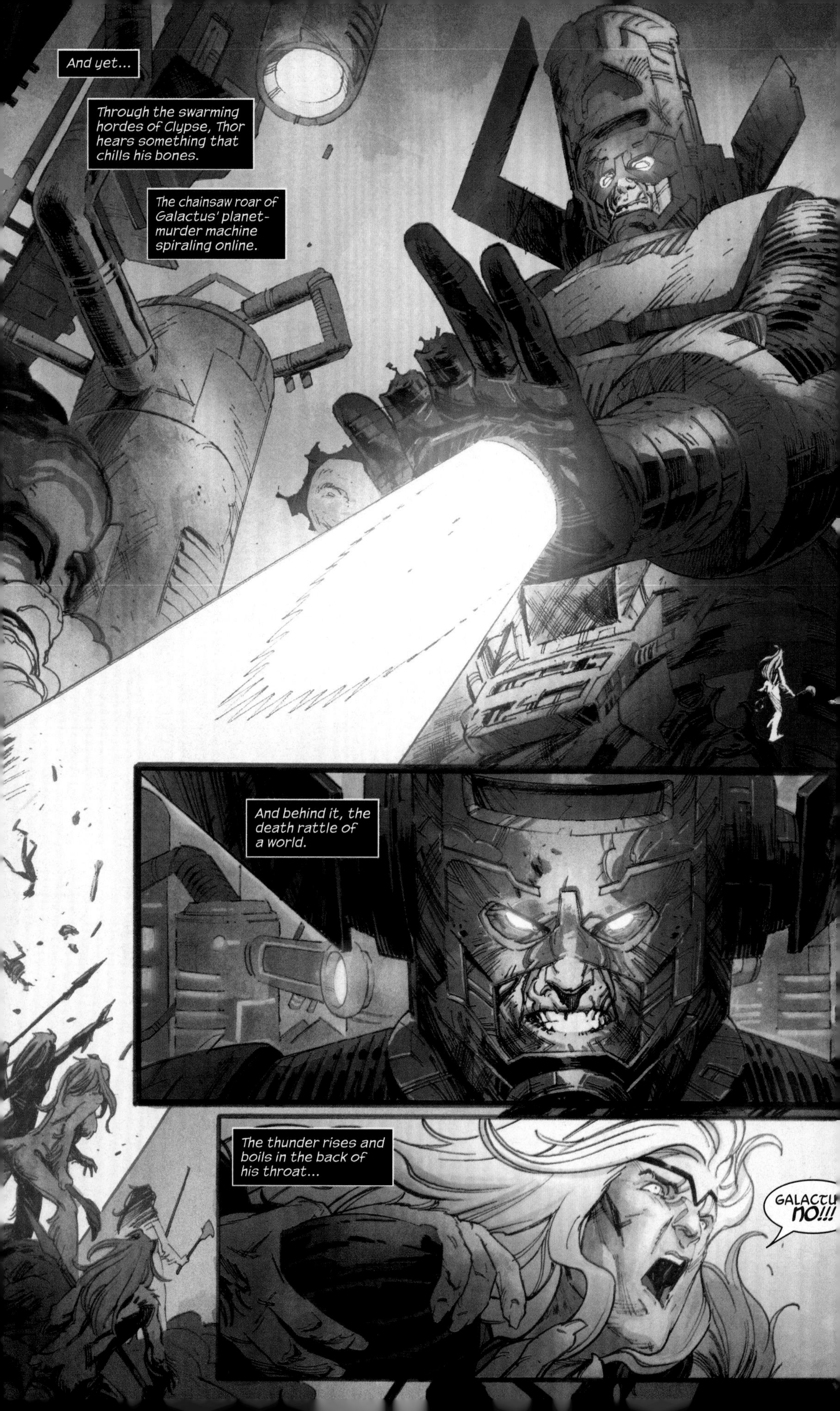
And yet...
Through the swarming hordes of Clypse, Thor hears something that chills his bones.
The chainsaw roar of Galactus' planet-murder machine spiraling online.
And behind it, the death rattle of a world.
The thunder rises and boils in the back of his throat...
GALACTU NO!!!

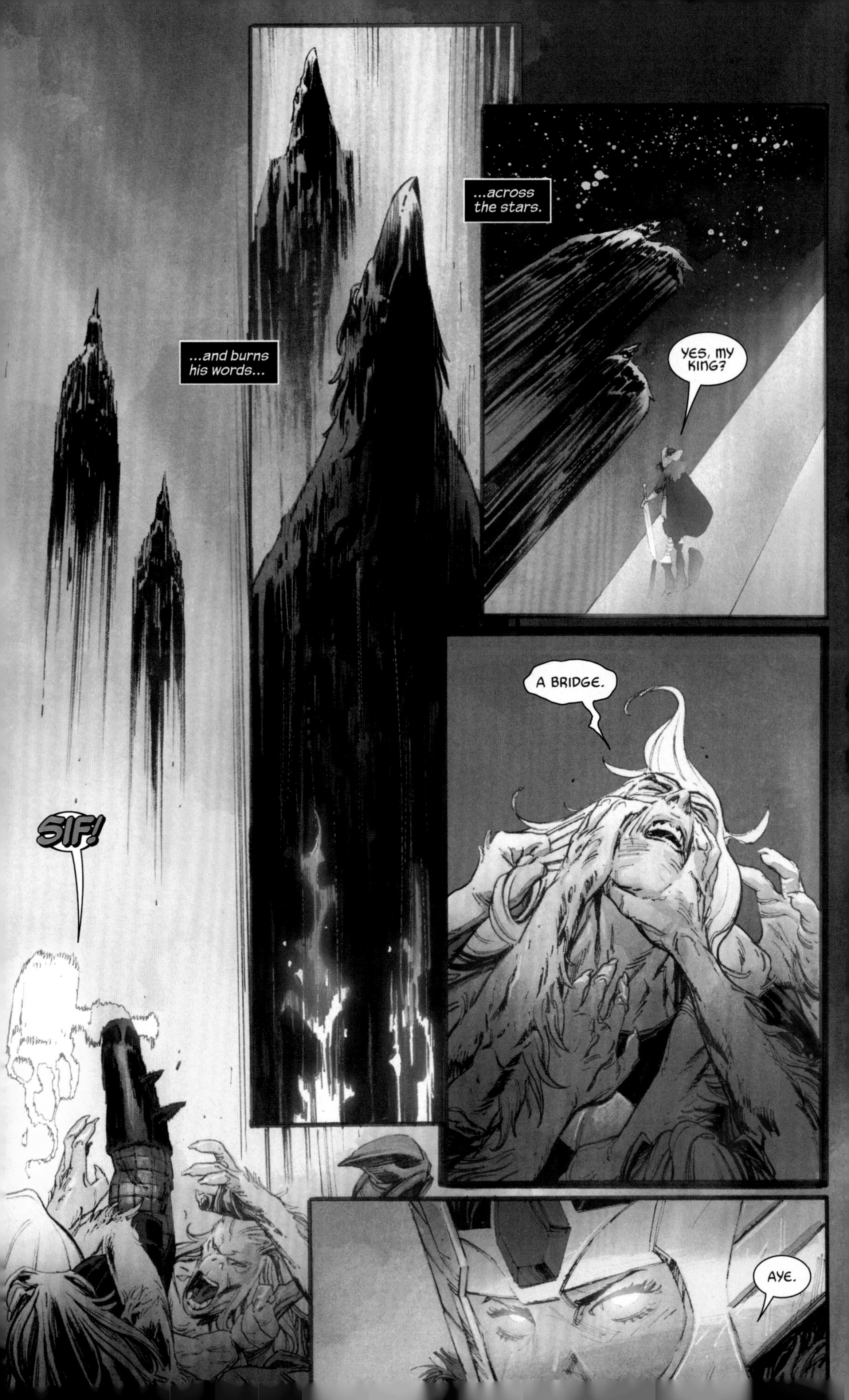
...and burns
his words...
...across
the stars.
YES, MY
KING?
SIF!
A BRIDGE.
AYE.

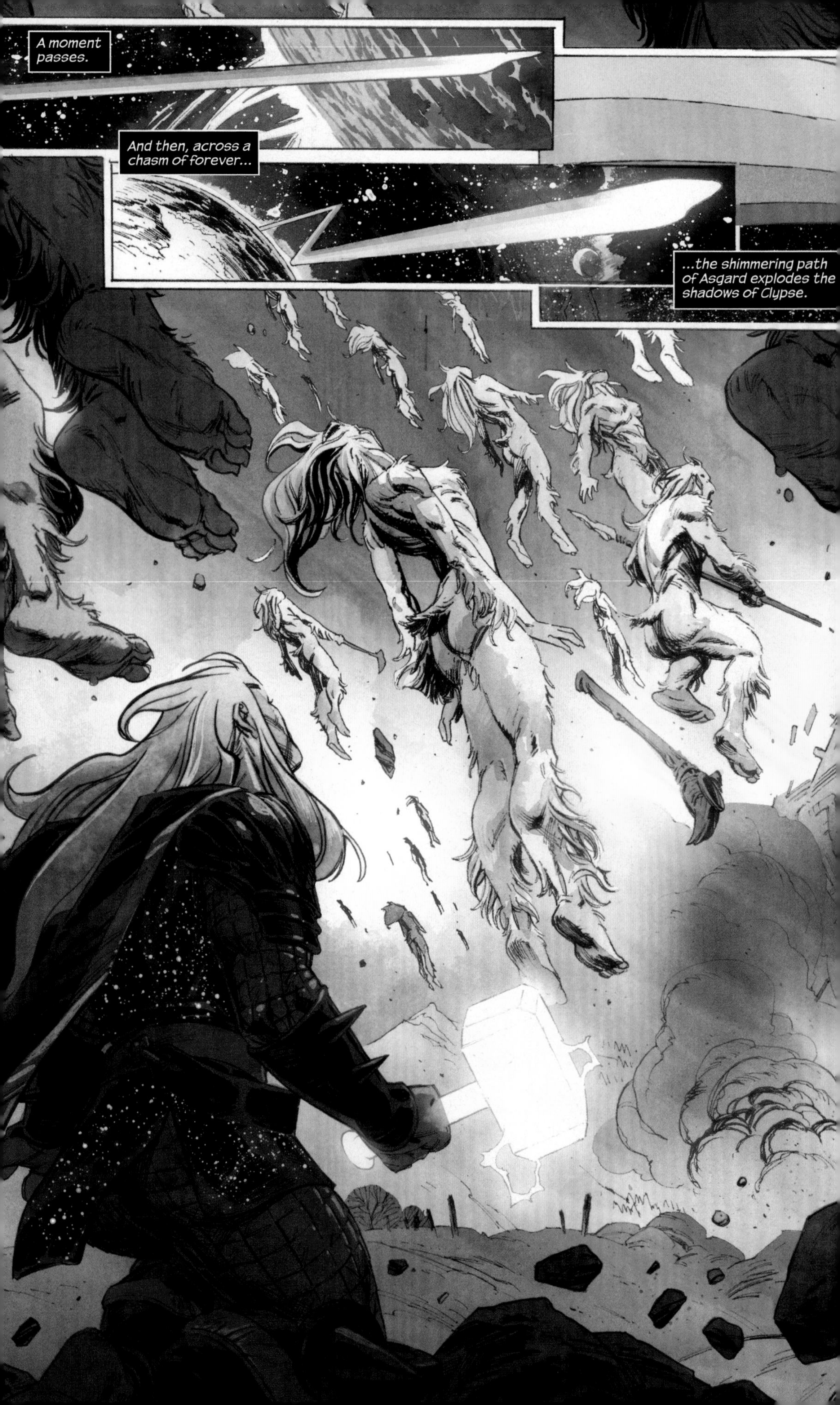
A moment passes.
And then, across a chasm of forever...
...the shimmering path of Asgard explodes the shadows of Clypse.

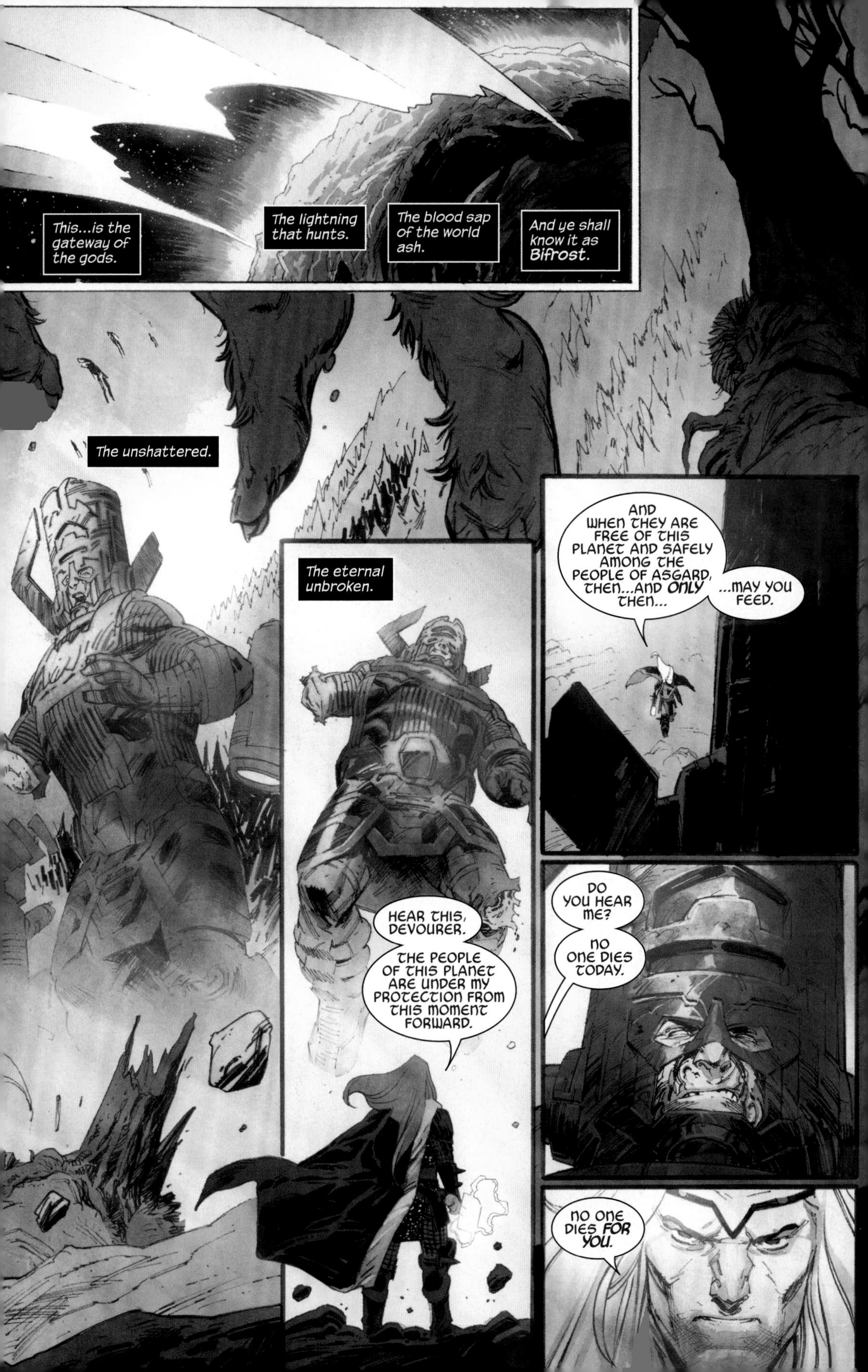
This...is the gateway of the gods.
The lightning that hunts.
The blood sap of the world ash.
And ye shall know it as Bifrost.
The unshattered.
The eternal unbroken.
HEAR THIS, DEVOURER.
THE PEOPLE OF THIS PLANET ARE UNDER MY PROTECTION FROM THIS MOMENT FORWARD.
AND WHEN THEY ARE FREE OF THIS PLANET AND SAFELY AMONG THE PEOPLE OF ASGARD, THEN...AND ONLY THEN...
...MAY YOU FEED.
DO YOU HEAR ME?
NO ONE DIES TODAY.
NO ONE DIES FOR YOU.

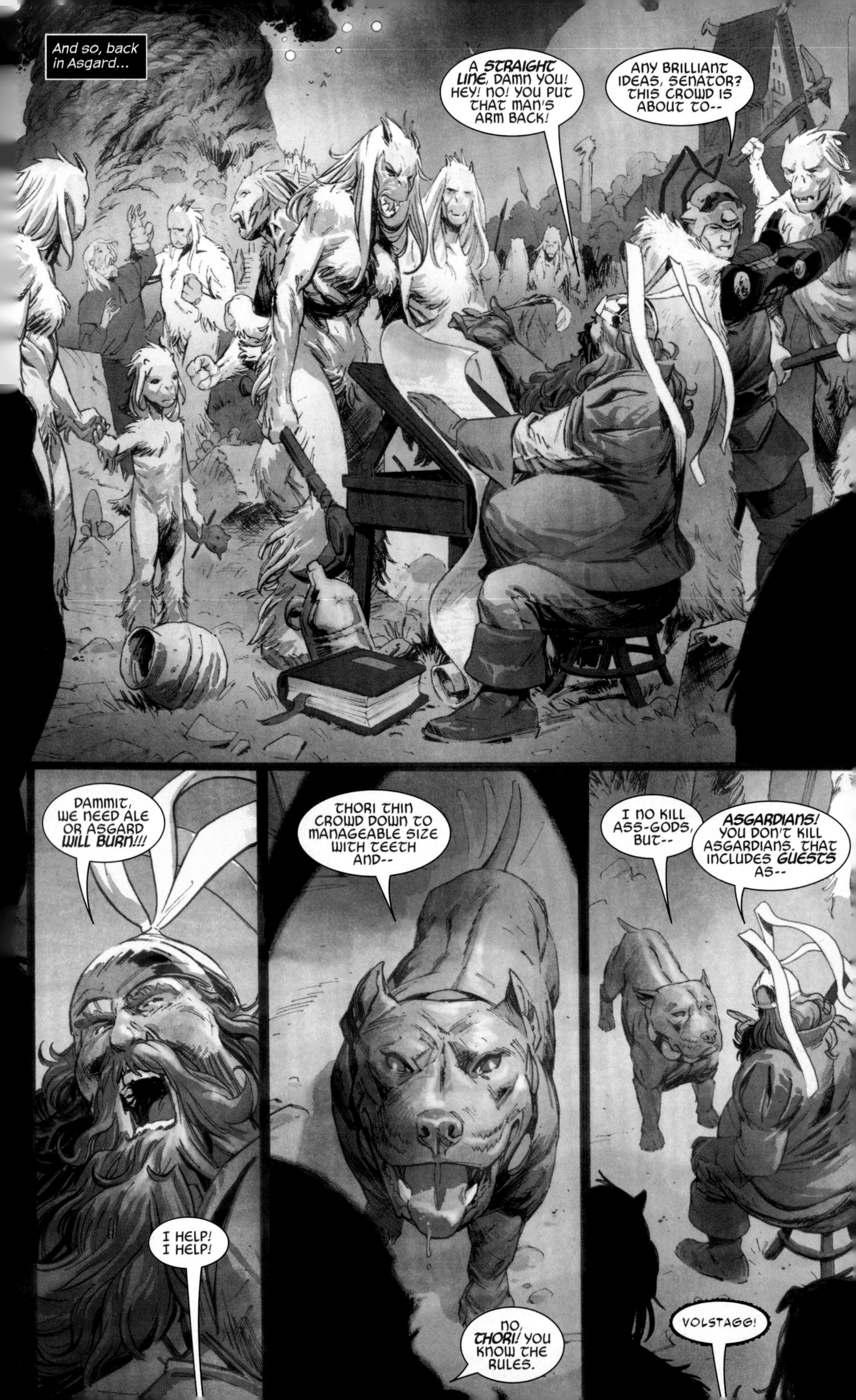
And so, back in Asgard...
A STRAIGHT LINE, DAMN YOU! HEY! NO! YOU PUT THAT MAN'S ARM BACK!
ANY BRILLIANT IDEAS, SENATOR? THIS CROWD IS ABOUT TO--
DAMMIT, WE NEED ALE OR ASGARD WILL BURN!!!
I HELP! I HELP!
THORI THIN CROWD DOWN TO MANAGEABLE SIZE WITH TEETH AND--
NO, THORI! YOU KNOW THE RULES.
I NO KILL ASS-GODS, BUT--
ASGARDIANS! YOU DON'T KILL ASGARDIANS. THAT INCLUDES GUESTS AS--
VOLSTAGG!

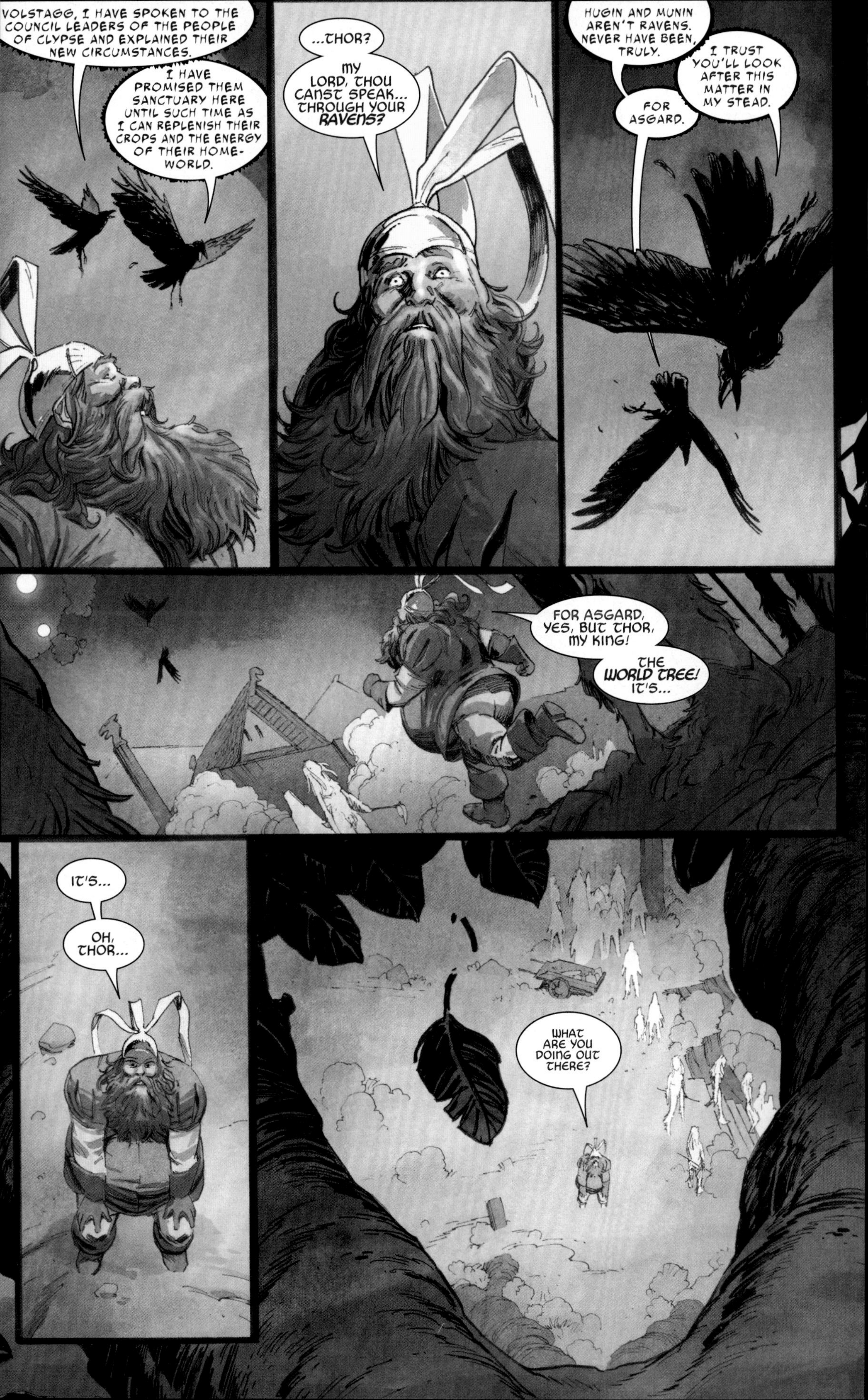
VOLSTAGG, I HAVE SPOKEN TO THE COUNCIL LEADERS OF THE PEOPLE OF CLYPSE AND EXPLAINED THEIR NEW CIRCUMSTANCES.
I HAVE PROMISED THEM SANCTUARY HERE UNTIL SUCH TIME AS I CAN REPLENISH THEIR CROPS AND THE ENERGY OF THEIR HOME-WORLD.
...THOR?
MY LORD, THOU CANST SPEAK... THROUGH YOUR RAVENS?
HUGIN AND MUNIN AREN'T RAVENS. NEVER HAVE BEEN, TRULY.
I TRUST YOU'LL LOOK AFTER THIS MATTER IN MY STEAD.
FOR ASGARD.
FOR ASGARD, YES, BUT THOR, MY KING!
THE WORLD TREE! IT'S...
IT'S...
OH, THOR...
WHAT ARE YOU DOING OUT THERE?

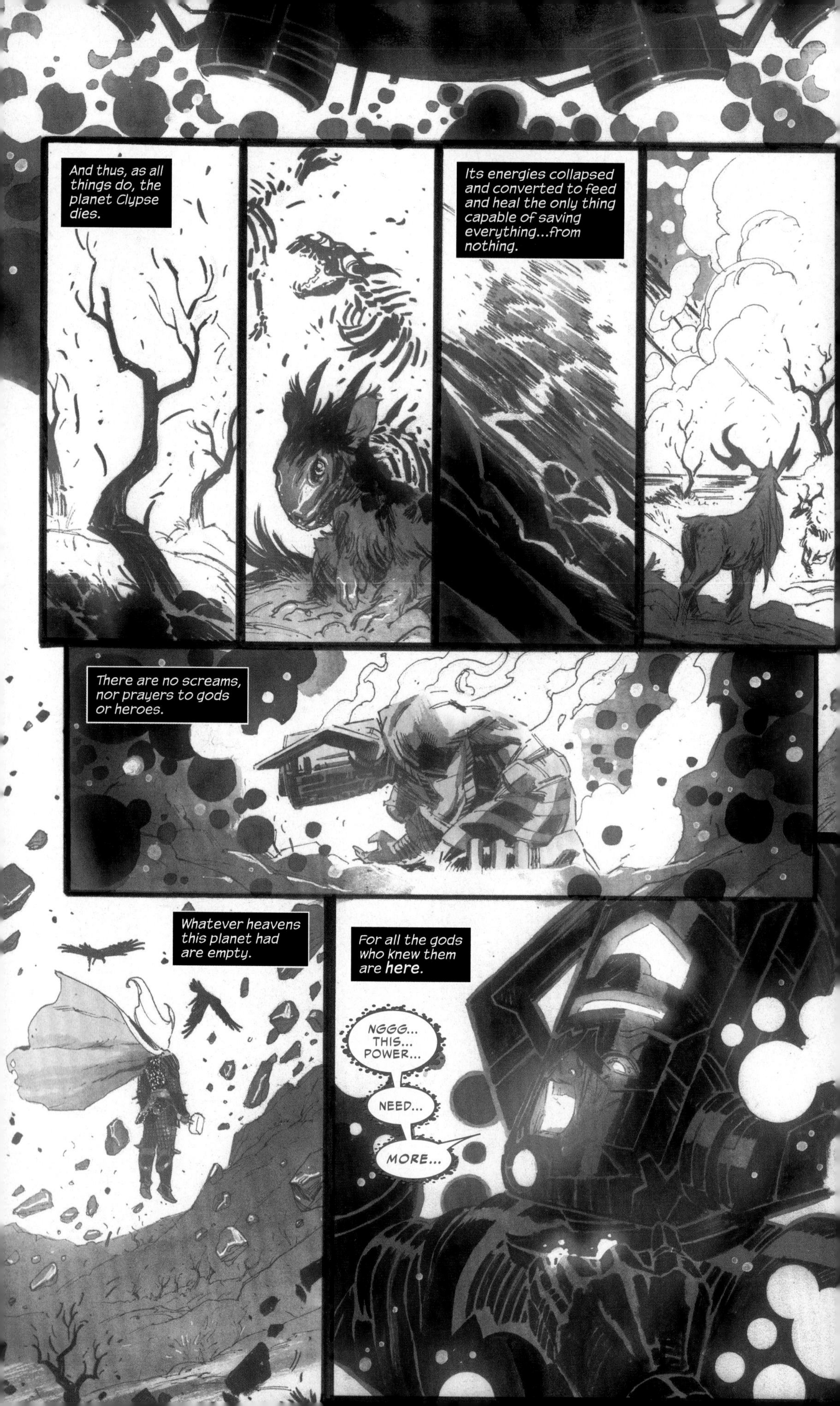
And thus, as all things do, the planet Clypse dies.
Its energies collapsed and converted to feed and heal the only thing capable of saving everything...from nothing.
There are no screams, nor prayers to gods or heroes.
Whatever heavens this planet had are empty.
For all the gods who knew them are here.
NGGG... THIS... POWER...
NEED...
MORE...

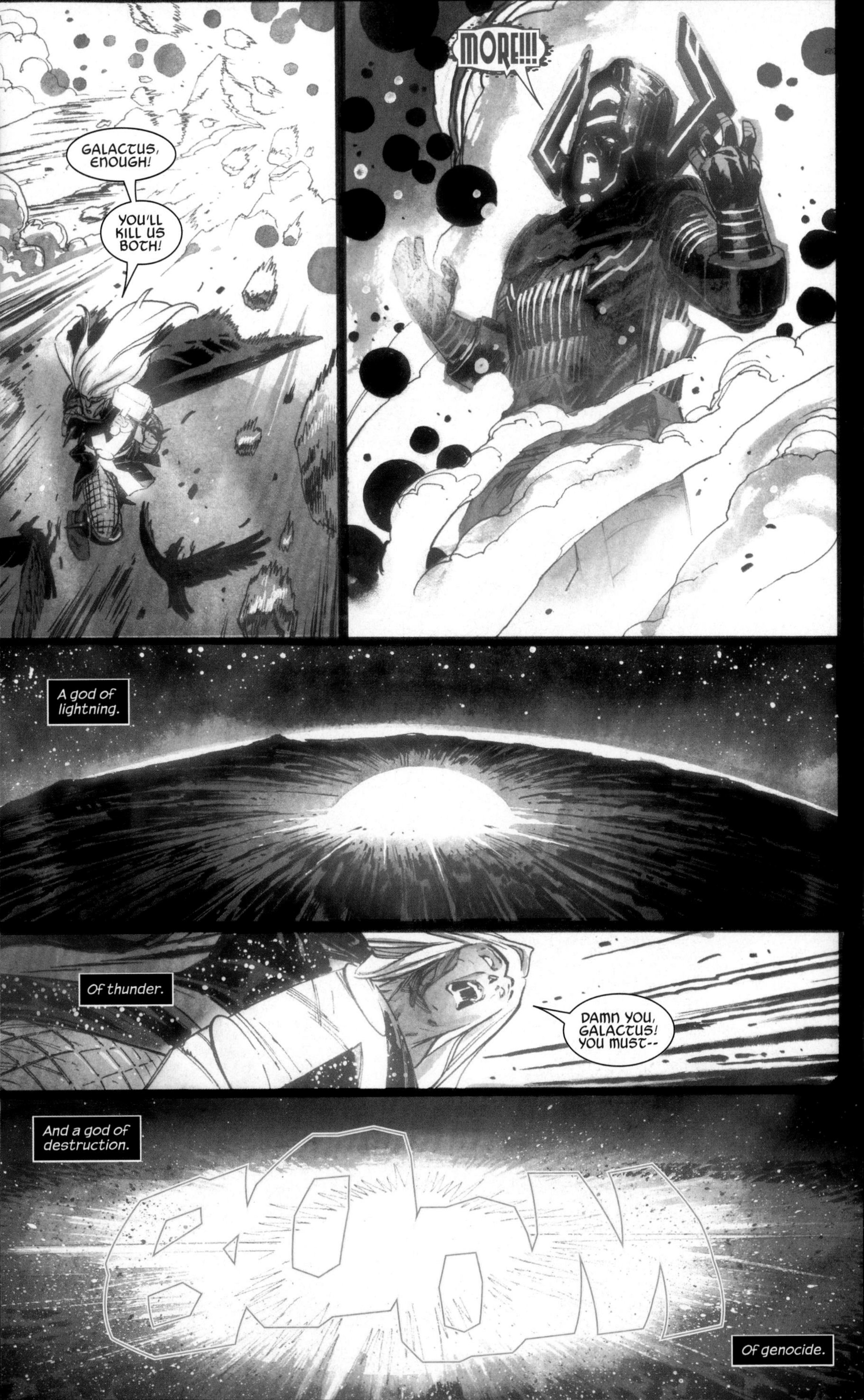
GALACTUS, ENOUGH!
YOU'LL KILL US BOTH!
MORE!!!
A god of lightning.
Of thunder.
DAMN YOU, GALACTUS! YOU MUST--
And a god of destruction.
BOOM
Of genocide.

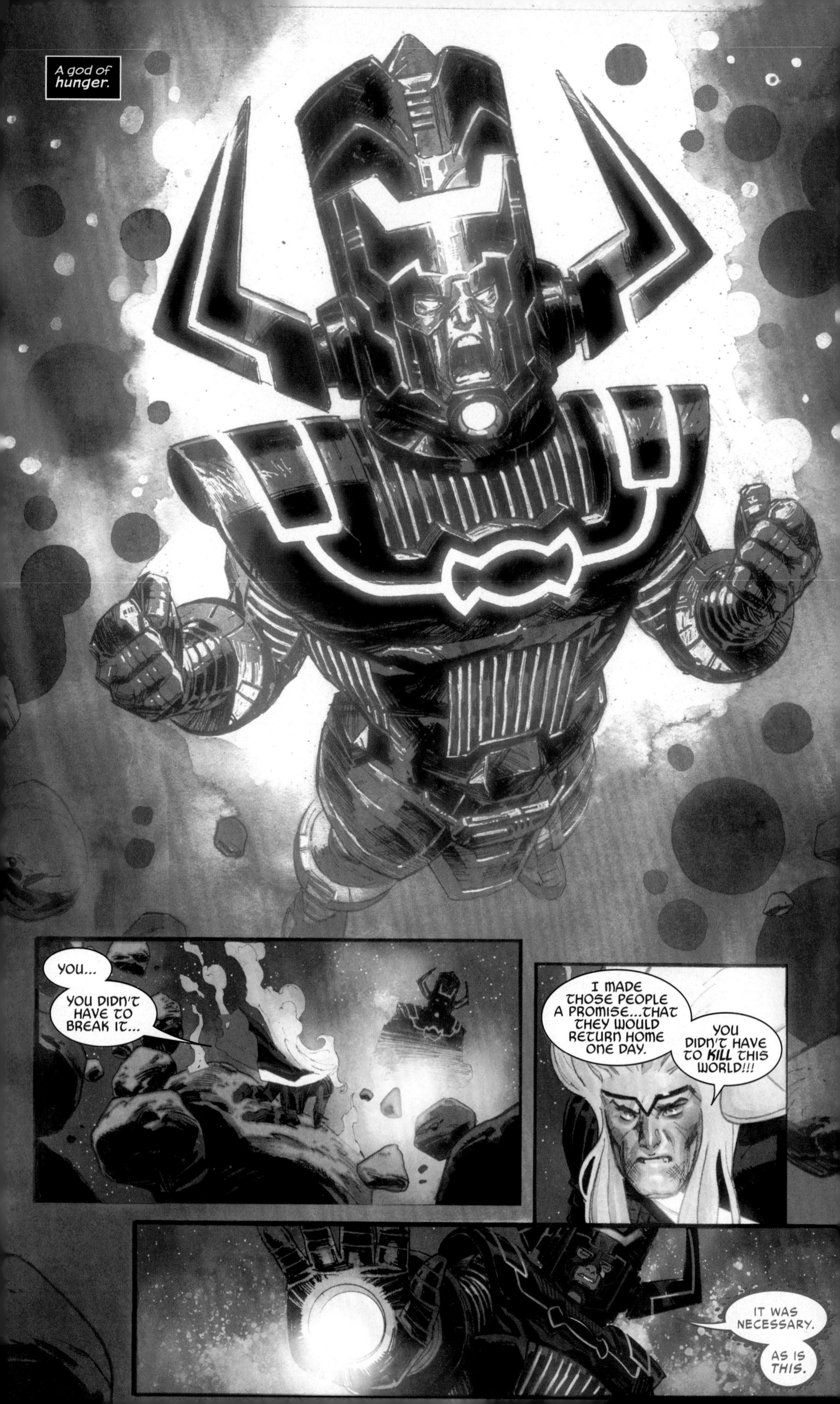

A god of hunger.
YOU...
YOU DIDN'T HAVE TO BREAK IT...
I MADE THOSE PEOPLE A PROMISE...THAT THEY WOULD RETURN HOME ONE DAY.
YOU DIDN'T HAVE TO KILL THIS WORLD!!!
IT WAS NECESSARY.
AS IS THIS.

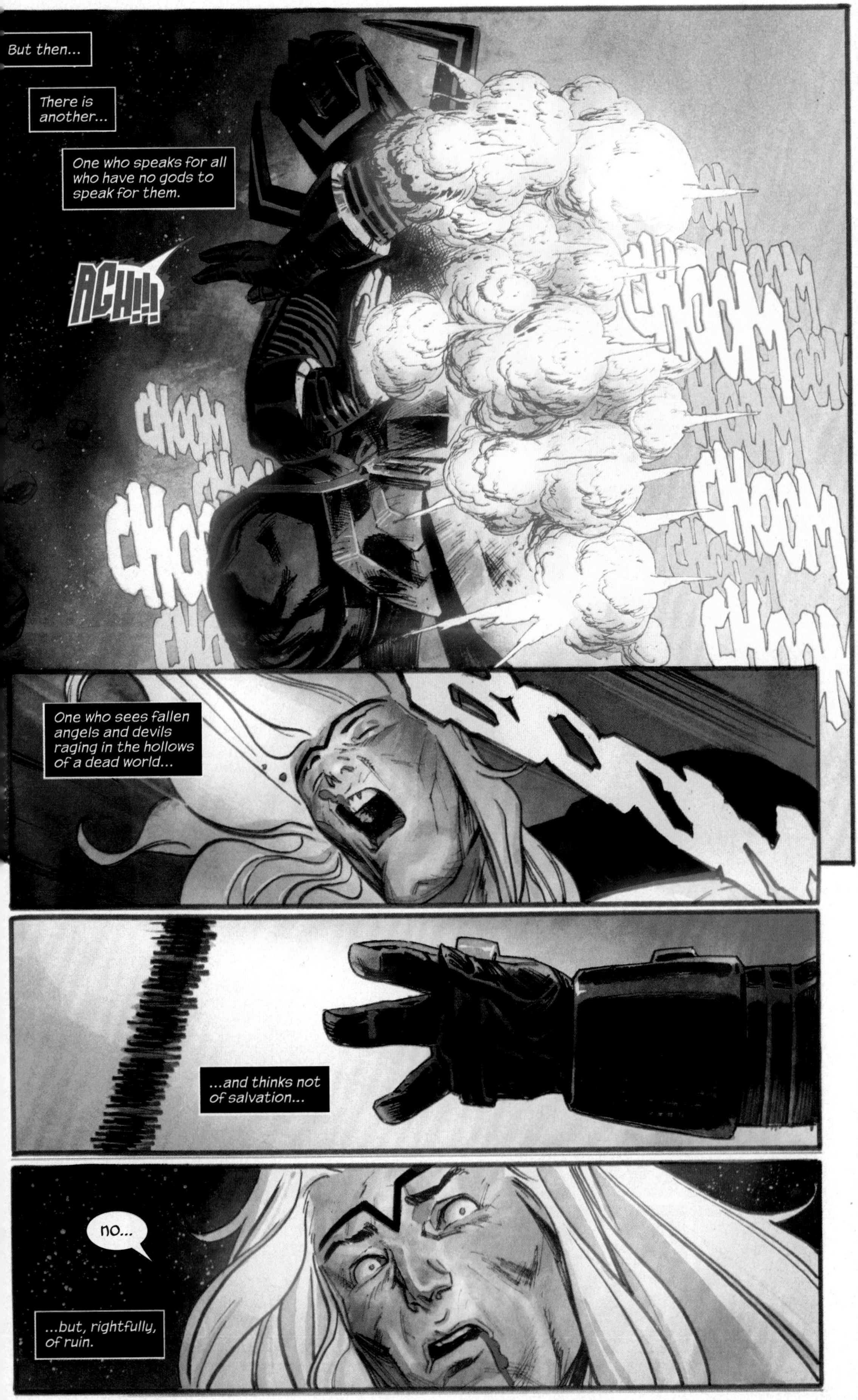

But then...
There is another...
One who speaks for all who have no gods to speak for them.
AGH!!!
CHOOM
CHOOM
CHOOM
CHOOM
One who sees fallen angels and devils raging in the hollows of a dead world...
...and thinks not of salvation...
no...
...but, rightfully, of ruin.

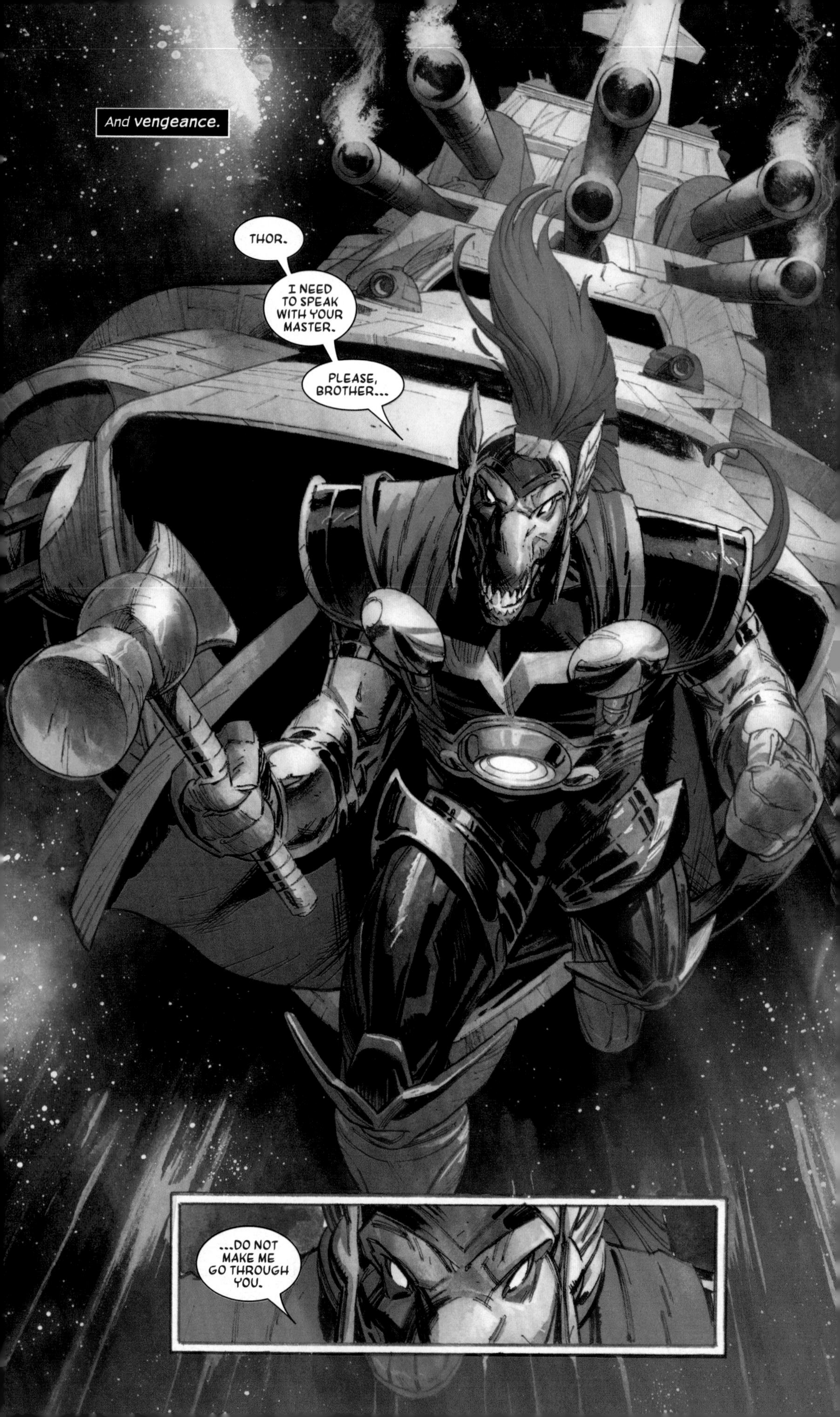
And vengeance.
THOR.
I NEED TO SPEAK WITH YOUR MASTER.
PLEASE, BROTHER...
...DO NOT MAKE ME GO THROUGH YOU.

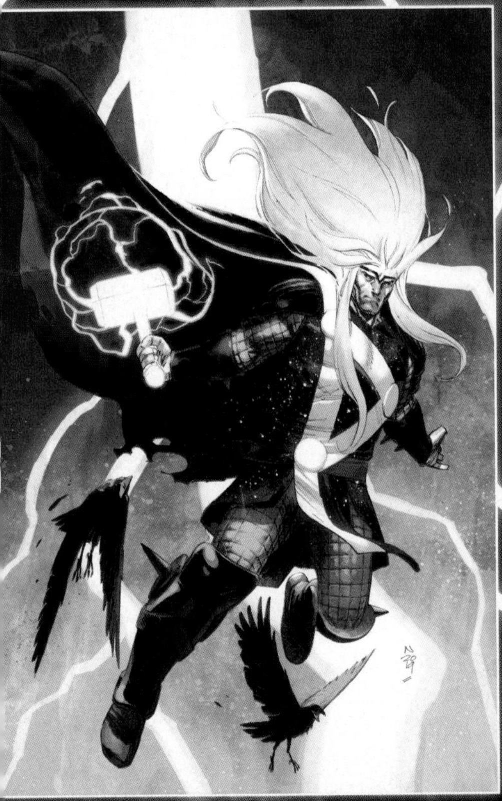

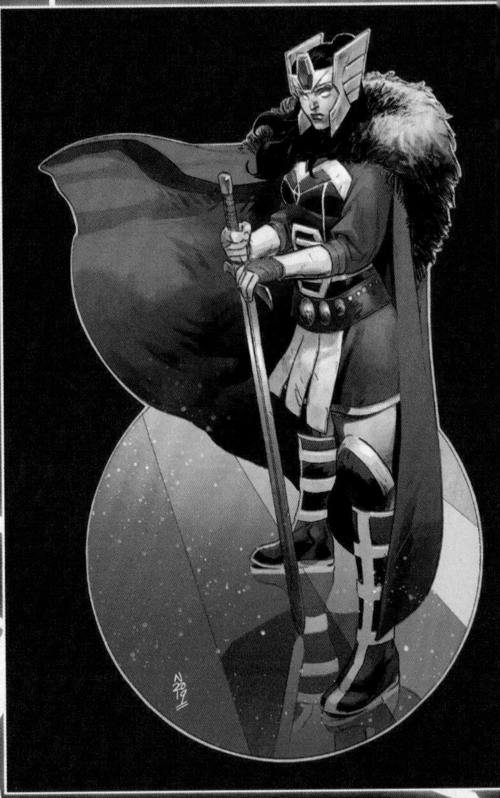

THOR 1 PARTY VARIANT BY
Nic Klein

THOR 1 SIF VARIANT BY
Nic Klein

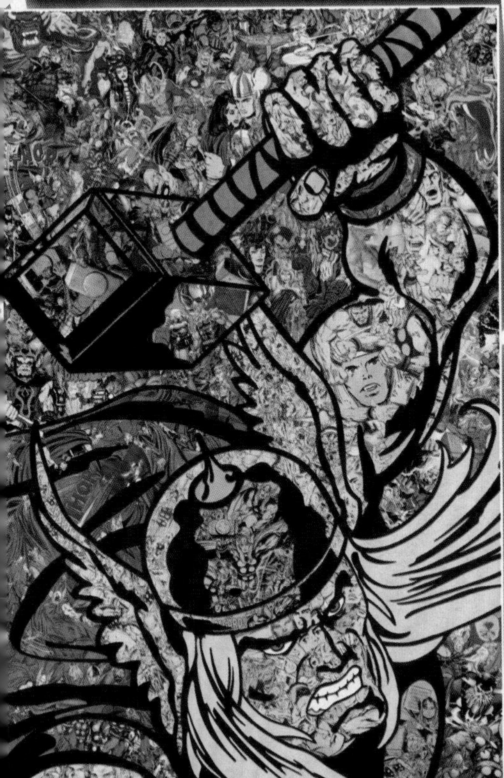

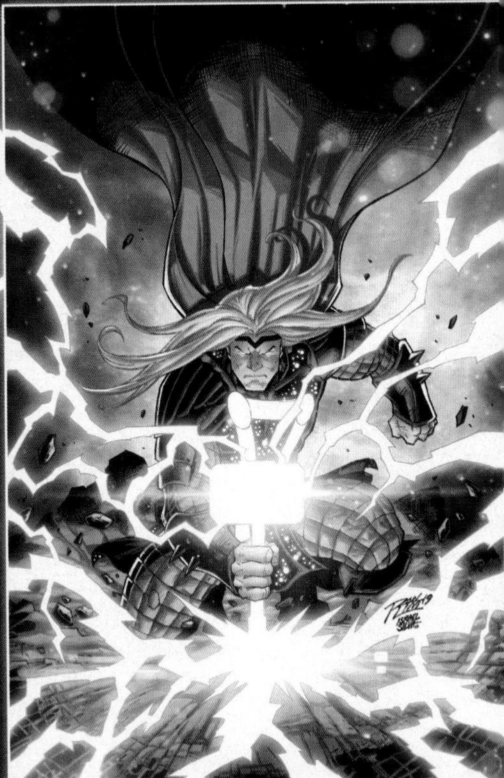

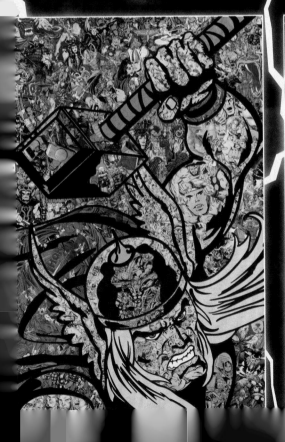

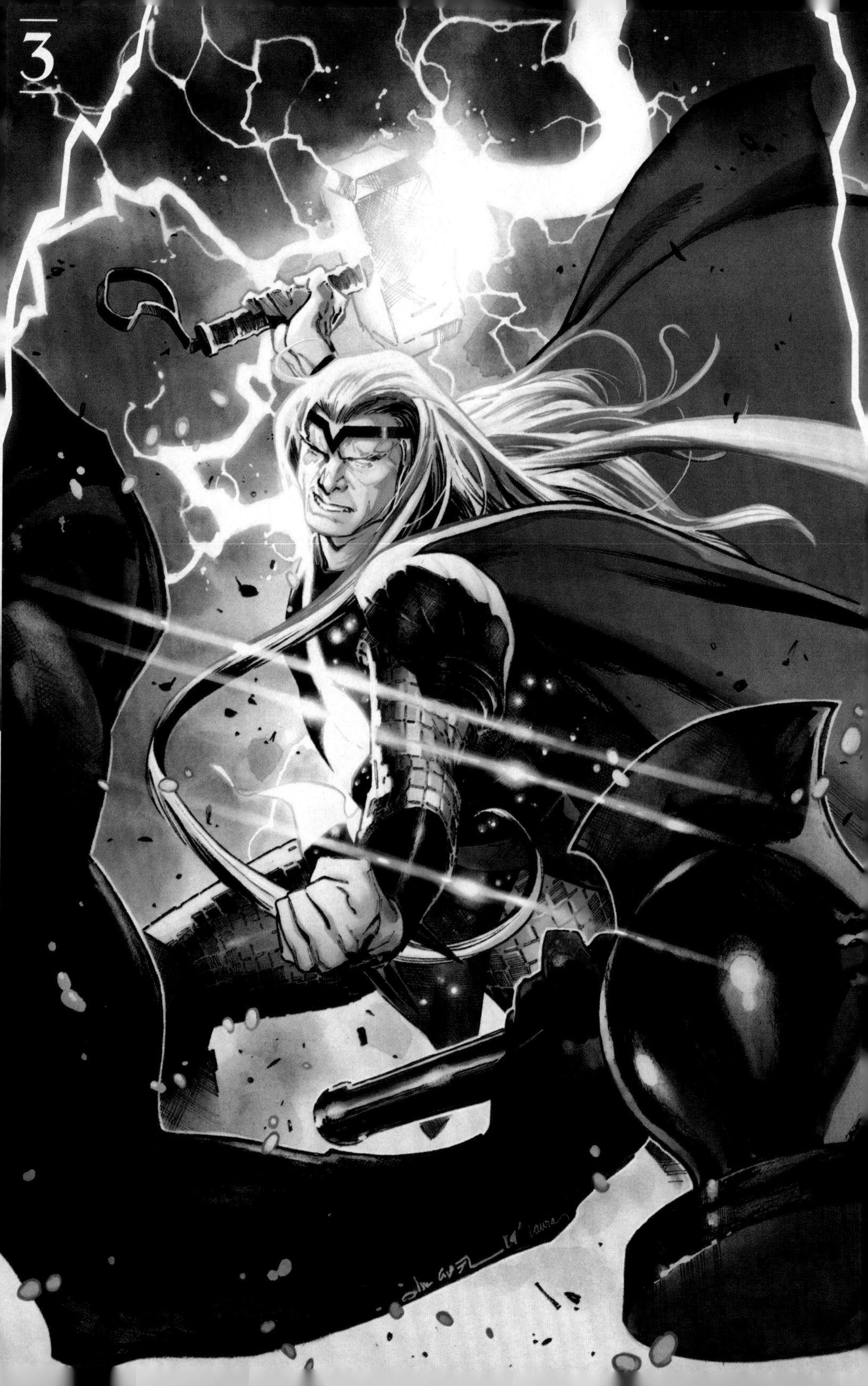
3

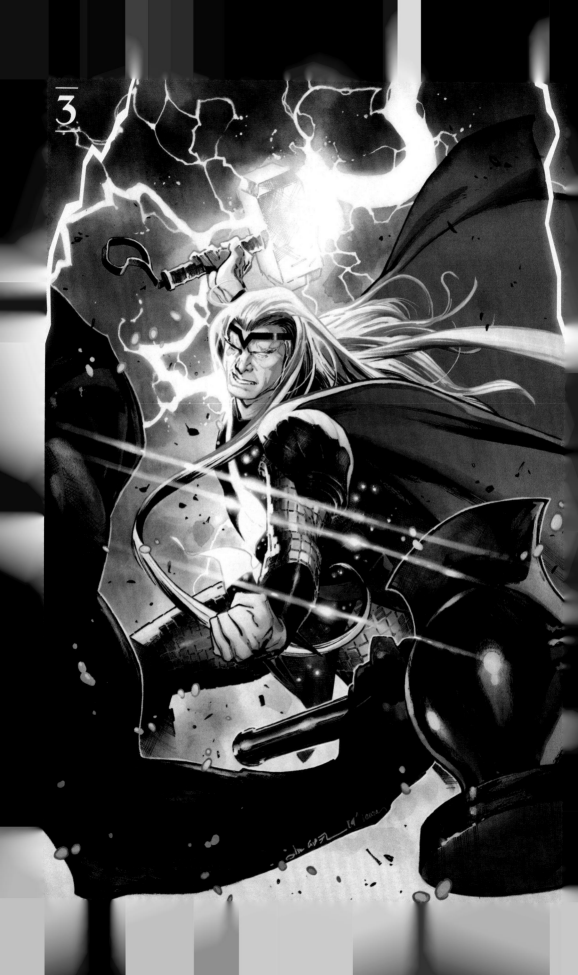

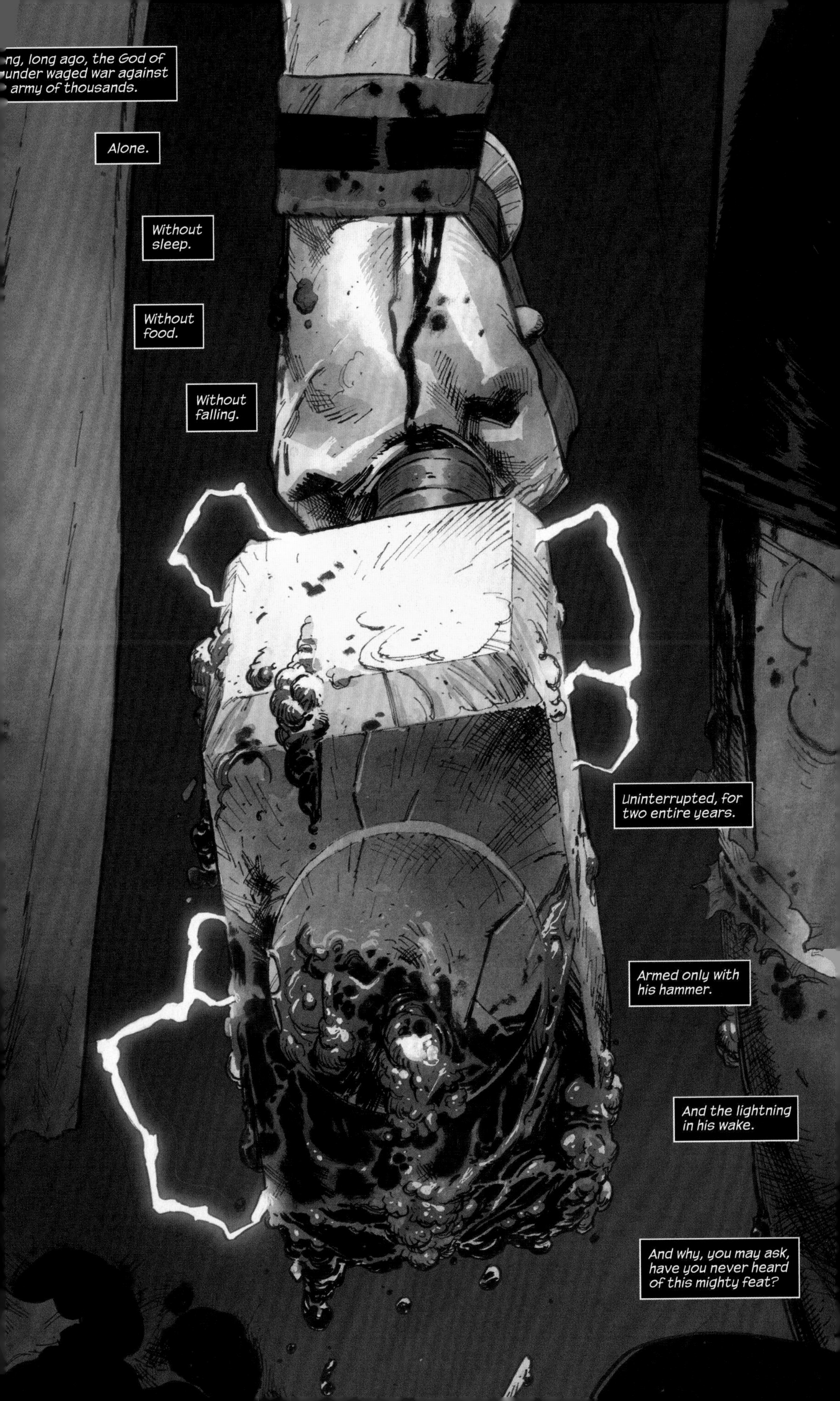
ng, long ago, the God of
under waged war against
army of thousands.
Alone.
Without sleep.
Without food.
Without falling.
Uninterrupted, for two entire years.
Armed only with his hammer.
And the lightning in his wake.
And why, you may ask, have you never heard of this mighty feat?

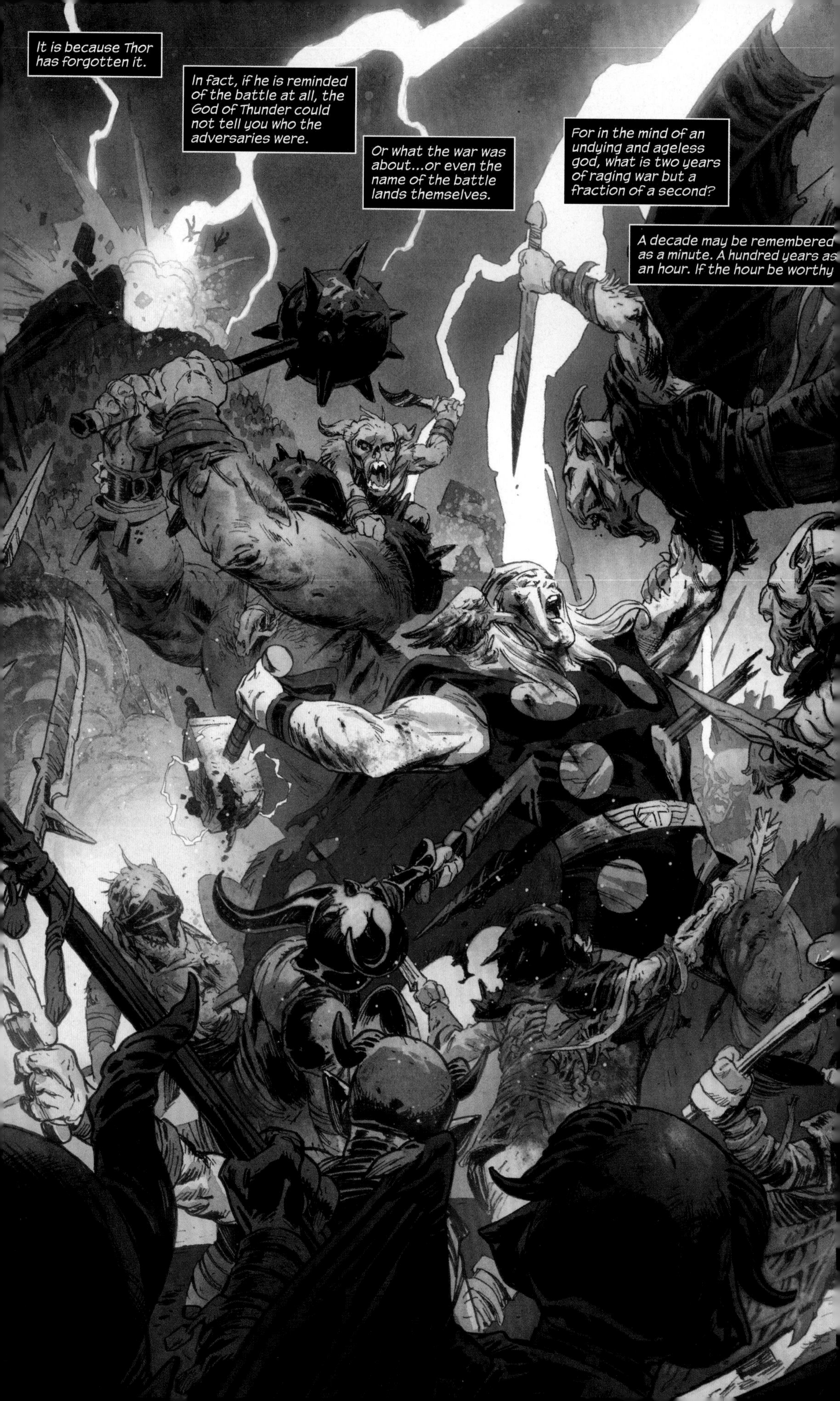
It is because Thor has forgotten it.
In fact, if he is reminded of the battle at all, the God of Thunder could not tell you who the adversaries were.
Or what the war was about...or even the name of the battle lands themselves.
For in the mind of an undying and ageless god, what is two years of raging war but a fraction of a second?
A decade may be remembered as a minute. A hundred years as an hour. If the hour be worthy

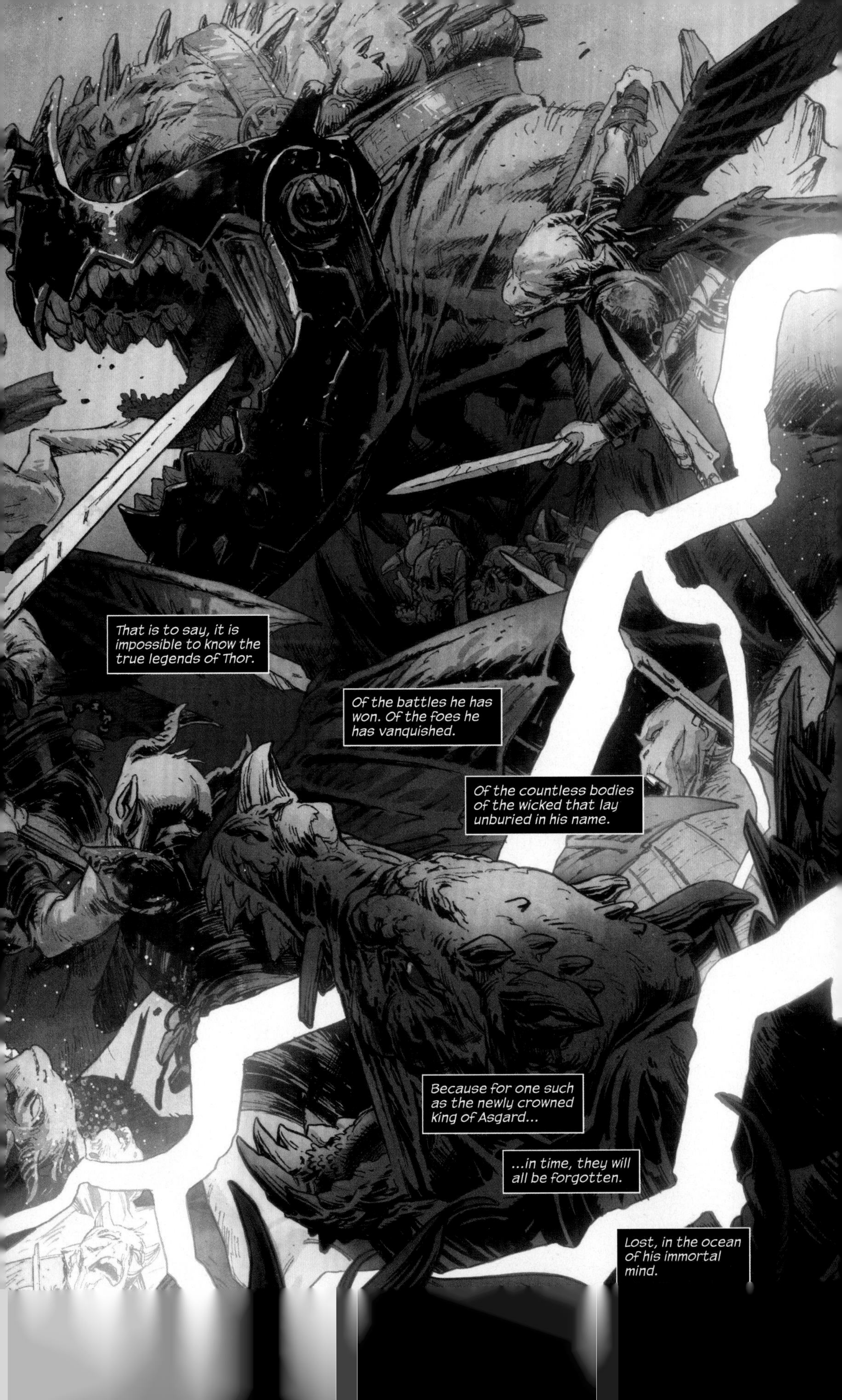
That is to say, it is impossible to know the true legends of Thor.
Of the battles he has won. Of the foes he has vanquished.
Of the countless bodies of the wicked that lay unburied in his name.
Because for one such as the newly crowned king of Asgard...
...in time, they will all be forgotten.
Lost, in the ocean of his immortal mind.

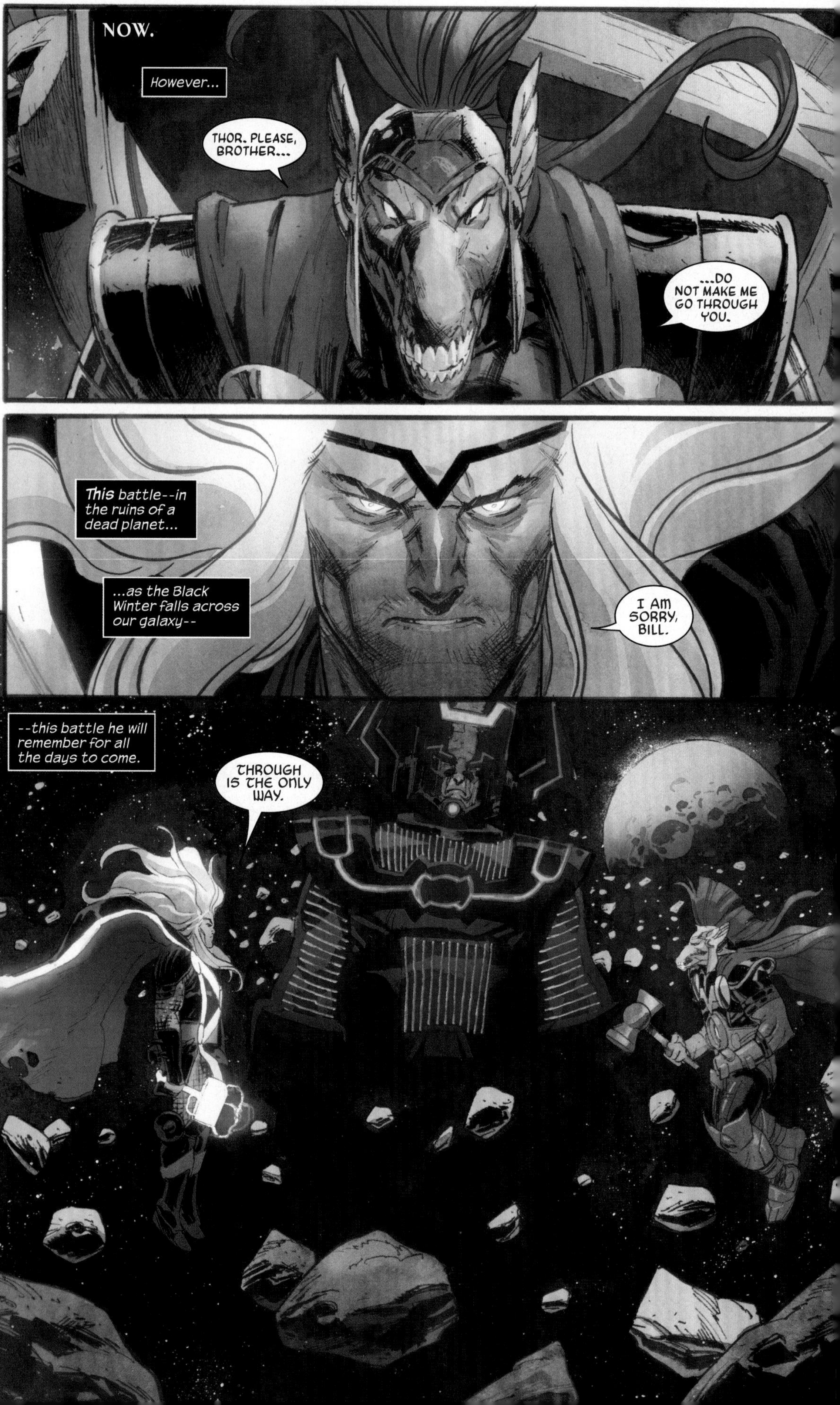

NOW.
However...
THOR. PLEASE, BROTHER...
...DO NOT MAKE ME GO THROUGH YOU.
This battle--in the ruins of a dead planet...
...as the Black Winter falls across our galaxy--
I AM SORRY, BILL.
--this battle he will remember for all the days to come.
THROUGH IS THE ONLY WAY.

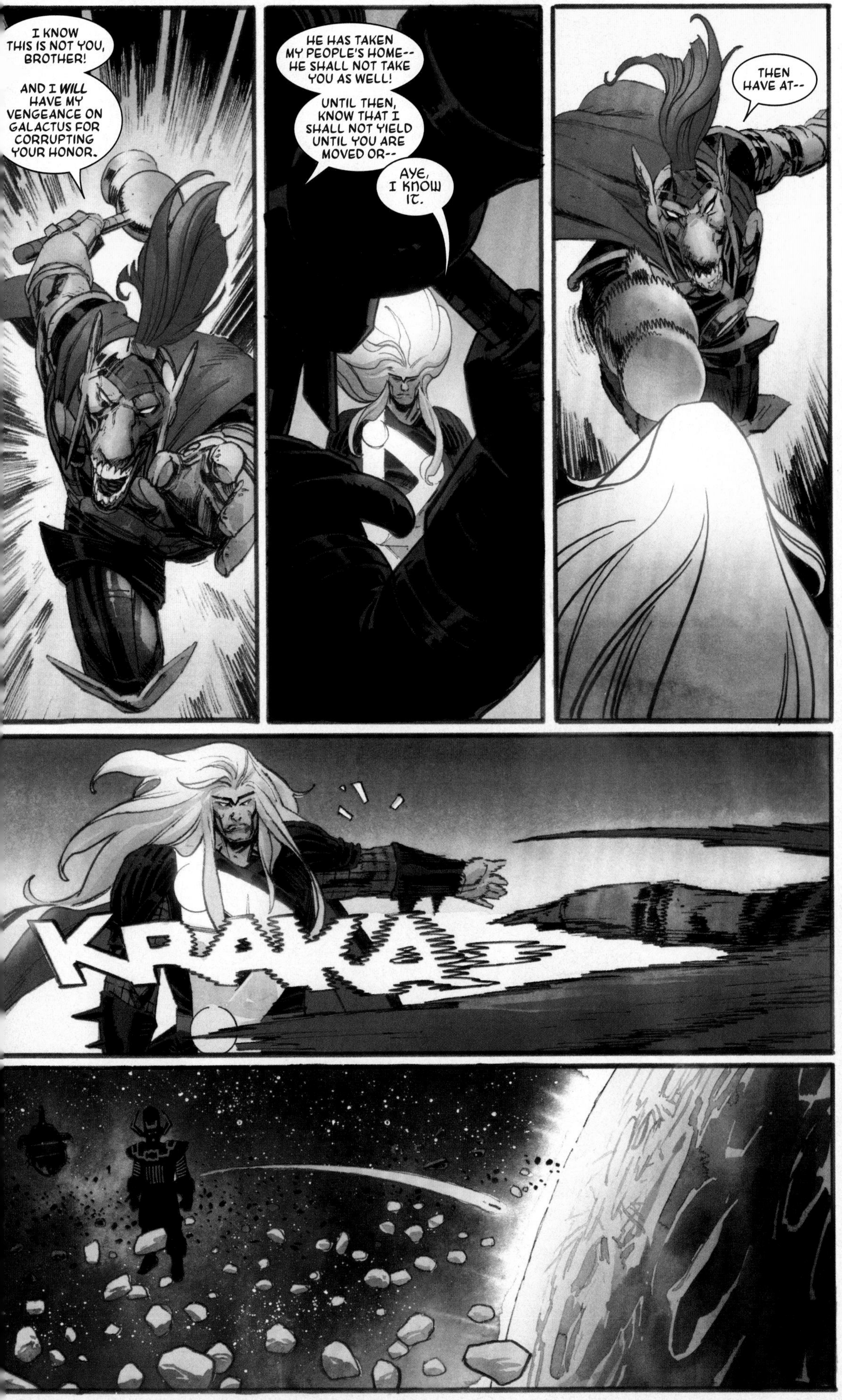
I KNOW THIS IS NOT YOU, BROTHER!
AND I *WILL* HAVE MY VENGEANCE ON GALACTUS FOR CORRUPTING YOUR HONOR.
HE HAS TAKEN MY PEOPLE'S HOME-- HE SHALL NOT TAKE YOU AS WELL!
UNTIL THEN, KNOW THAT I SHALL NOT YIELD UNTIL YOU ARE MOVED OR--
AYE, I KNOW IT.
THEN HAVE AT--
KRAKA

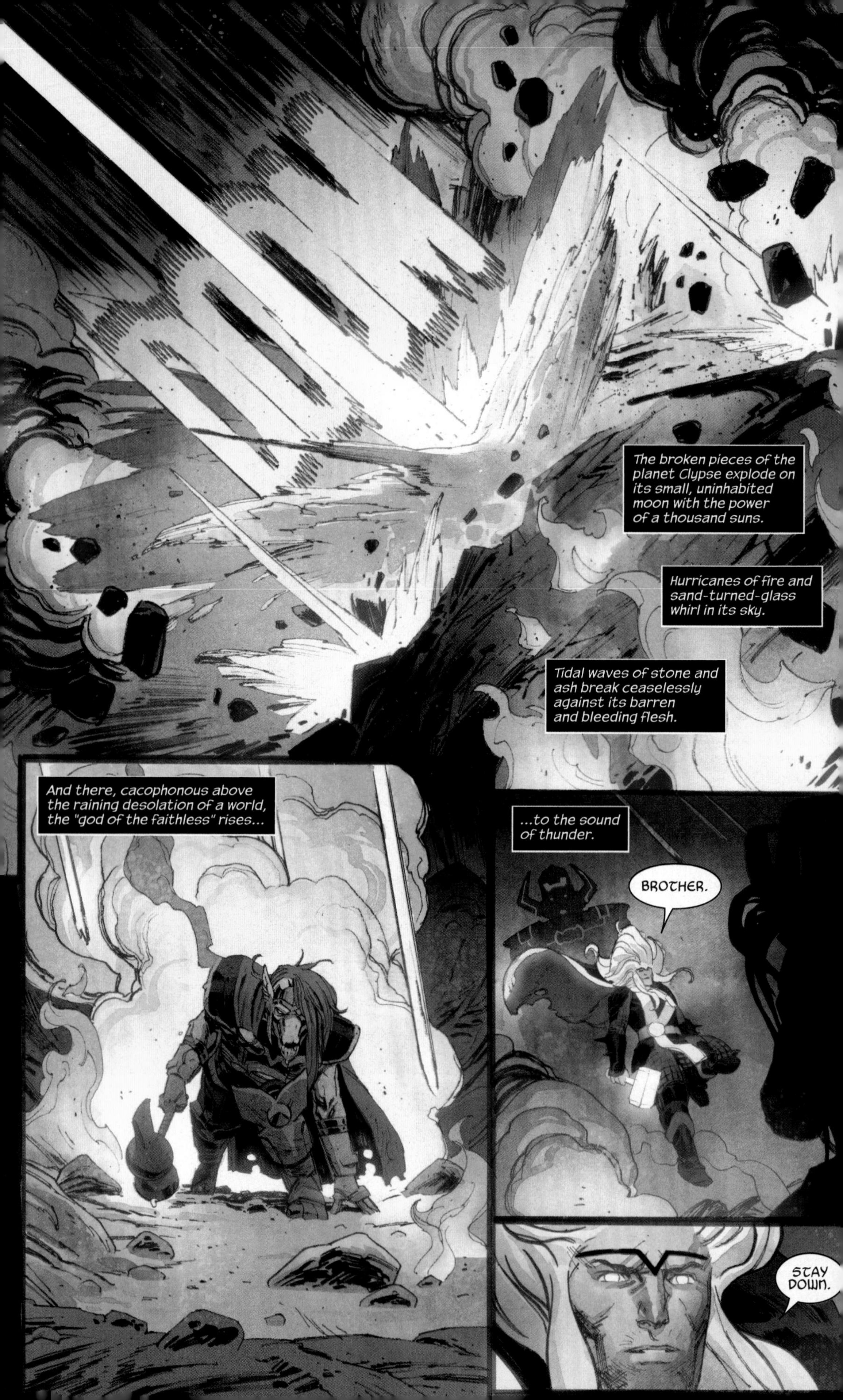
The broken pieces of the planet Clypse explode on its small, uninhabited moon with the power of a thousand suns.
Hurricanes of fire and sand-turned-glass whirl in its sky.
Tidal waves of stone and ash break ceaselessly against its barren and bleeding flesh.
And there, cacophonous above the raining desolation of a world, the "god of the faithless" rises...
...to the sound of thunder.
BROTHER.
STAY DOWN.

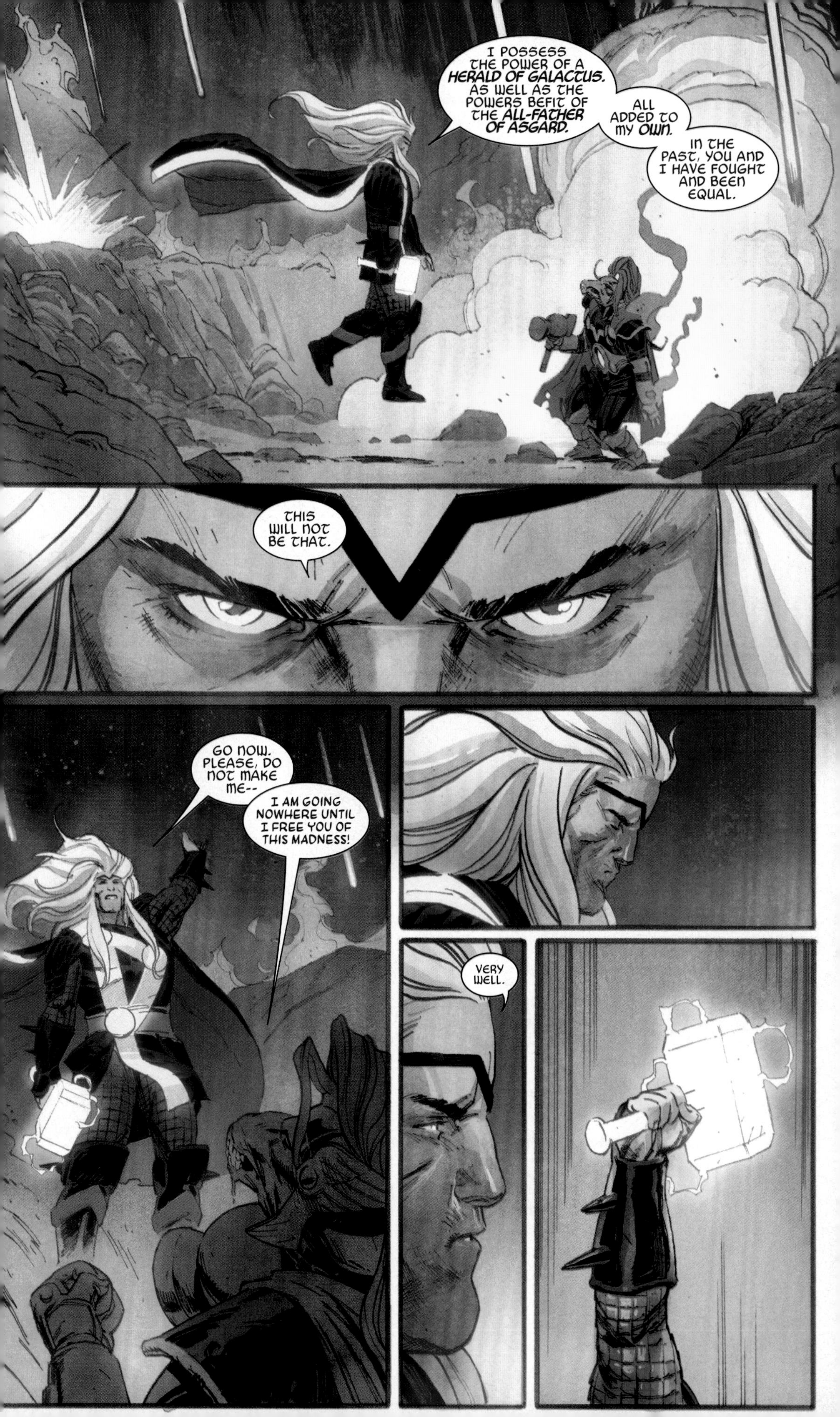

I POSSESS THE POWER OF A **HERALD OF GALACTUS.** AS WELL AS THE POWERS BEFIT OF THE **ALL-FATHER OF ASGARD.**
ALL ADDED TO MY **OWN.**
IN THE PAST, YOU AND I HAVE FOUGHT AND BEEN EQUAL.
THIS WILL NOT BE THAT.
GO NOW. PLEASE, DO NOT MAKE ME--
I AM GOING NOWHERE UNTIL I FREE YOU OF THIS MADNESS!
VERY WELL.

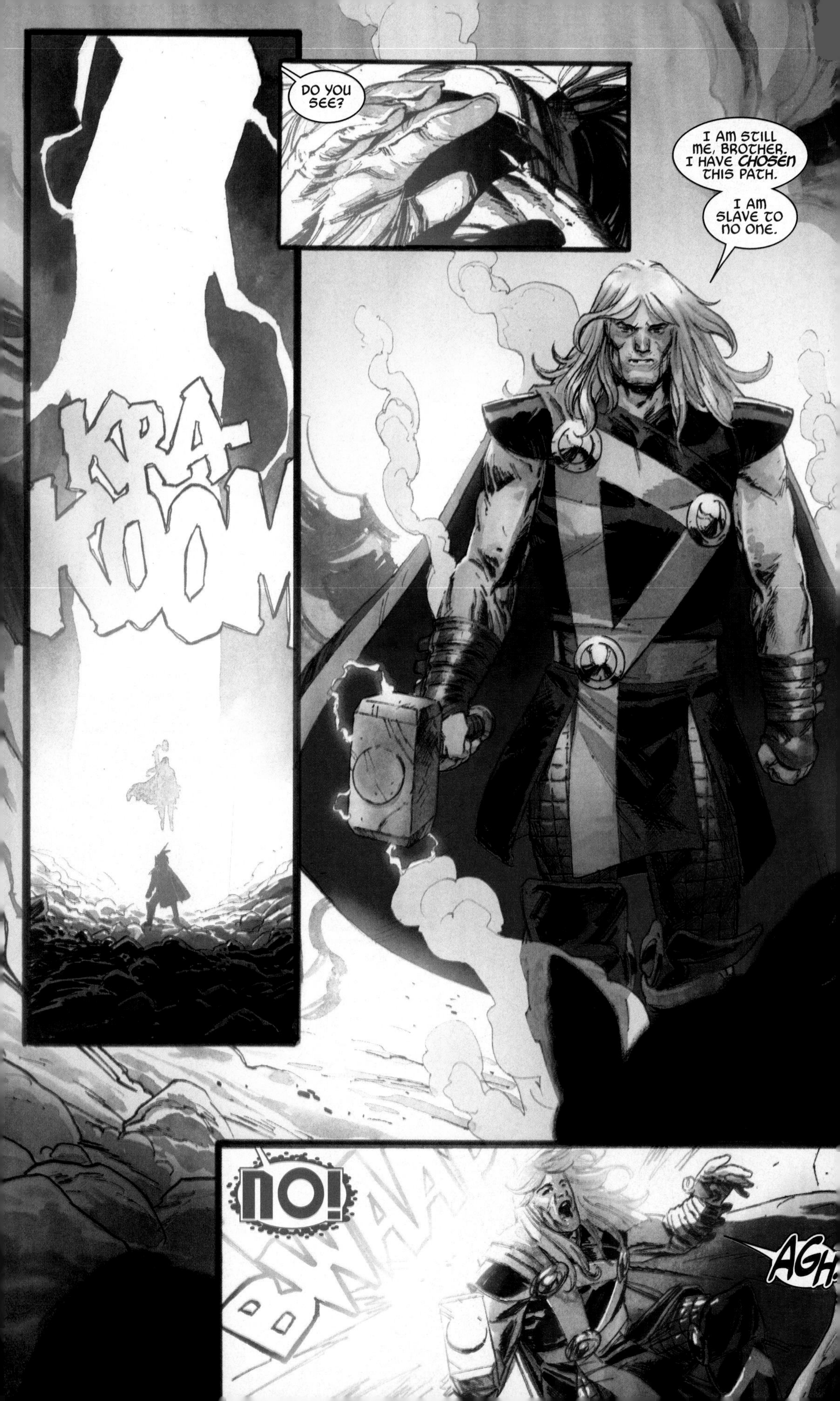
DO YOU SEE?
I AM STILL ME, BROTHER. I HAVE CHOSEN THIS PATH.
I AM SLAVE TO NO ONE.
KRA-KOOOM
NO!
AGH!

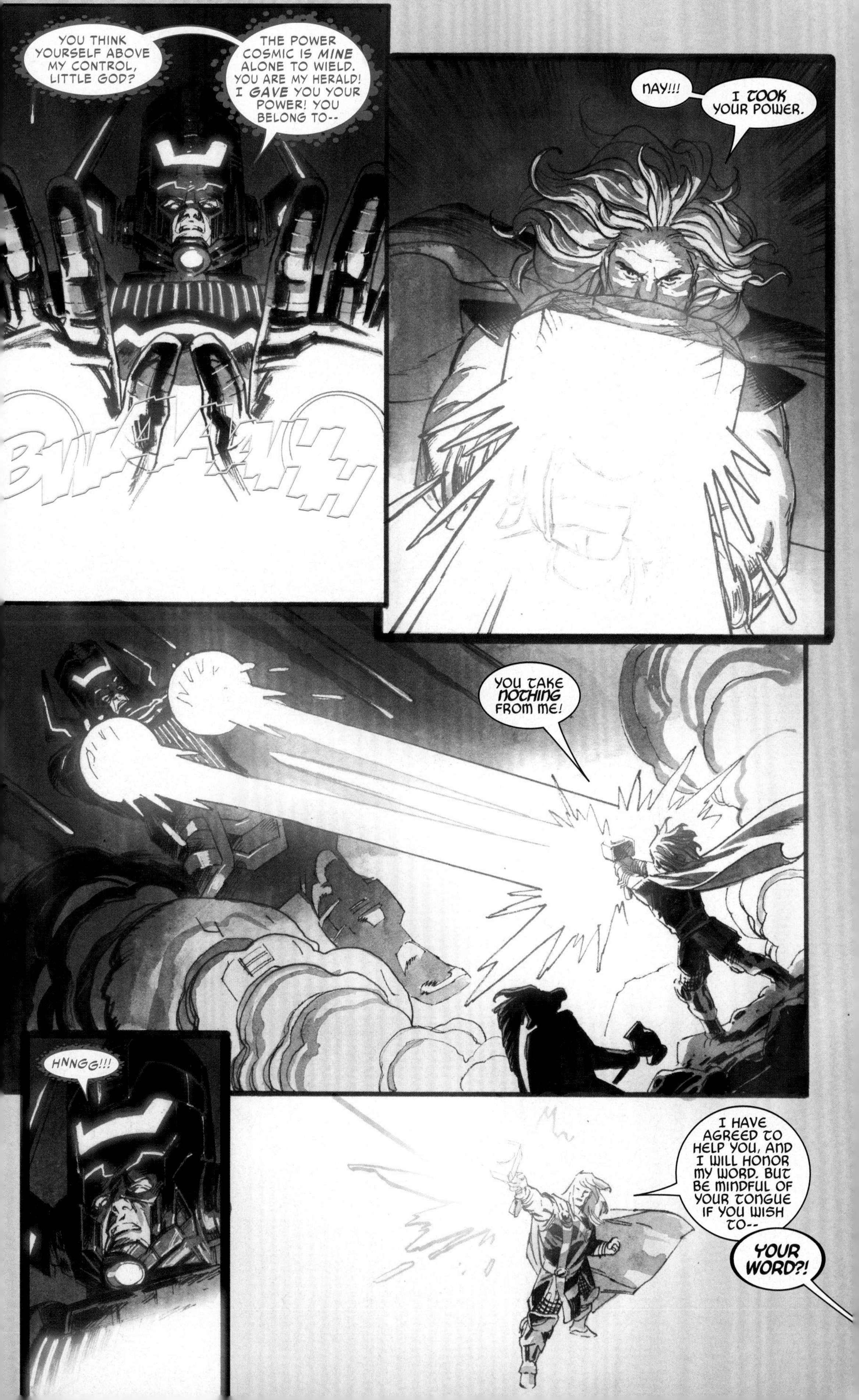
YOU THINK YOURSELF ABOVE MY CONTROL, LITTLE GOD?
THE POWER COSMIC IS MINE ALONE TO WIELD. YOU ARE MY HERALD! I GAVE YOU YOUR POWER! YOU BELONG TO--
BWAAAAH
NAY!!!
I TOOK YOUR POWER.
YOU TAKE NOTHING FROM ME!
HNNGG!!!
I HAVE AGREED TO HELP YOU, AND I WILL HONOR MY WORD. BUT BE MINDFUL OF YOUR TONGUE IF YOU WISH TO--
YOUR WORD?!

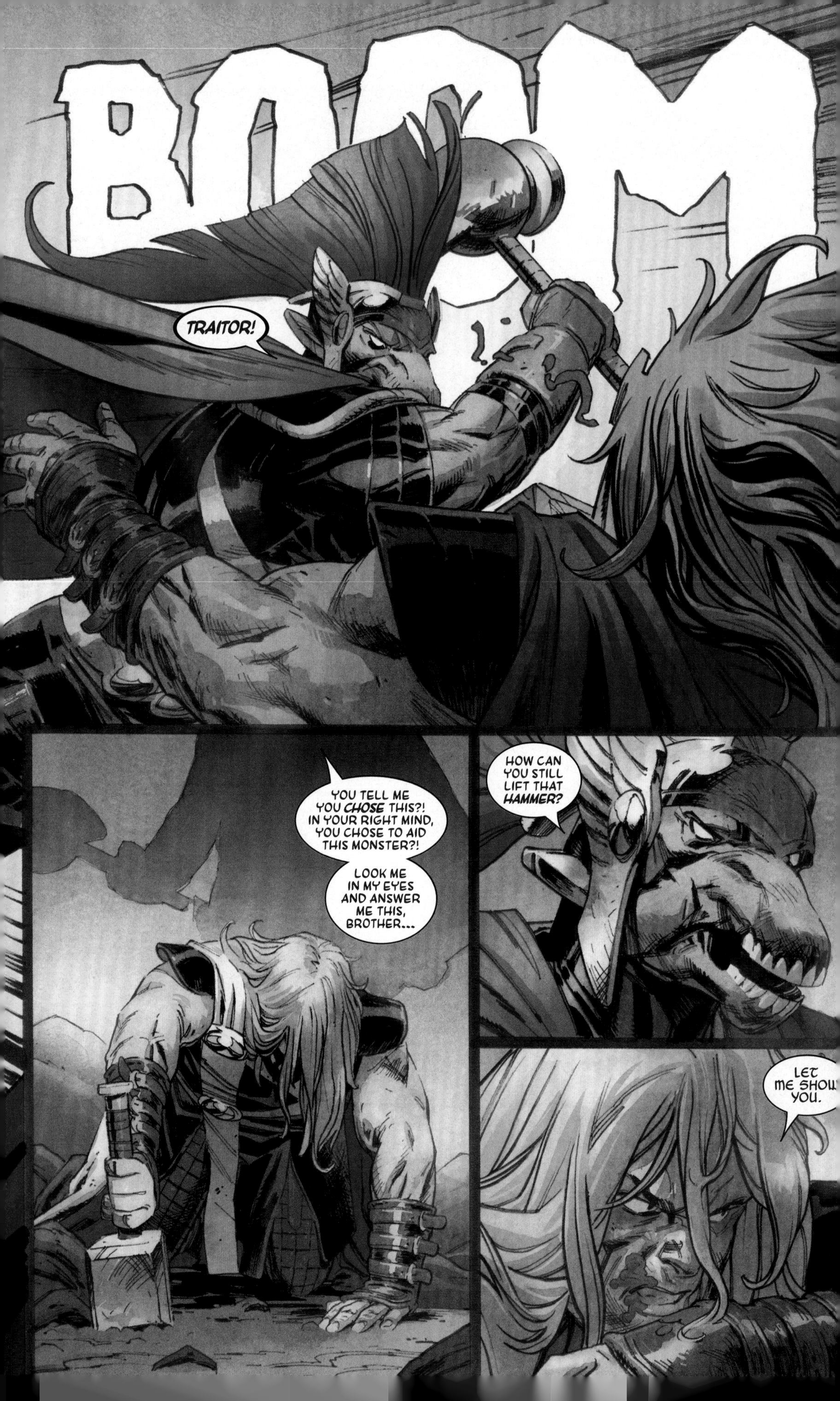
BOOM
TRAITOR!
YOU TELL ME YOU CHOSE THIS?! IN YOUR RIGHT MIND, YOU CHOSE TO AID THIS MONSTER?!
LOOK ME IN MY EYES AND ANSWER ME THIS, BROTHER...
HOW CAN YOU STILL LIFT THAT HAMMER?
LET ME SHOW YOU.

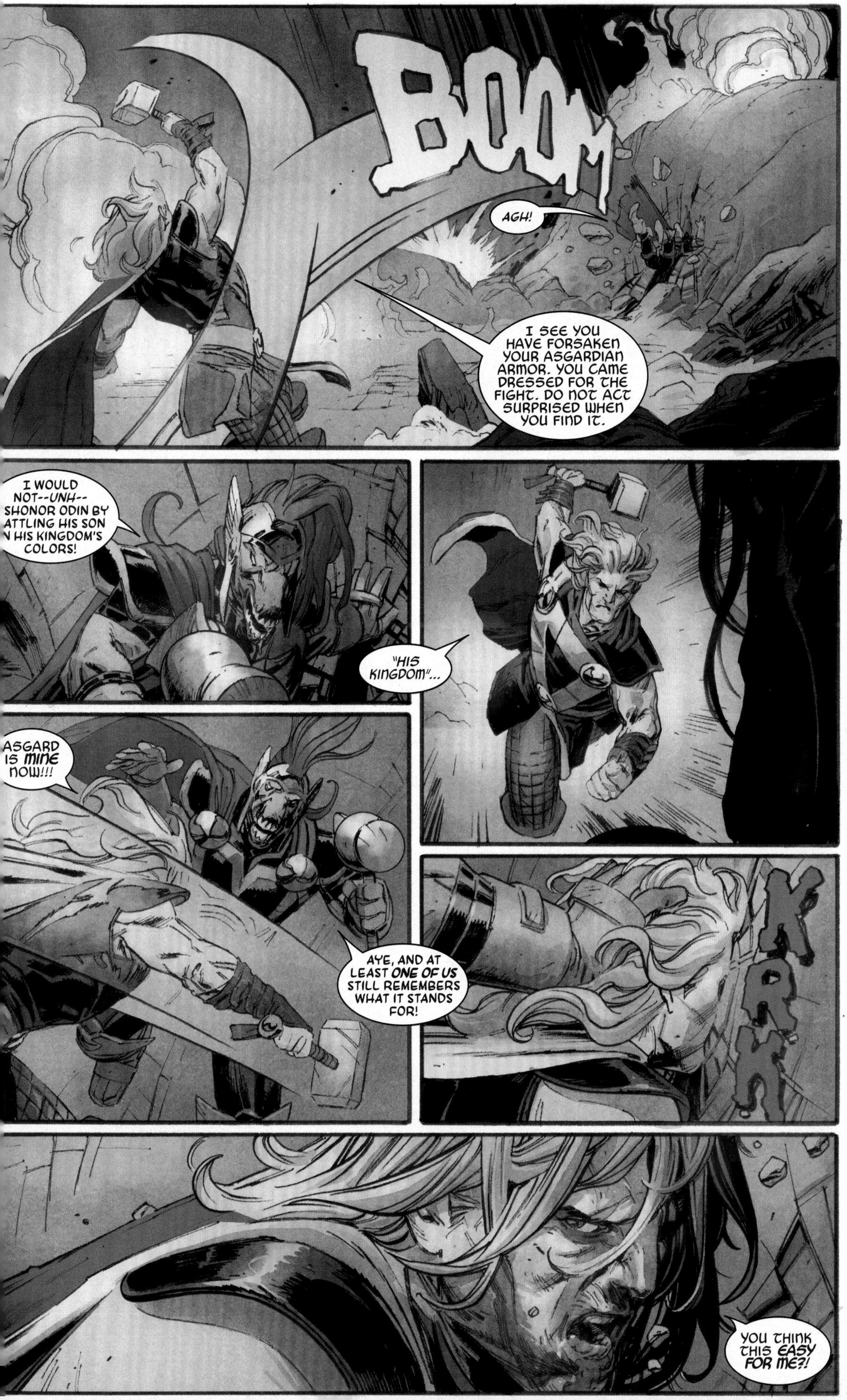
BOOM
AGH!
I SEE YOU HAVE FORSAKEN YOUR ASGARDIAN ARMOR. YOU CAME DRESSED FOR THE FIGHT. DO NOT ACT SURPRISED WHEN YOU FIND IT.
I WOULD NOT--UNH--SHONOR ODIN BY ATTLING HIS SON N HIS KINGDOM'S COLORS!
"HIS KINGDOM"...
ASGARD IS MINE NOW!!!
AYE, AND AT LEAST ONE OF US STILL REMEMBERS WHAT IT STANDS FOR!
KRAK
YOU THINK THIS EASY FOR ME?!

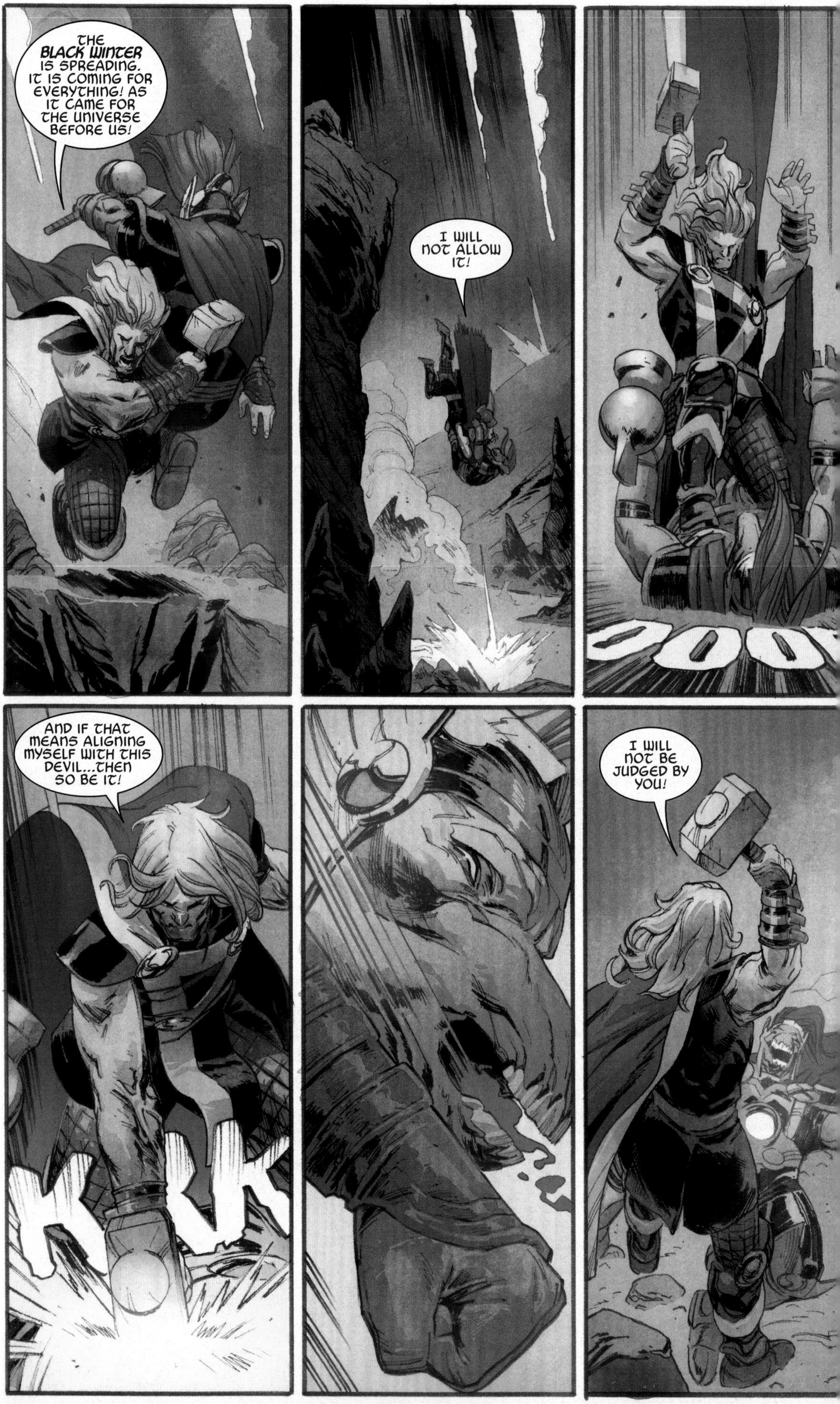
THE BLACK WINTER IS SPREADING. IT IS COMING FOR EVERYTHING! AS IT CAME FOR THE UNIVERSE BEFORE US!
I WILL NOT ALLOW IT!
AND IF THAT MEANS ALIGNING MYSELF WITH THIS DEVIL...THEN SO BE IT!
I WILL NOT BE JUDGED BY YOU!

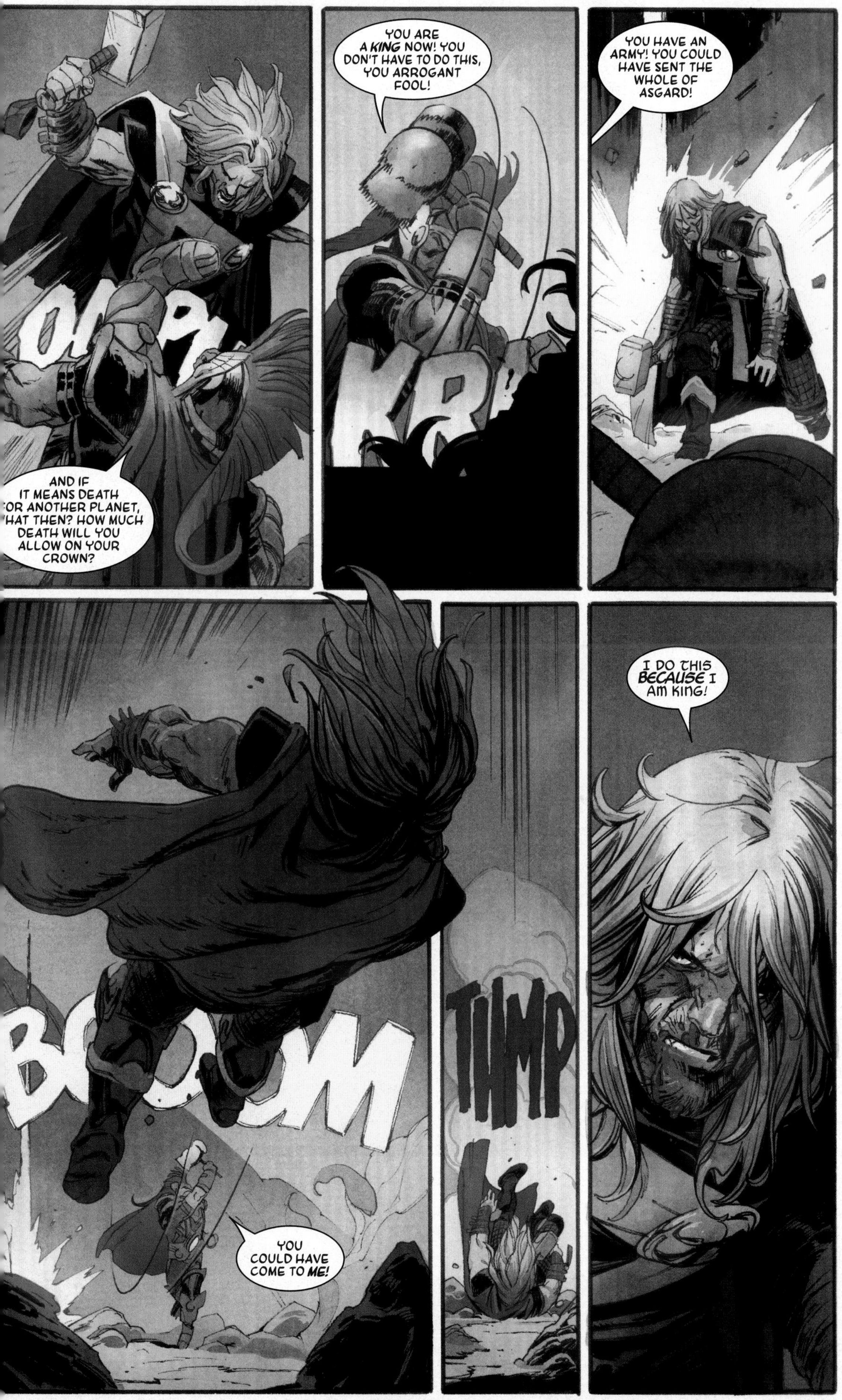
AND IF IT MEANS DEATH FOR ANOTHER PLANET, WHAT THEN? HOW MUCH DEATH WILL YOU ALLOW ON YOUR CROWN?
YOU ARE A KING NOW! YOU DON'T HAVE TO DO THIS, YOU ARROGANT FOOL!
YOU HAVE AN ARMY! YOU COULD HAVE SENT THE WHOLE OF ASGARD!
BOOOM
YOU COULD HAVE COME TO ME!
THMP
I DO THIS BECAUSE I AM KING!

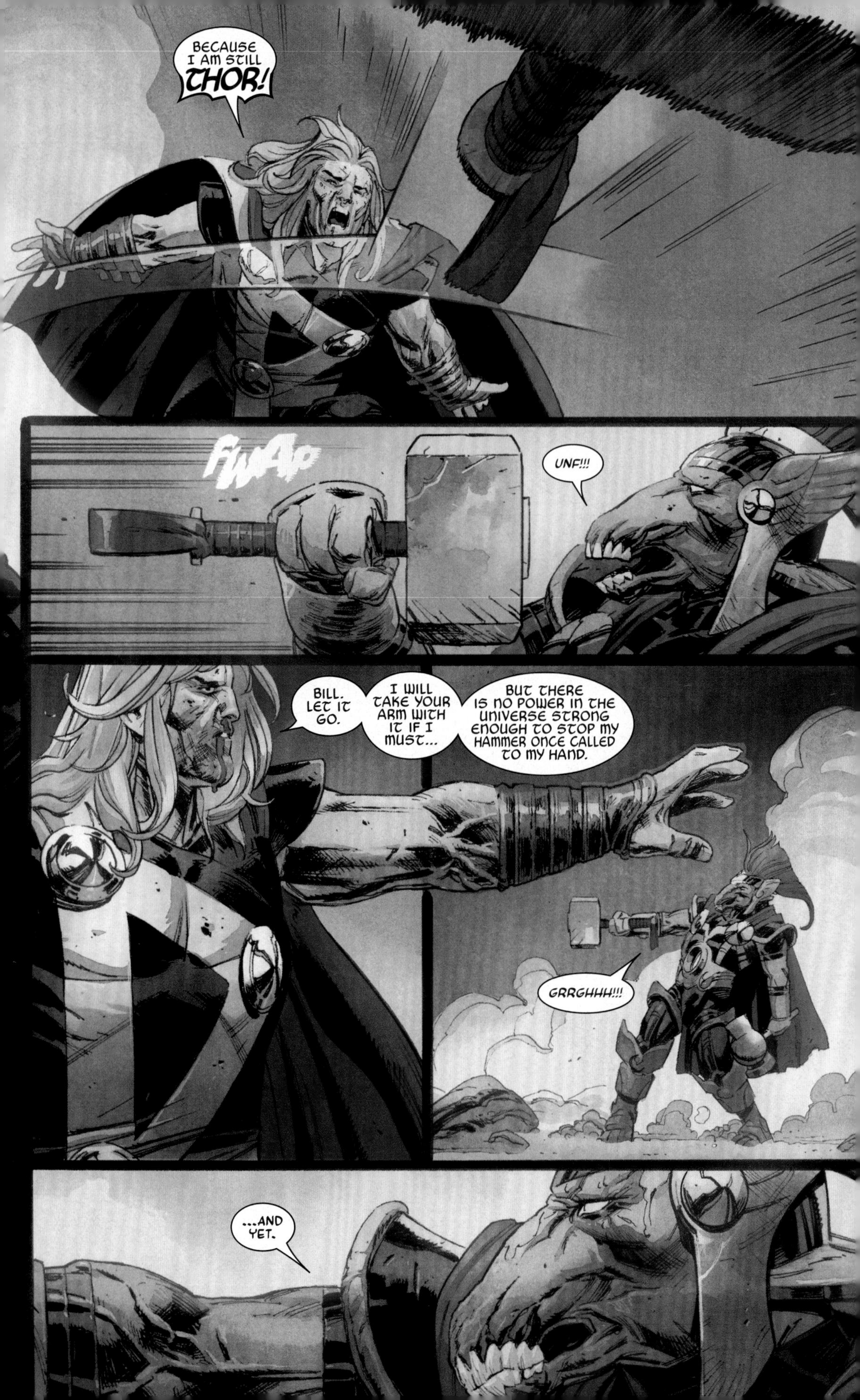
BECAUSE I AM STILL THOR!
FWAP
UNF!!!
BILL. LET IT GO.
I WILL TAKE YOUR ARM WITH IT IF I MUST...
BUT THERE IS NO POWER IN THE UNIVERSE STRONG ENOUGH TO STOP MY HAMMER ONCE CALLED TO MY HAND.
GRRGHHH!!!
...AND YET.

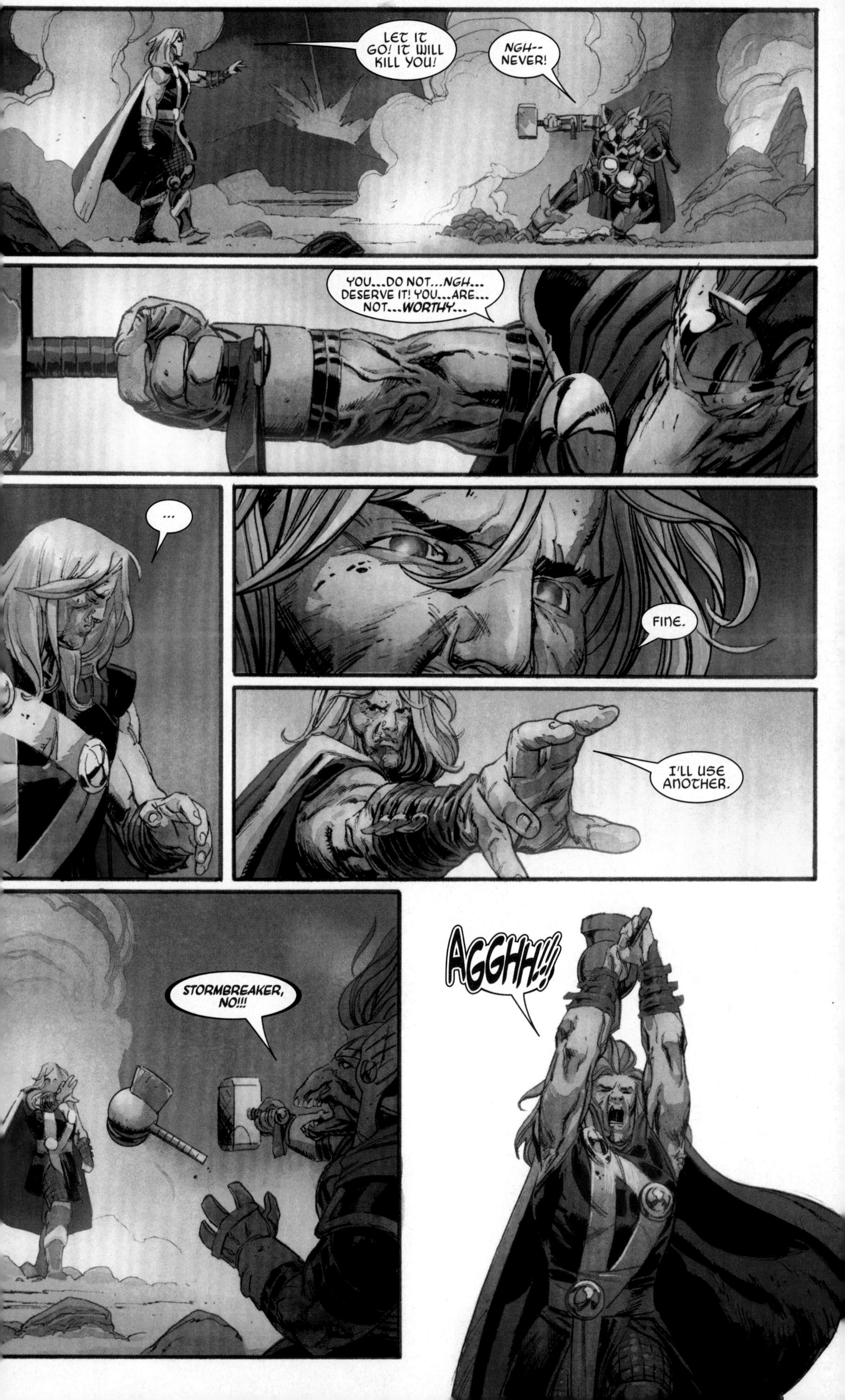
LET IT GO! IT WILL KILL YOU!
NGH-- NEVER!
YOU...DO NOT...NGH... DESERVE IT! YOU...ARE... NOT...WORTHY...
...
FINE.
I'LL USE ANOTHER.
STORMBREAKER, NO!!!
AGGHH!!!

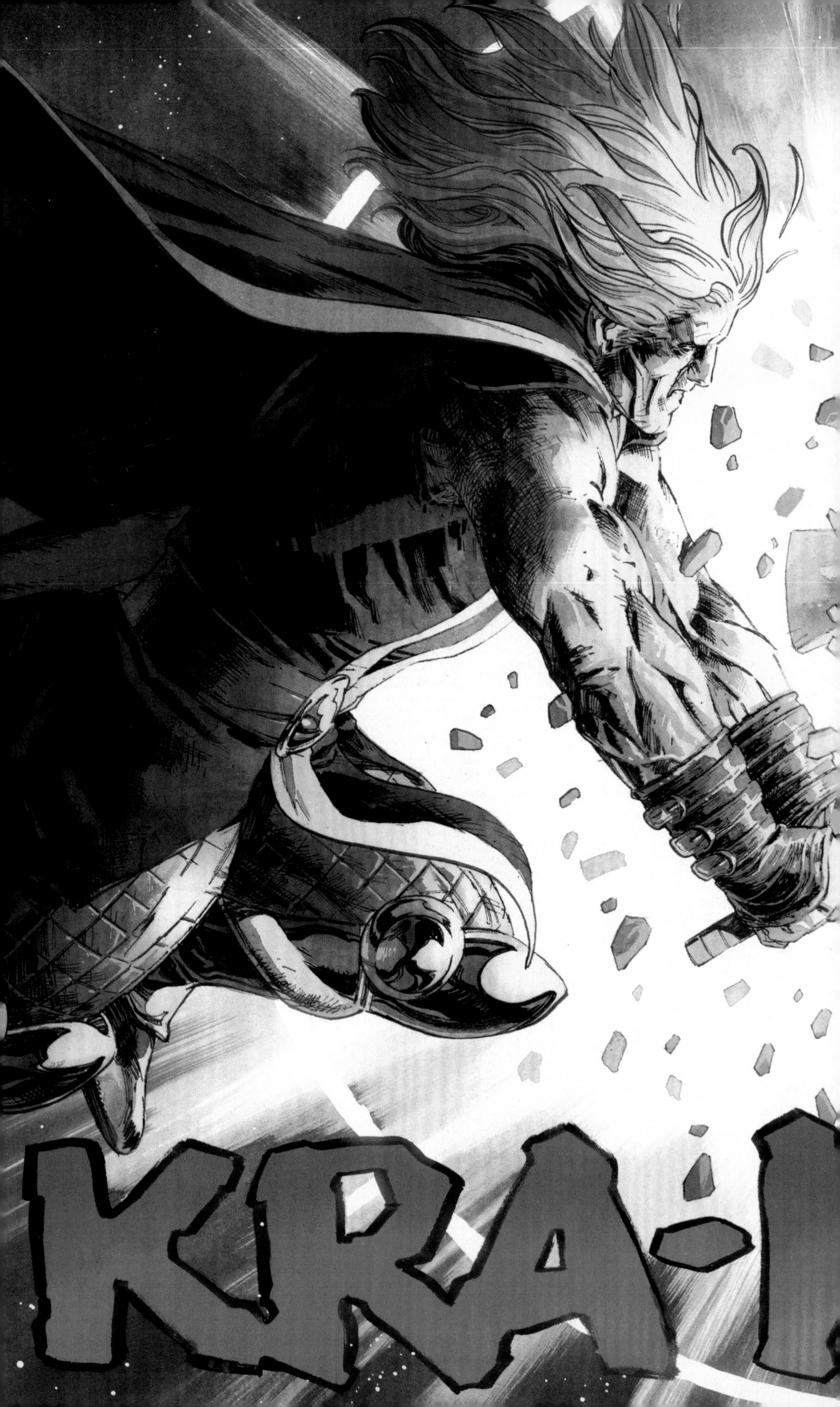
KRA-

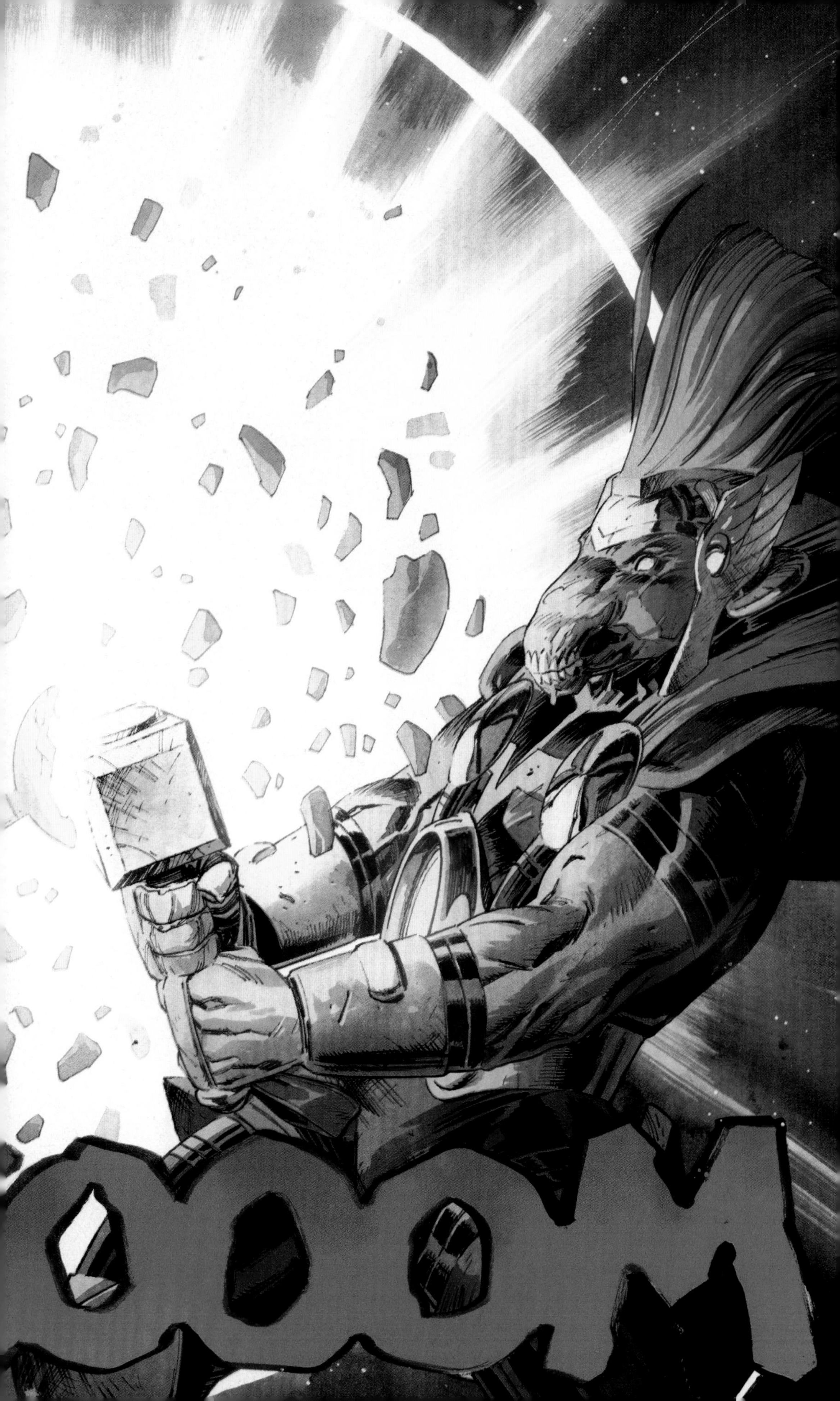
OOOM

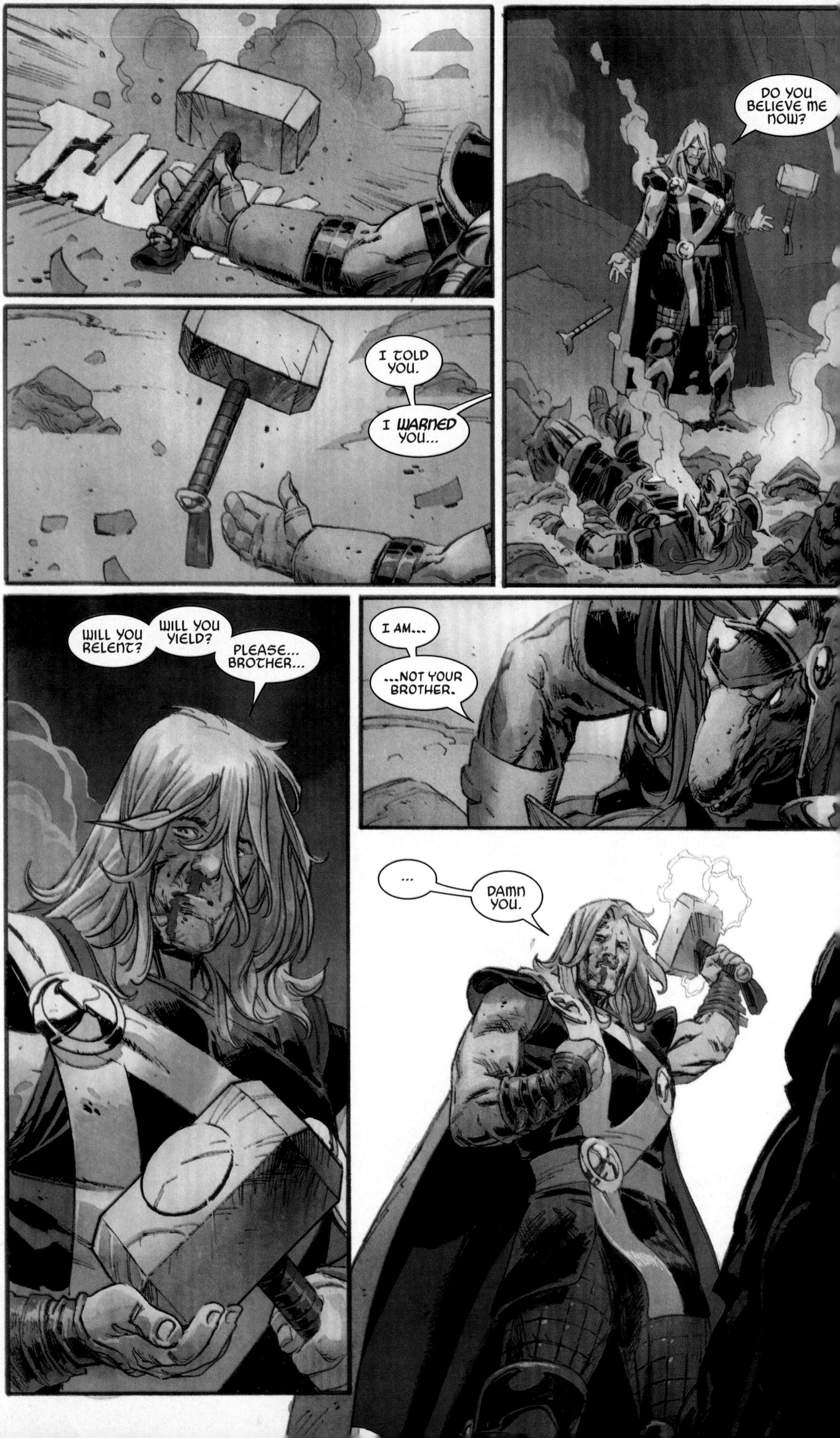
THU
I TOLD YOU.
I WARNED YOU...
DO YOU BELIEVE ME NOW?
WILL YOU RELENT?
WILL YOU YIELD?
PLEASE... BROTHER...
I AM...
...NOT YOUR BROTHER.
...
DAMN YOU.

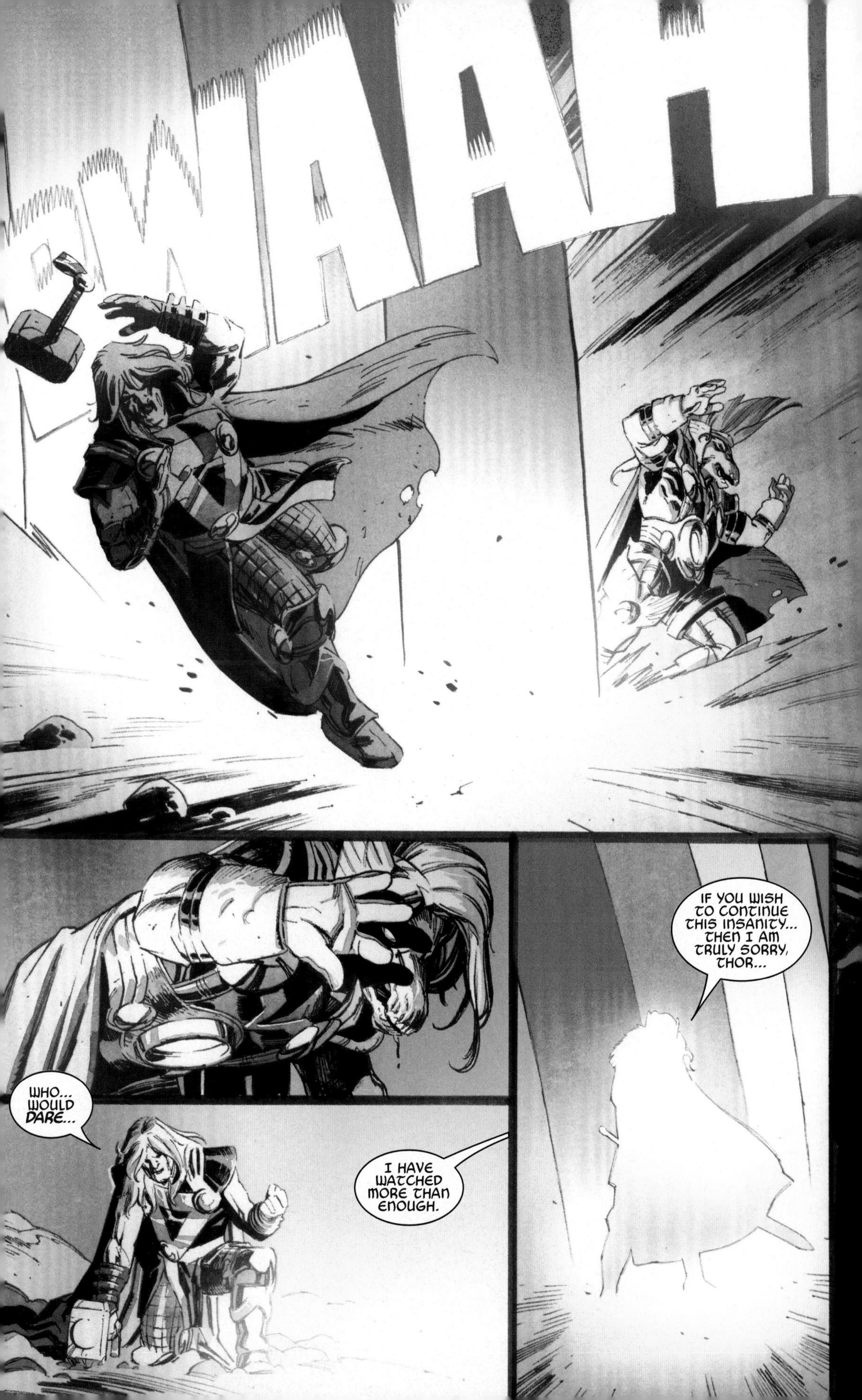
WHO... WOULD *DARE*...
I HAVE WATCHED MORE THAN ENOUGH.
IF YOU WISH TO CONTINUE THIS INSANITY... THEN I AM TRULY SORRY, THOR...

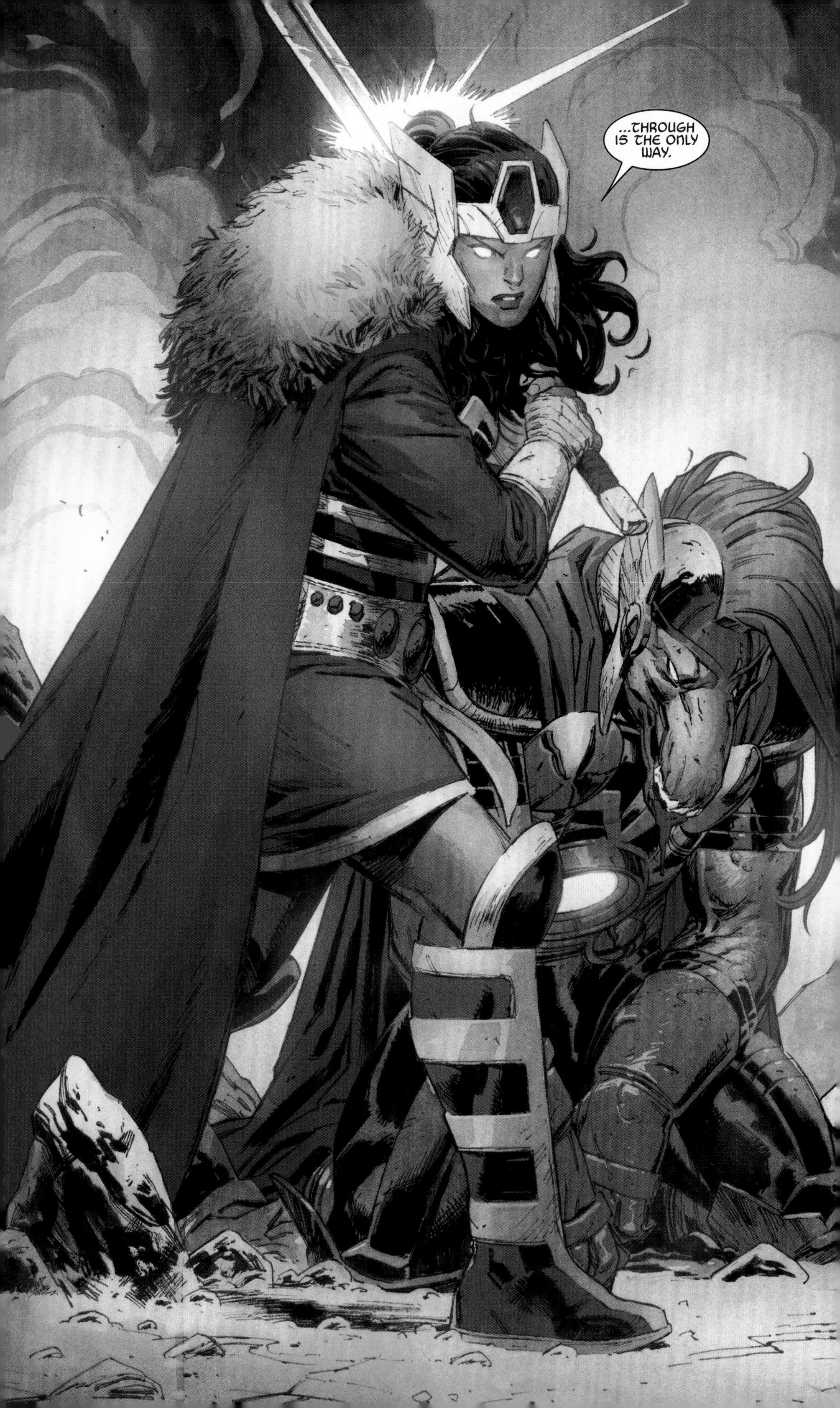
...THROUGH IS THE ONLY WAY.

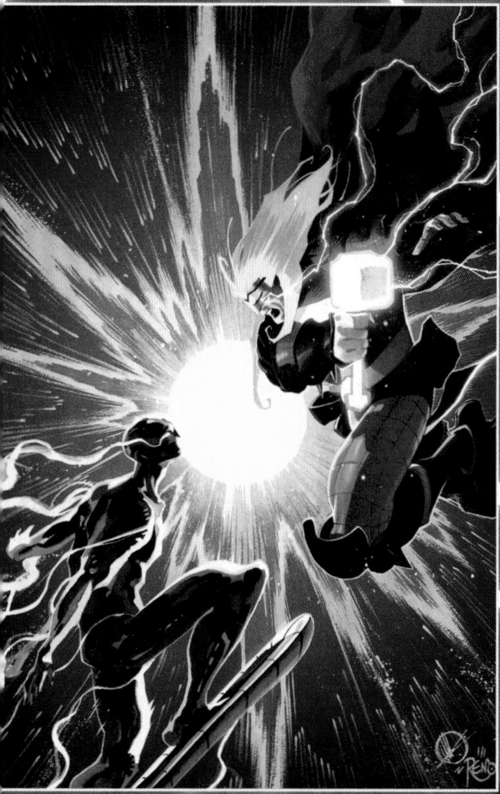

THOR 1 VARIANT BY
Matteo Scalera & Moreno Dinisio

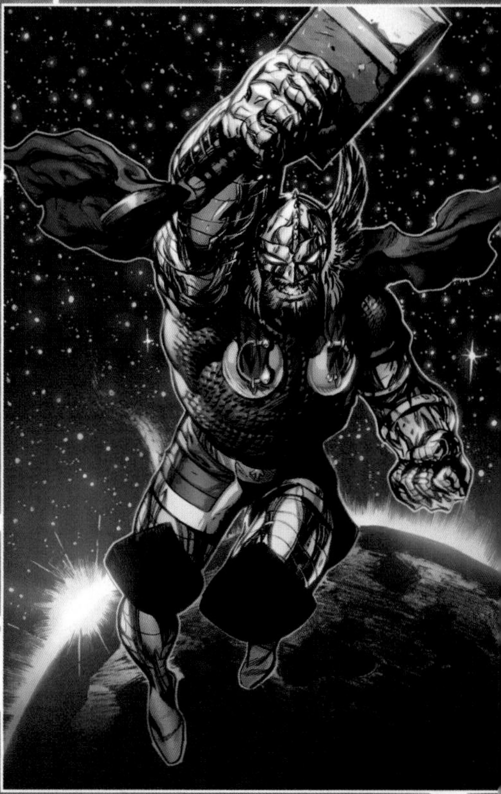

THOR 1 VARIANT BY
Ryan Stegman & Jason Keith

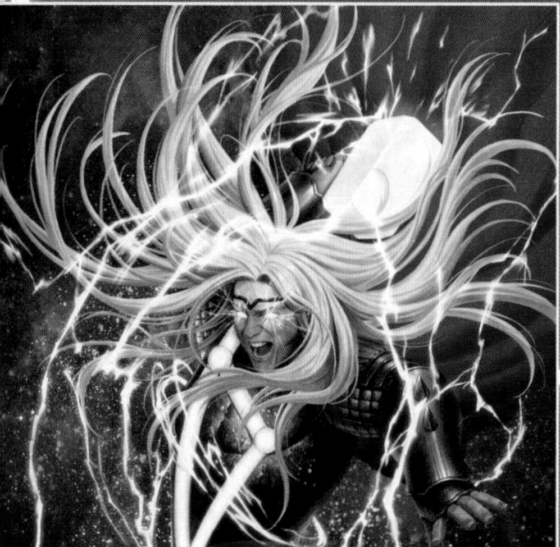

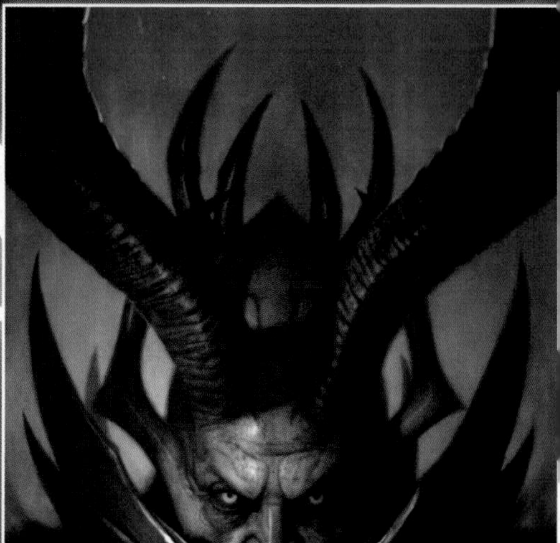

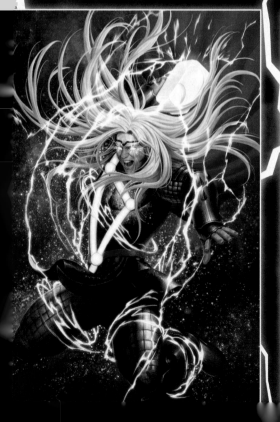

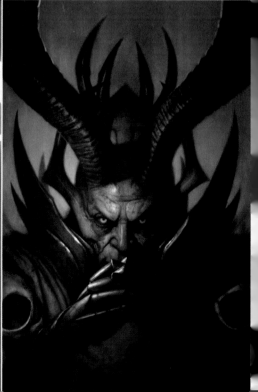

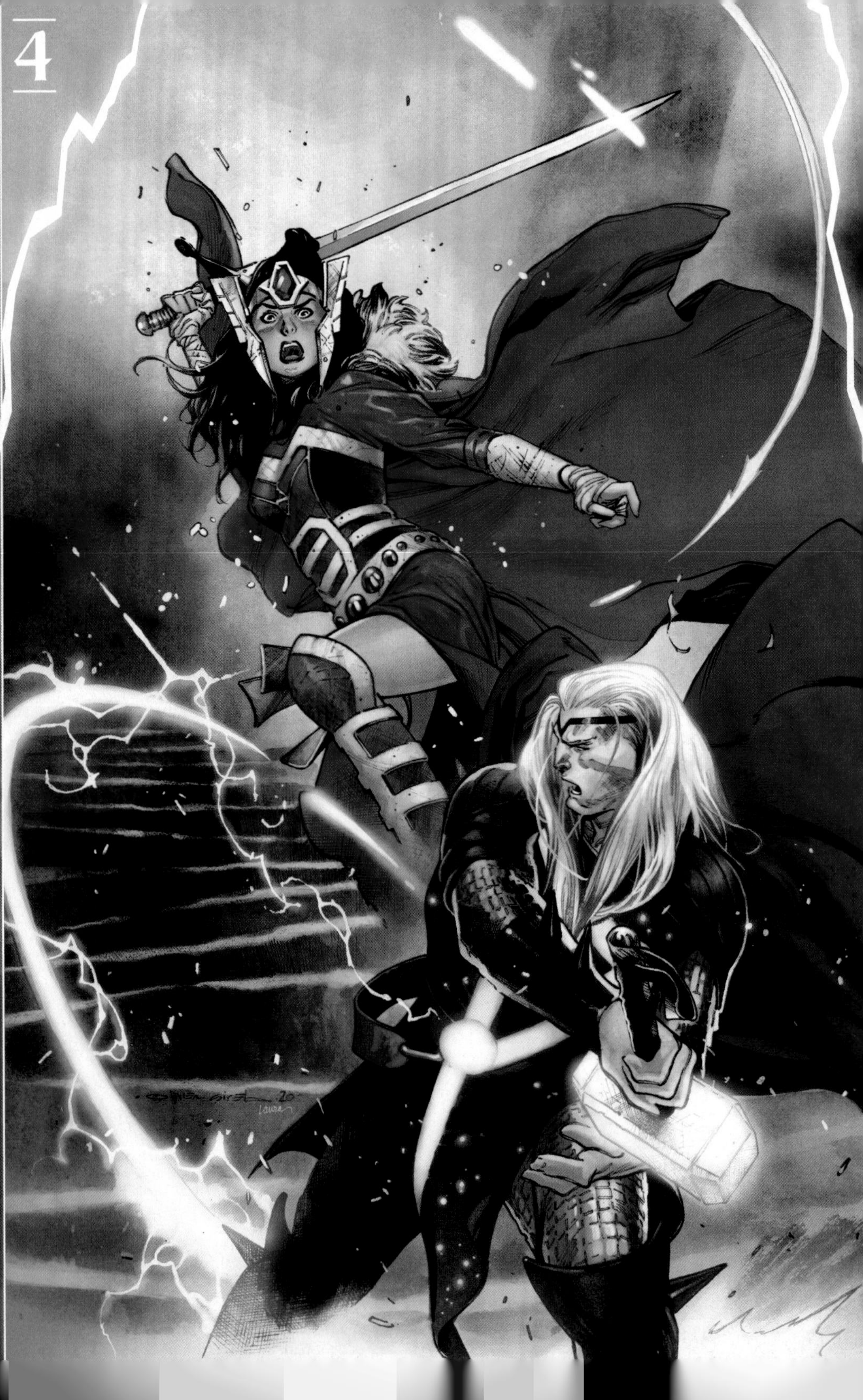
4

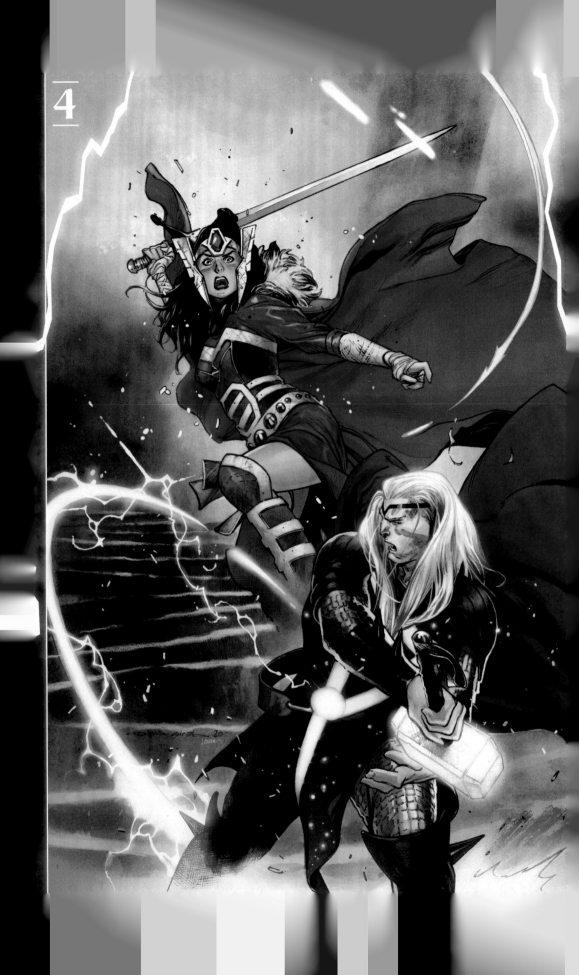

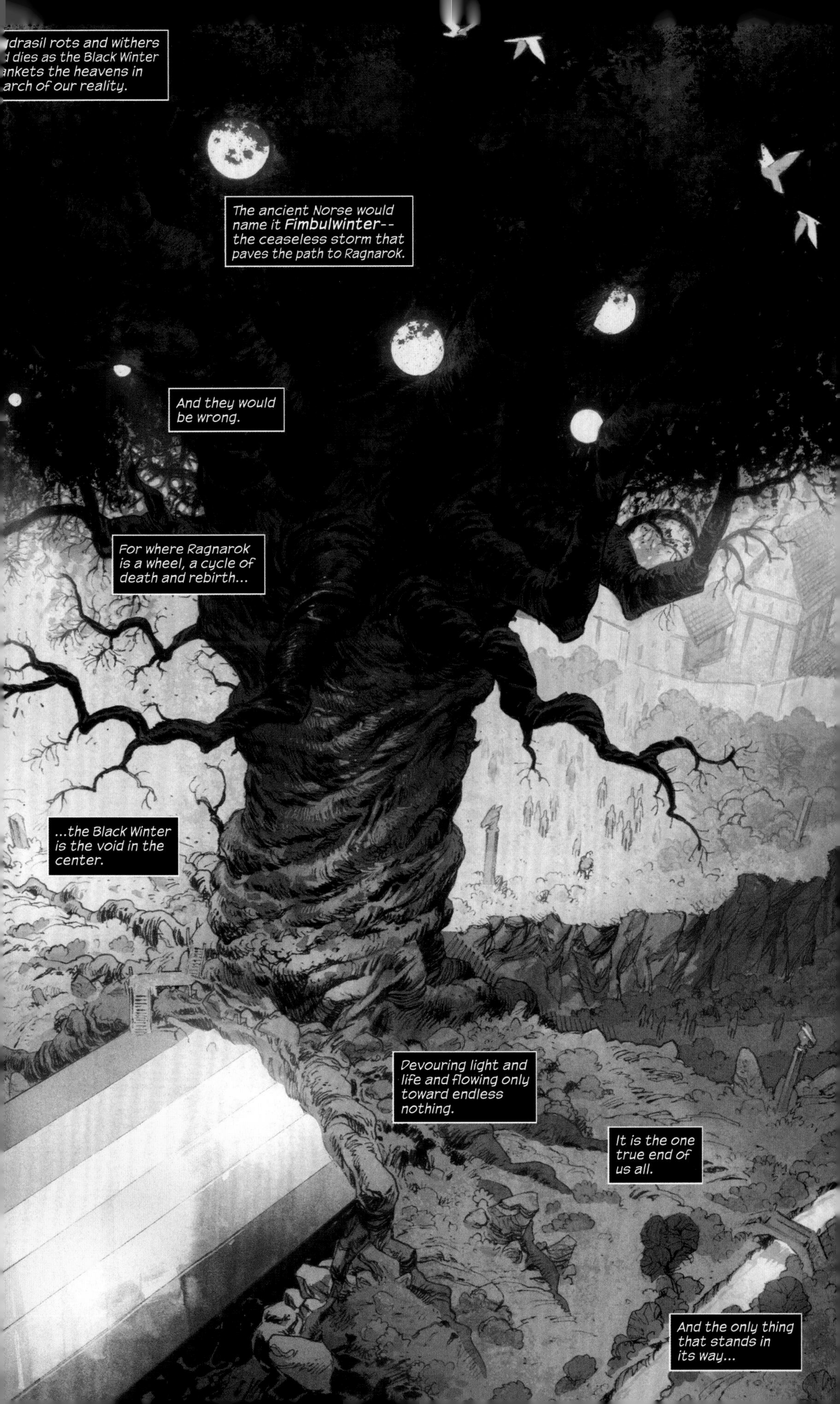

.drasil rots and withers
.d dies as the Black Winter
.ankets the heavens in
.arch of our reality.
The ancient Norse would name it Fimbulwinter-- the ceaseless storm that paves the path to Ragnarok.
And they would be wrong.
For where Ragnarok is a wheel, a cycle of death and rebirth...
...the Black Winter is the void in the center.
Devouring light and life and flowing only toward endless nothing.
It is the one true end of us all.
And the only thing that stands in its way...

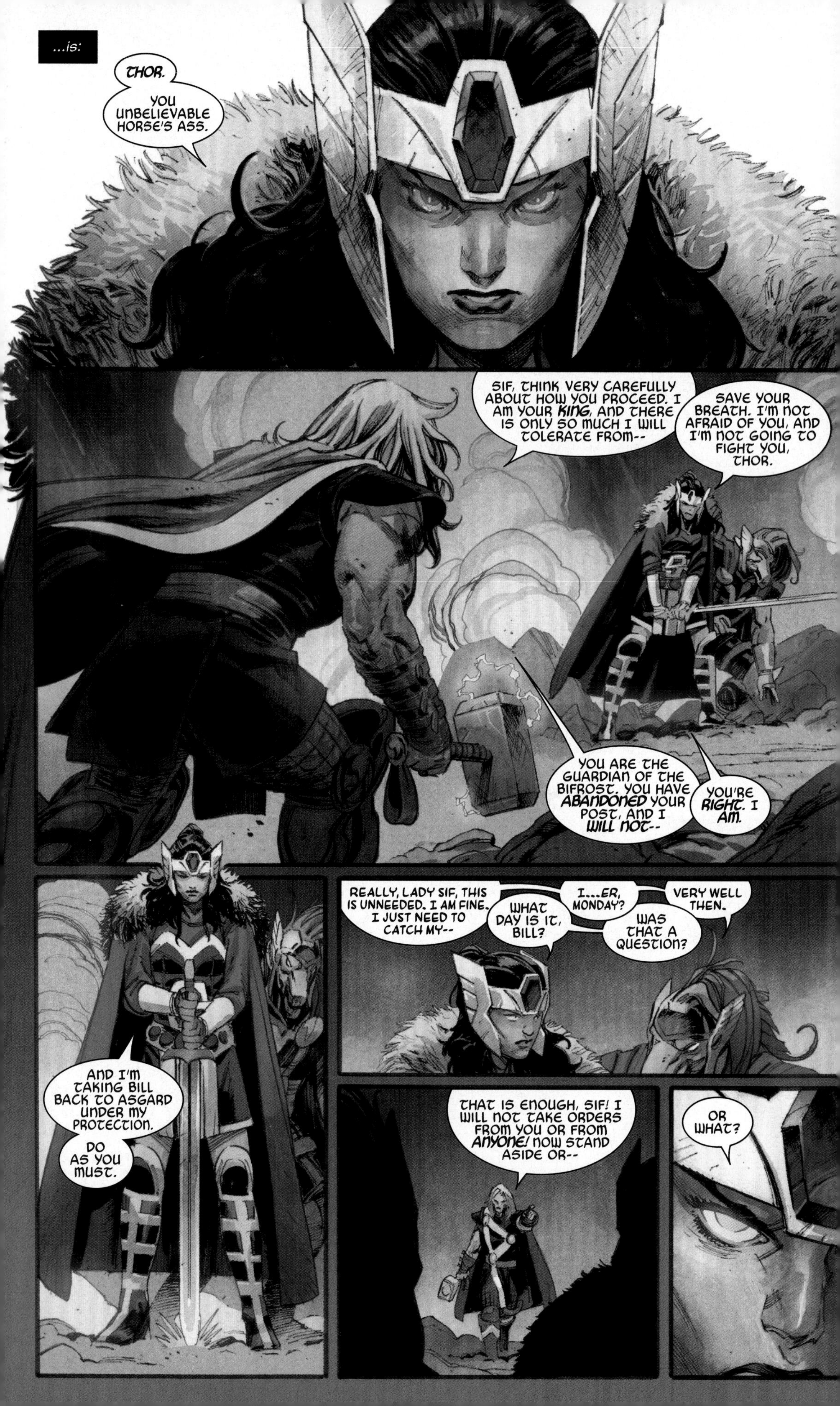
...is:
THOR.
YOU UNBELIEVABLE HORSE'S ASS.
SIF, THINK VERY CAREFULLY ABOUT HOW YOU PROCEED. I AM YOUR KING, AND THERE IS ONLY SO MUCH I WILL TOLERATE FROM--
SAVE YOUR BREATH. I'M NOT AFRAID OF YOU, AND I'M NOT GOING TO FIGHT YOU, THOR.
YOU ARE THE GUARDIAN OF THE BIFROST. YOU HAVE ABANDONED YOUR POST, AND I WILL NOT--
YOU'RE RIGHT. I AM.
AND I'M TAKING BILL BACK TO ASGARD UNDER MY PROTECTION.
DO AS YOU MUST.
REALLY, LADY SIF, THIS IS UNNEEDED. I AM FINE. I JUST NEED TO CATCH MY--
WHAT DAY IS IT, BILL?
I...ER, MONDAY?
WAS THAT A QUESTION?
VERY WELL THEN.
THAT IS ENOUGH, SIF! I WILL NOT TAKE ORDERS FROM YOU OR FROM ANYONE! NOW STAND ASIDE OR--
OR WHAT?

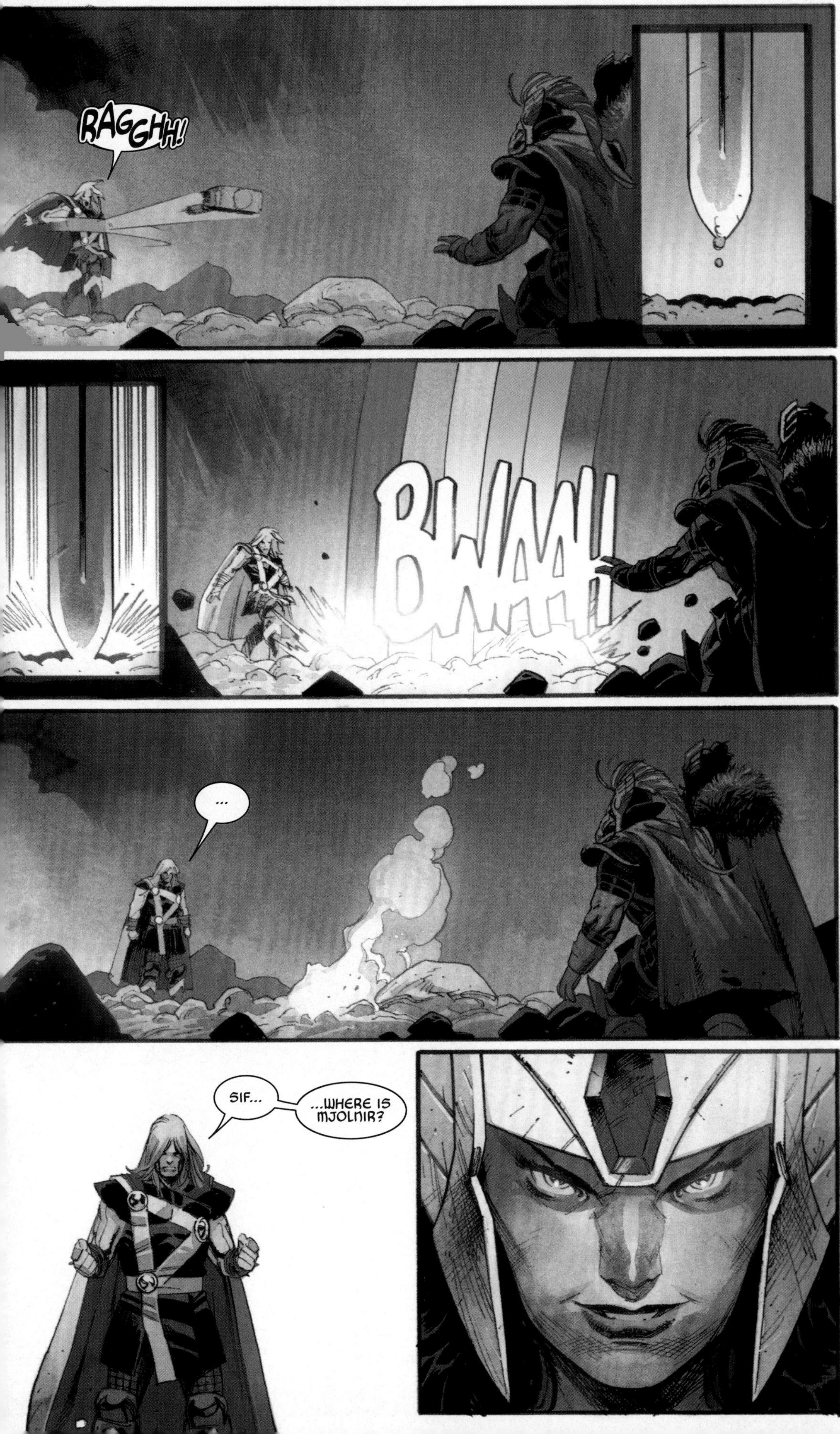
RAGGHH!
BWAAM
...
SIF...
...WHERE IS MJOLNIR?

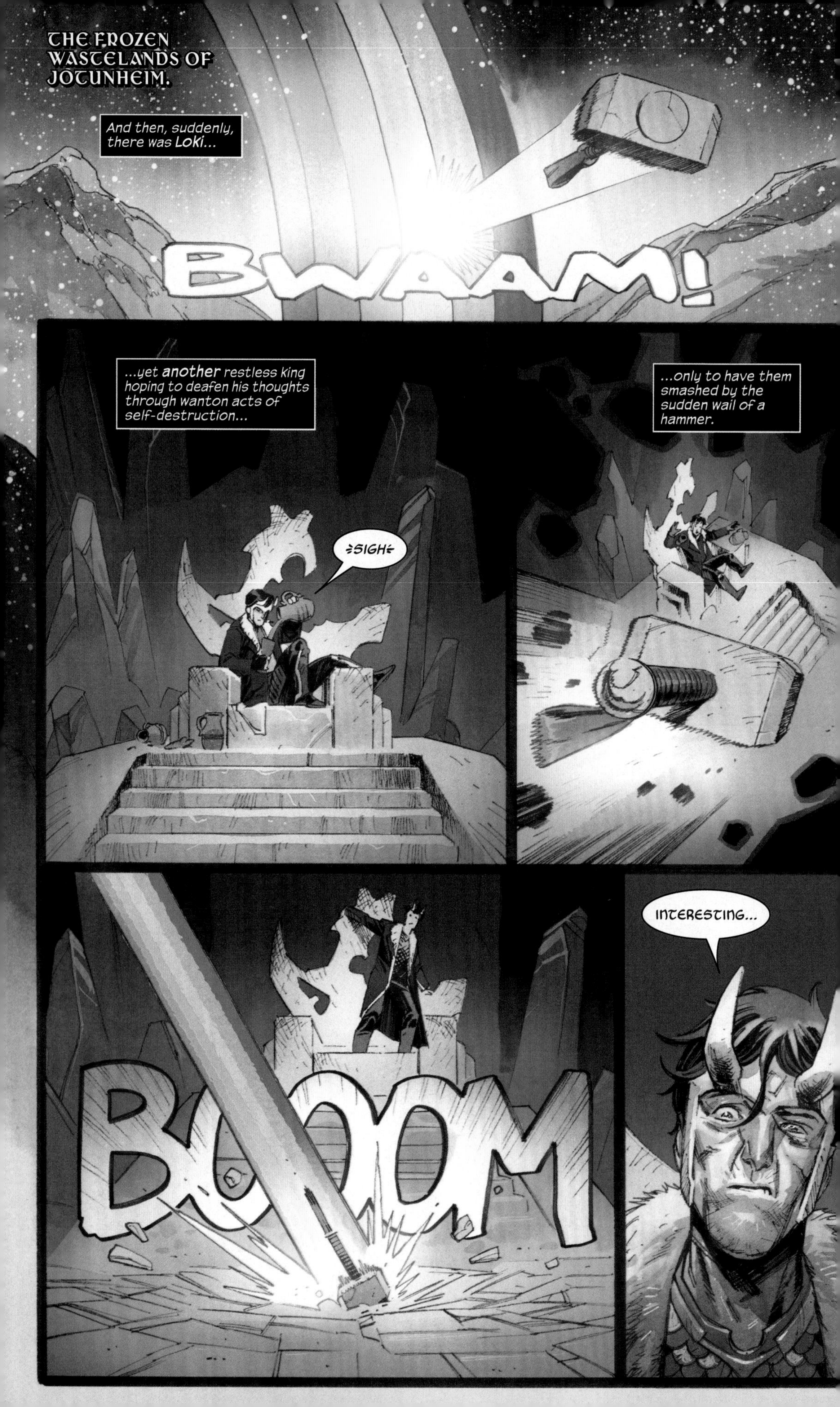
THE FROZEN WASTELANDS OF JOTUNHEIM.
And then, suddenly, there was Loki...
BWAAM!
...yet another restless king hoping to deafen his thoughts through wanton acts of self-destruction...
SIGH
...only to have them smashed by the sudden wail of a hammer.
BOOOM
INTERESTING...

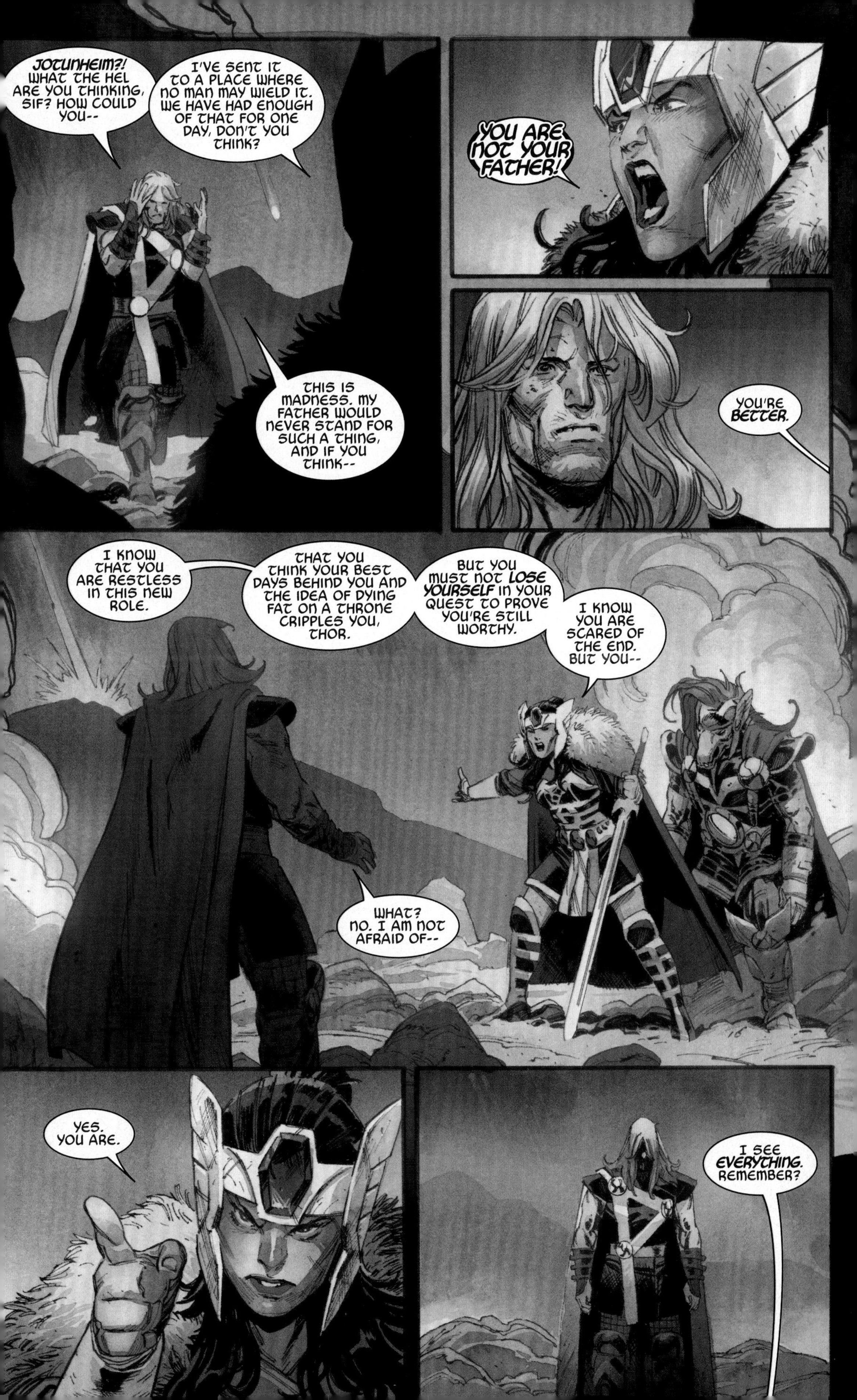

JOTUNHEIM?! WHAT THE HEL ARE YOU THINKING, SIF? HOW COULD YOU--
I'VE SENT IT TO A PLACE WHERE NO MAN MAY WIELD IT. WE HAVE HAD ENOUGH OF THAT FOR ONE DAY, DON'T YOU THINK?
THIS IS MADNESS. MY FATHER WOULD NEVER STAND FOR SUCH A THING, AND IF YOU THINK--
YOU ARE NOT YOUR FATHER!
YOU'RE BETTER.
I KNOW THAT YOU ARE RESTLESS IN THIS NEW ROLE.
THAT YOU THINK YOUR BEST DAYS BEHIND YOU AND THE IDEA OF DYING FAT ON A THRONE CRIPPLES YOU, THOR.
BUT YOU MUST NOT LOSE YOURSELF IN YOUR QUEST TO PROVE YOU'RE STILL WORTHY.
I KNOW YOU ARE SCARED OF THE END. BUT YOU--
WHAT? NO. I AM NOT AFRAID OF--
YES. YOU ARE.
I SEE EVERYTHING. REMEMBER?

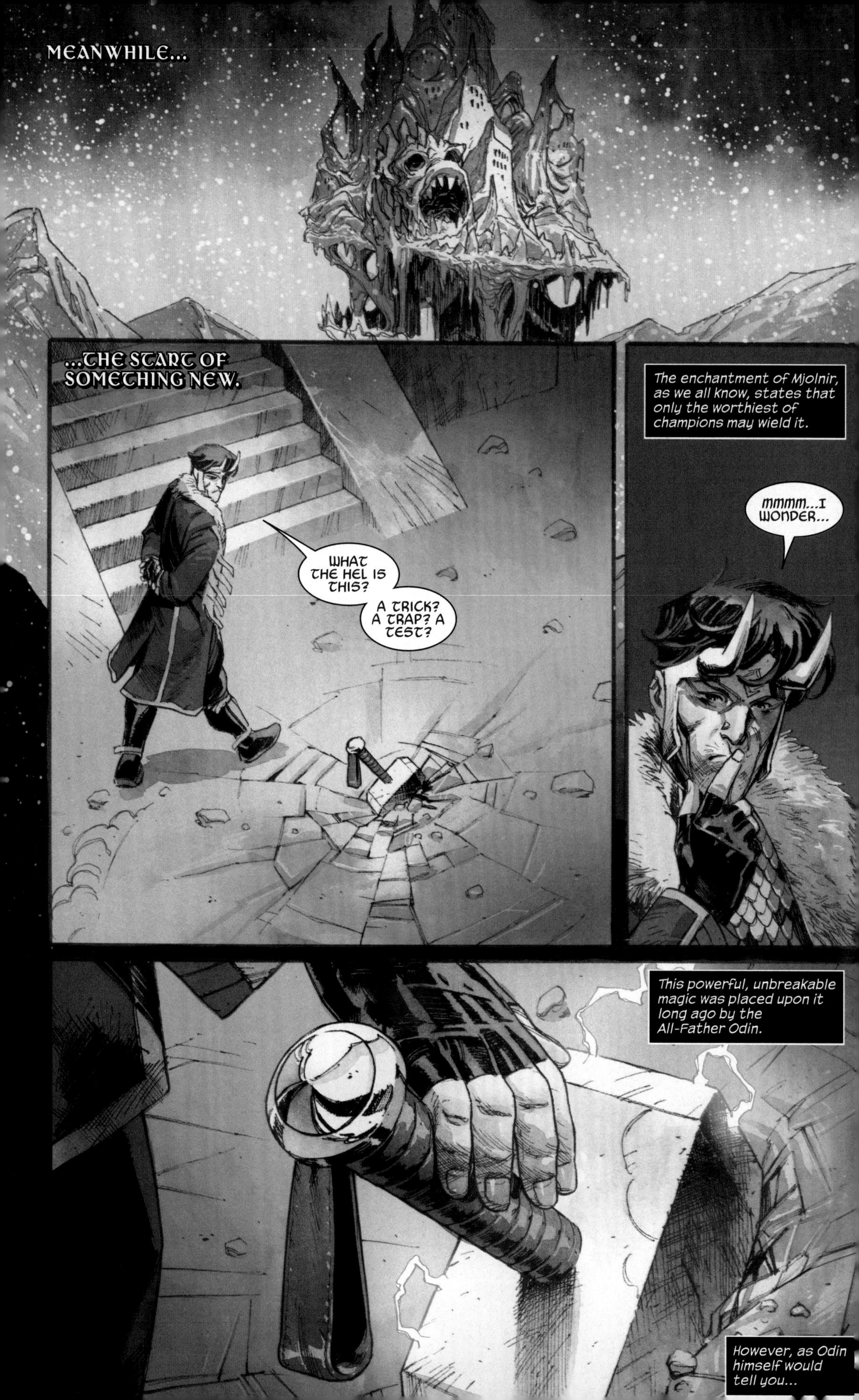
MEANWHILE...
...THE START OF SOMETHING NEW.
WHAT THE HEL IS THIS?
A TRICK? A TRAP? A TEST?
The enchantment of Mjolnir, as we all know, states that only the worthiest of champions may wield it.
mmmm...I WONDER...
This powerful, unbreakable magic was placed upon it long ago by the All-Father Odin.
However, as Odin himself would tell you...

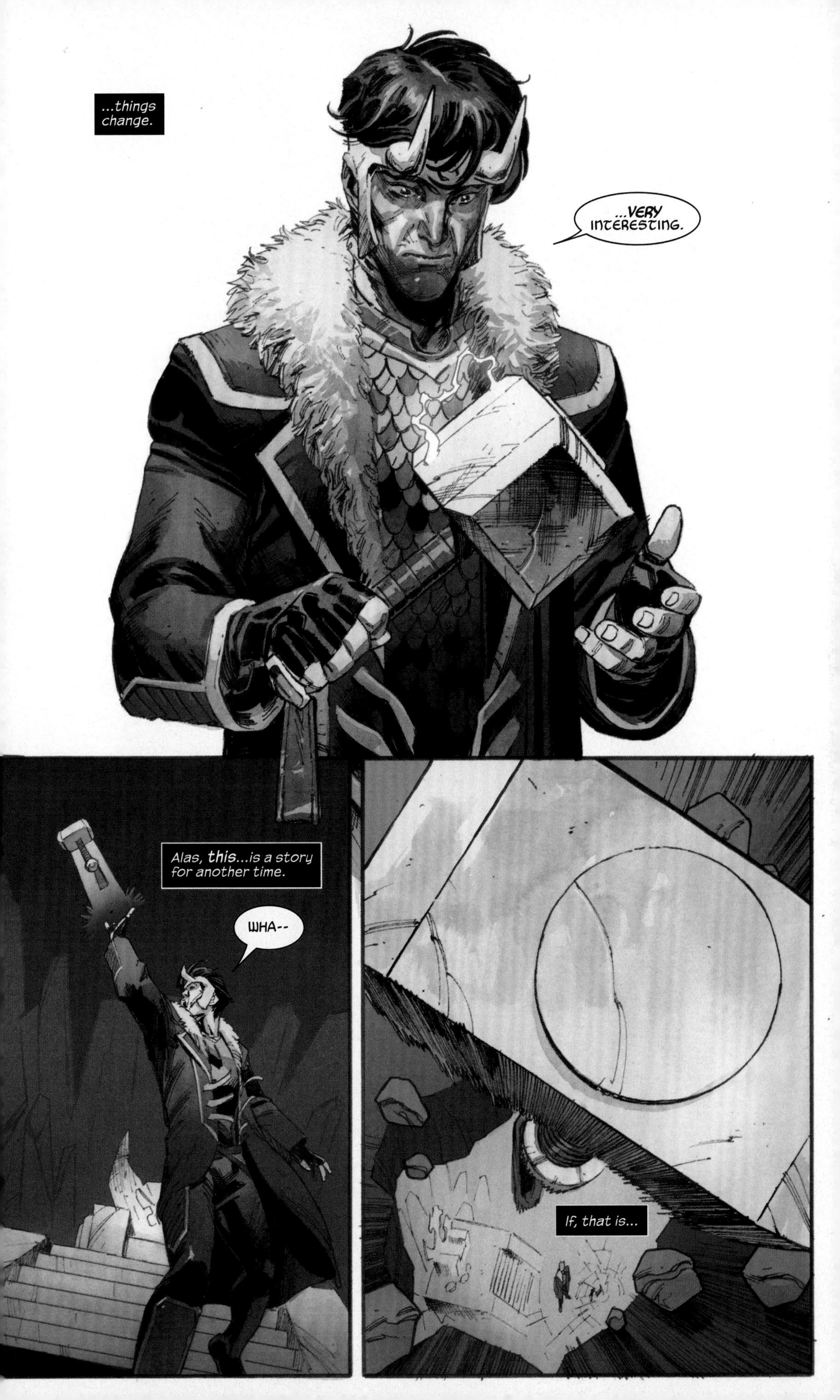
...things change.
...VERY INTERESTING.
Alas, this...is a story for another time.
WHA--
If, that is...

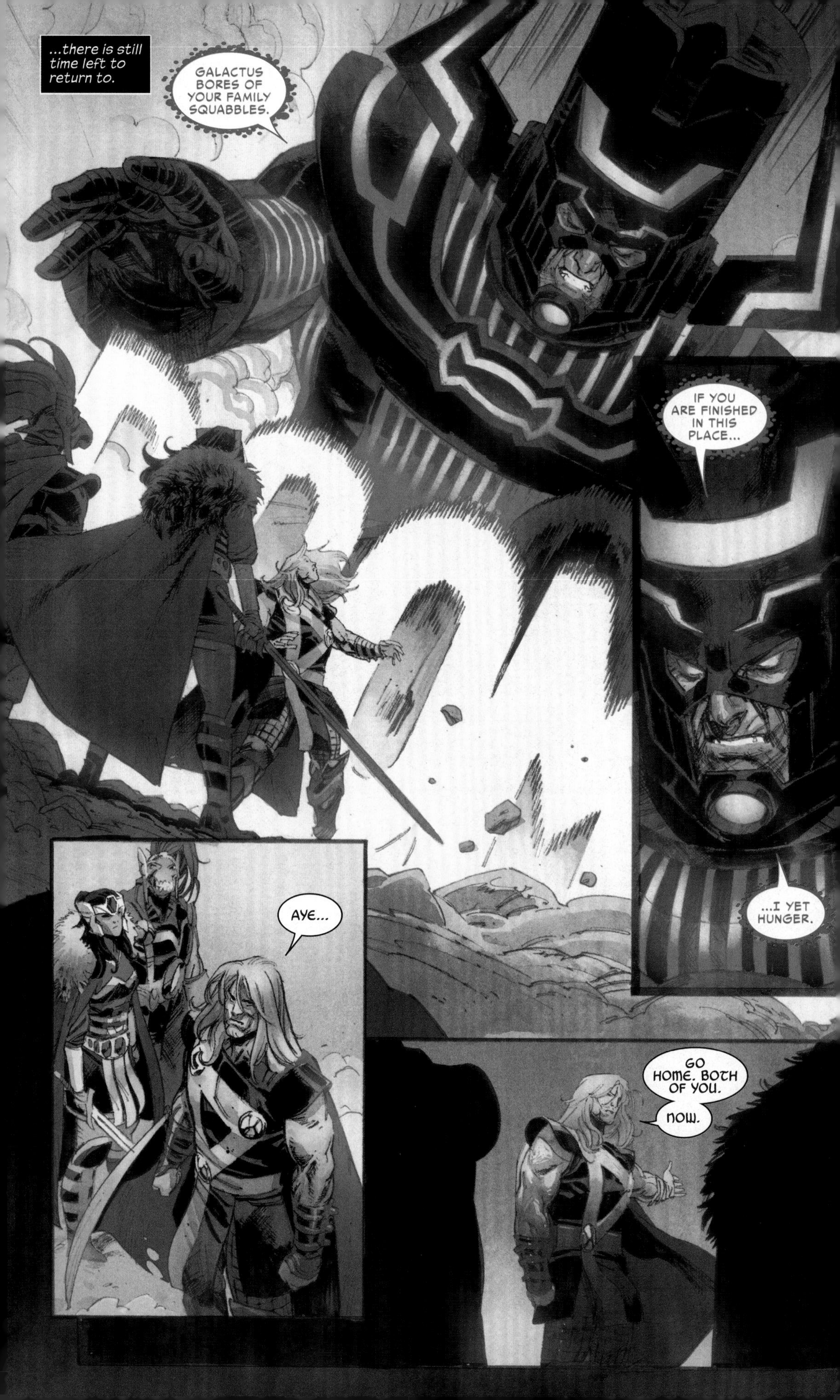
...there is still time left to return to.
GALACTUS BORES OF YOUR FAMILY SQUABBLES.
IF YOU ARE FINISHED IN THIS PLACE...
...I YET HUNGER.
AYE...
GO HOME. BOTH OF YOU.
NOW.

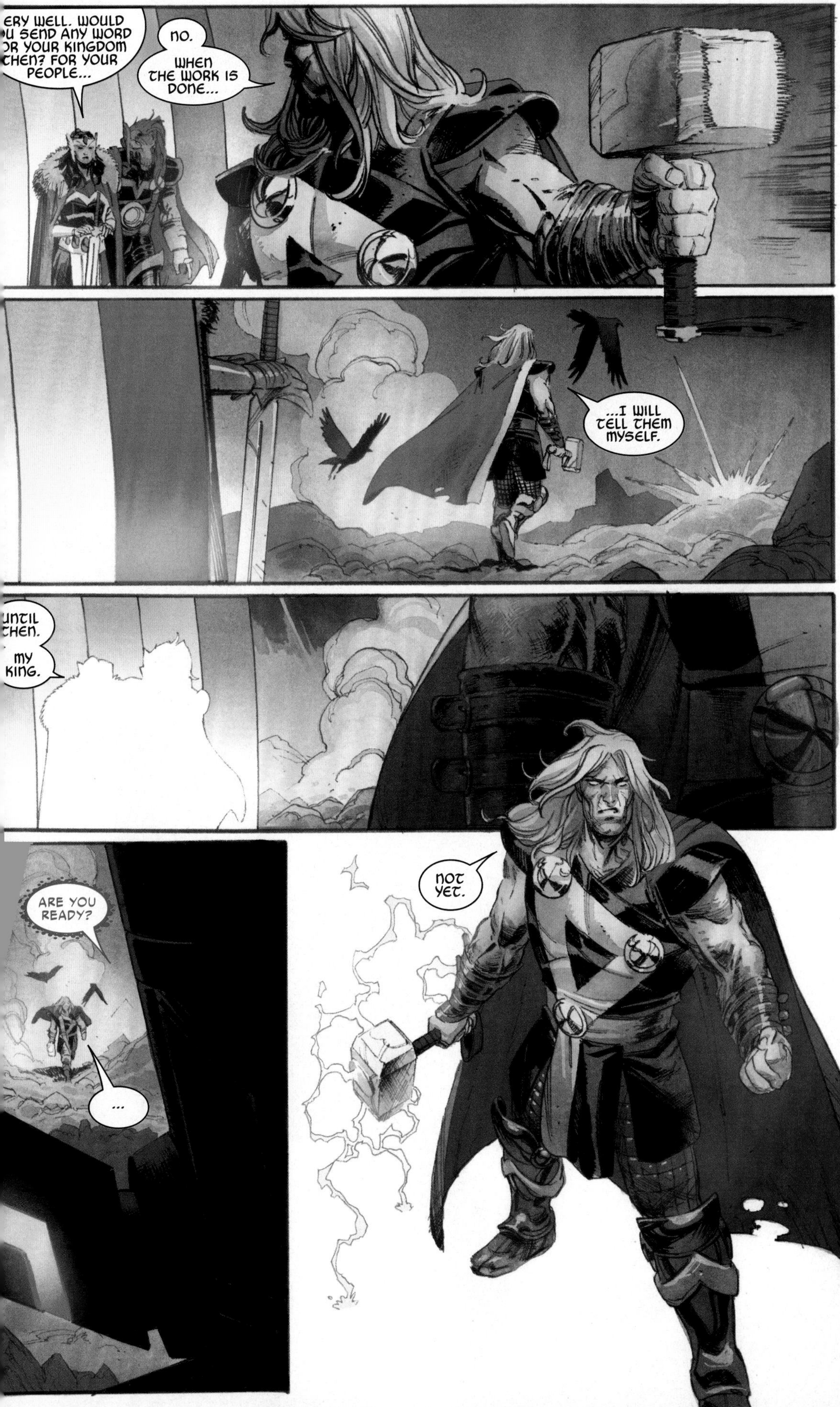
ERY WELL. WOULD
OU SEND ANY WORD
OR YOUR KINGDOM
THEN? FOR YOUR
PEOPLE...
NO.
WHEN
THE WORK IS
DONE...
...I WILL
TELL THEM
MYSELF.
UNTIL
THEN.
MY
KING.
ARE YOU
READY?
...
NOT
YET.

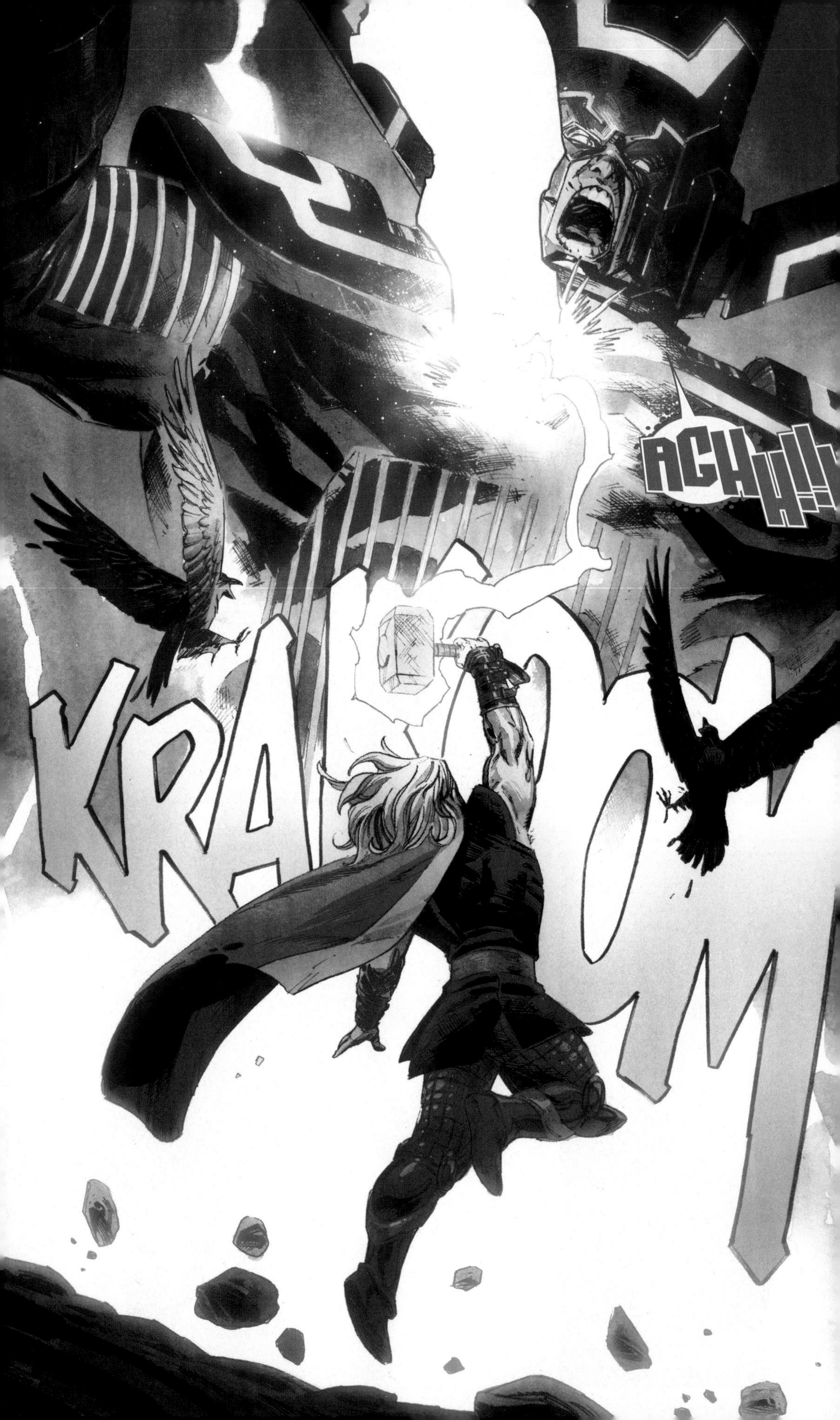
AGHHH!!
KRA OM

GGHH!!!

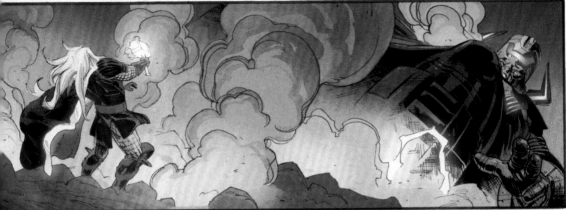

UHF...MY... MY POWER COSMIC...YOU HAVE TAKEN IT...

...YOU DARE...

AYE. AND NOW I AM READY.

LET'S END THIS.

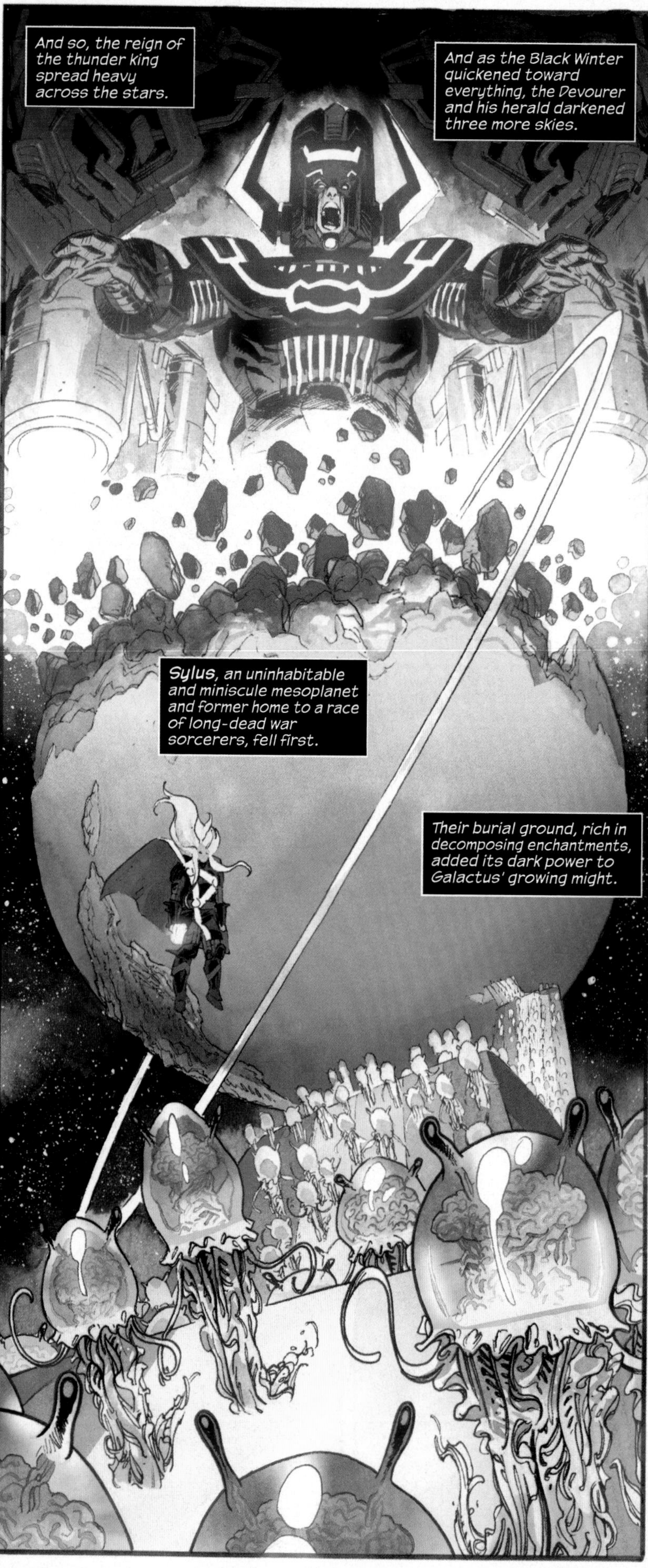

And so, the reign of the thunder king spread heavy across the stars.
And as the Black Winter quickened toward everything, the Devourer and his herald darkened three more skies.
Sylus, an uninhabitable and miniscule mesoplanet and former home to a race of long-dead war sorcerers, fell first.
Their burial ground, rich in decomposing enchantments, added its dark power to Galactus' growing might.

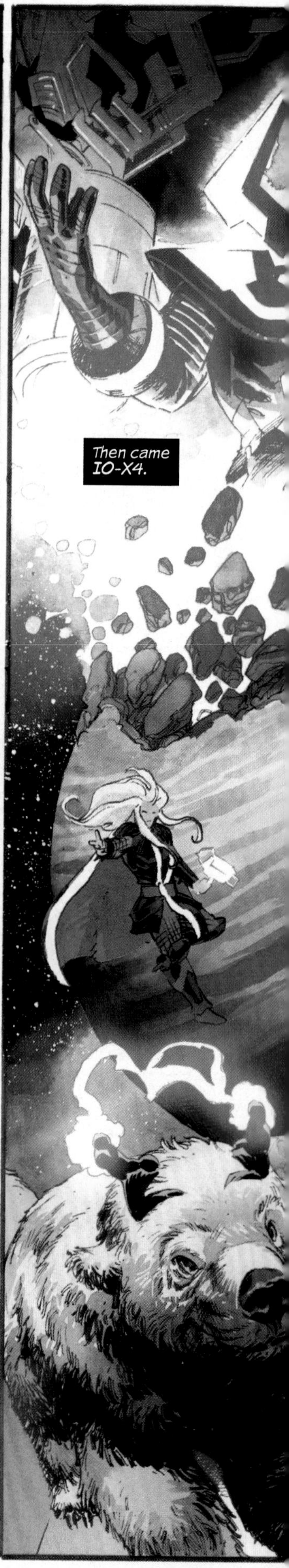

Then came IO-X4.

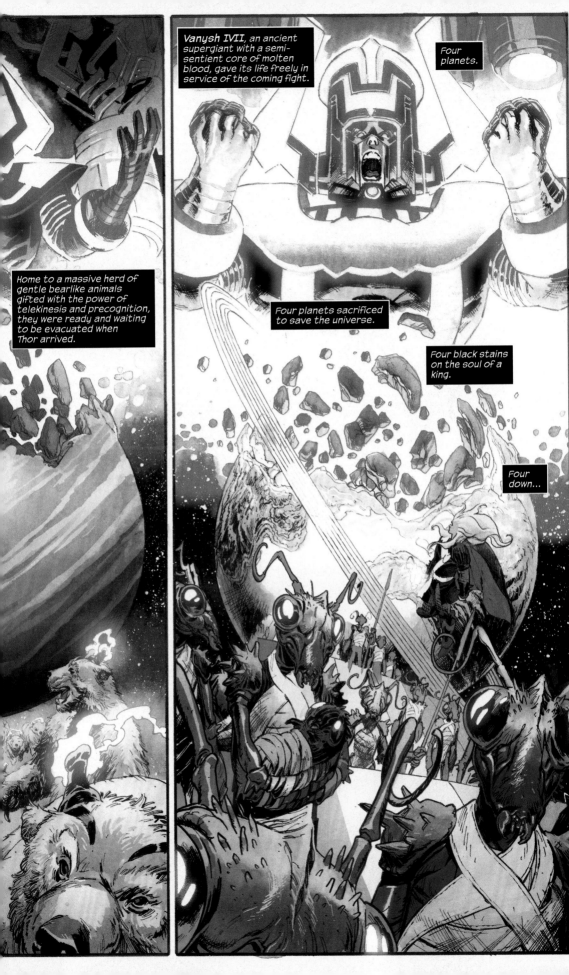

Home to a massive herd of gentle bearlike animals gifted with the power of telekinesis and precognition, they were ready and waiting to be evacuated when Thor arrived.

Vanysh IVII, an ancient supergiant with a semi-sentient core of molten blood, gave its life freely in service of the coming fight.

Four planets.

Four planets sacrificed to save the universe.

Four black stains on the soul of a king.

Four down...

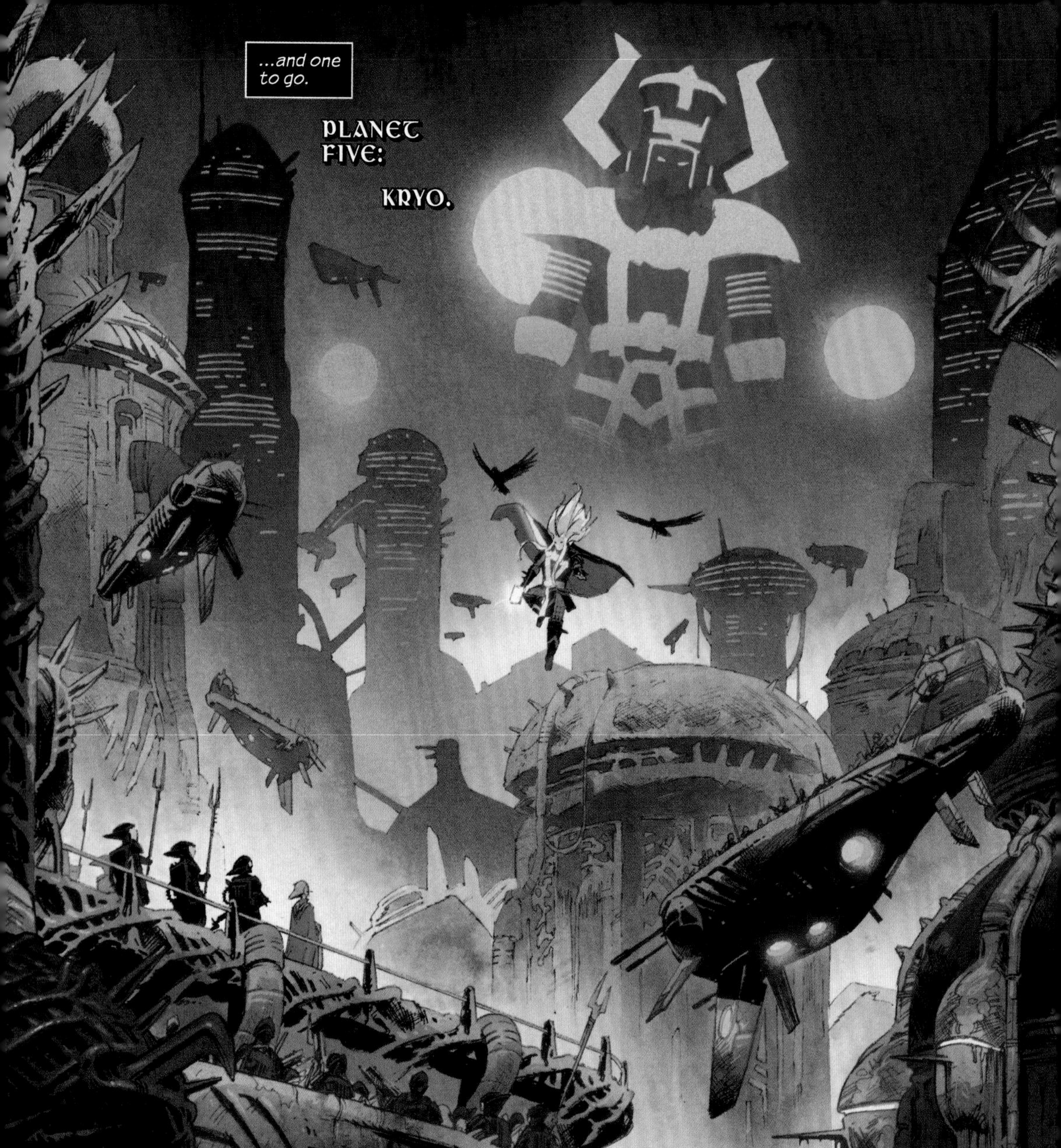
...and one to go.
PLANET FIVE:
KRYO.

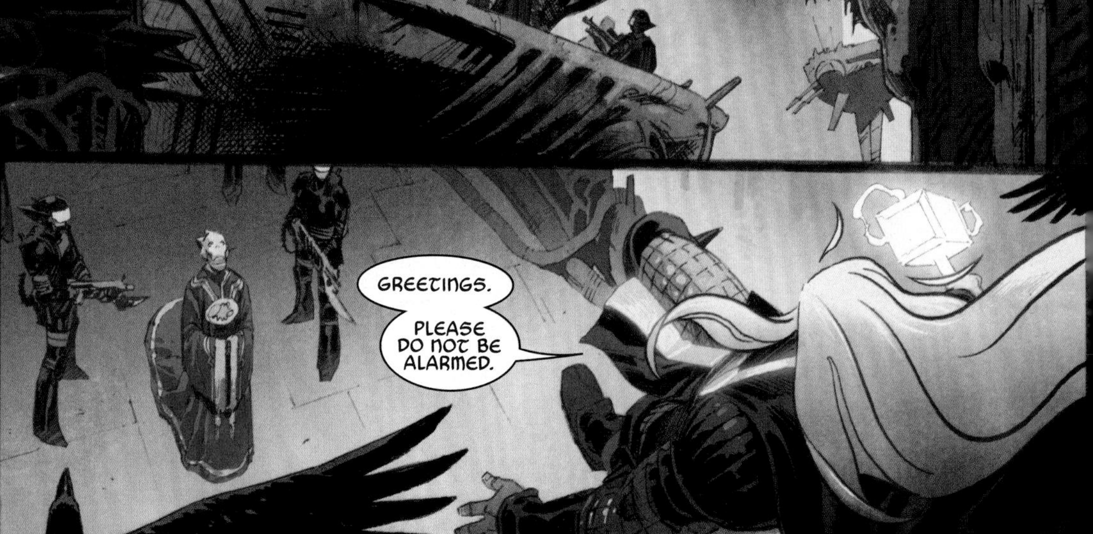
GREETINGS.
PLEASE DO NOT BE ALARMED.

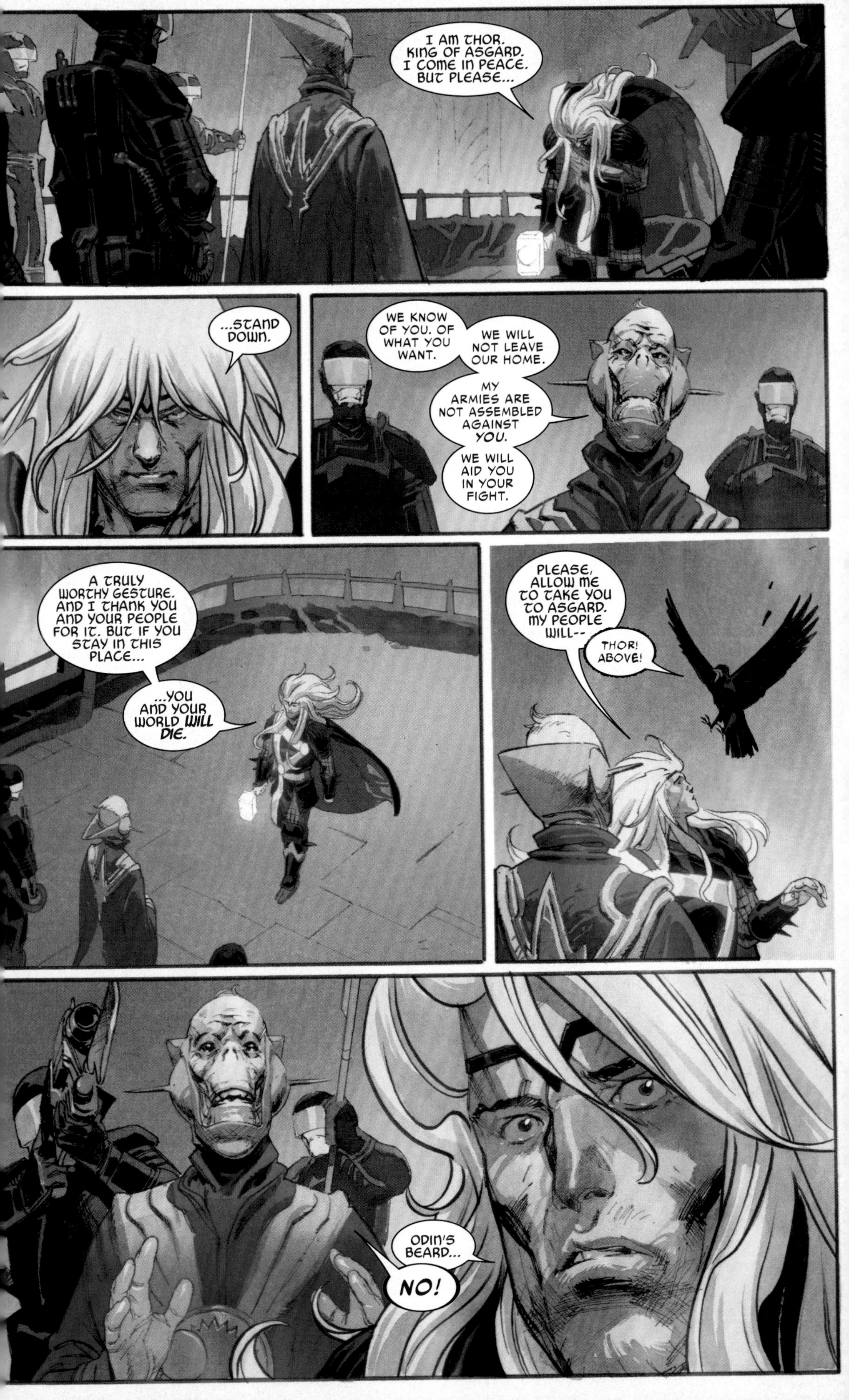

I AM THOR. KING OF ASGARD. I COME IN PEACE. BUT PLEASE...
...STAND DOWN.
WE KNOW OF YOU. OF WHAT YOU WANT.
WE WILL NOT LEAVE OUR HOME.
MY ARMIES ARE NOT ASSEMBLED AGAINST YOU.
WE WILL AID YOU IN YOUR FIGHT.
A TRULY WORTHY GESTURE. AND I THANK YOU AND YOUR PEOPLE FOR IT. BUT IF YOU STAY IN THIS PLACE...
...YOU AND YOUR WORLD WILL DIE.
PLEASE, ALLOW ME TO TAKE YOU TO ASGARD. MY PEOPLE WILL--
THOR! ABOVE!
ODIN'S BEARD...
NO!

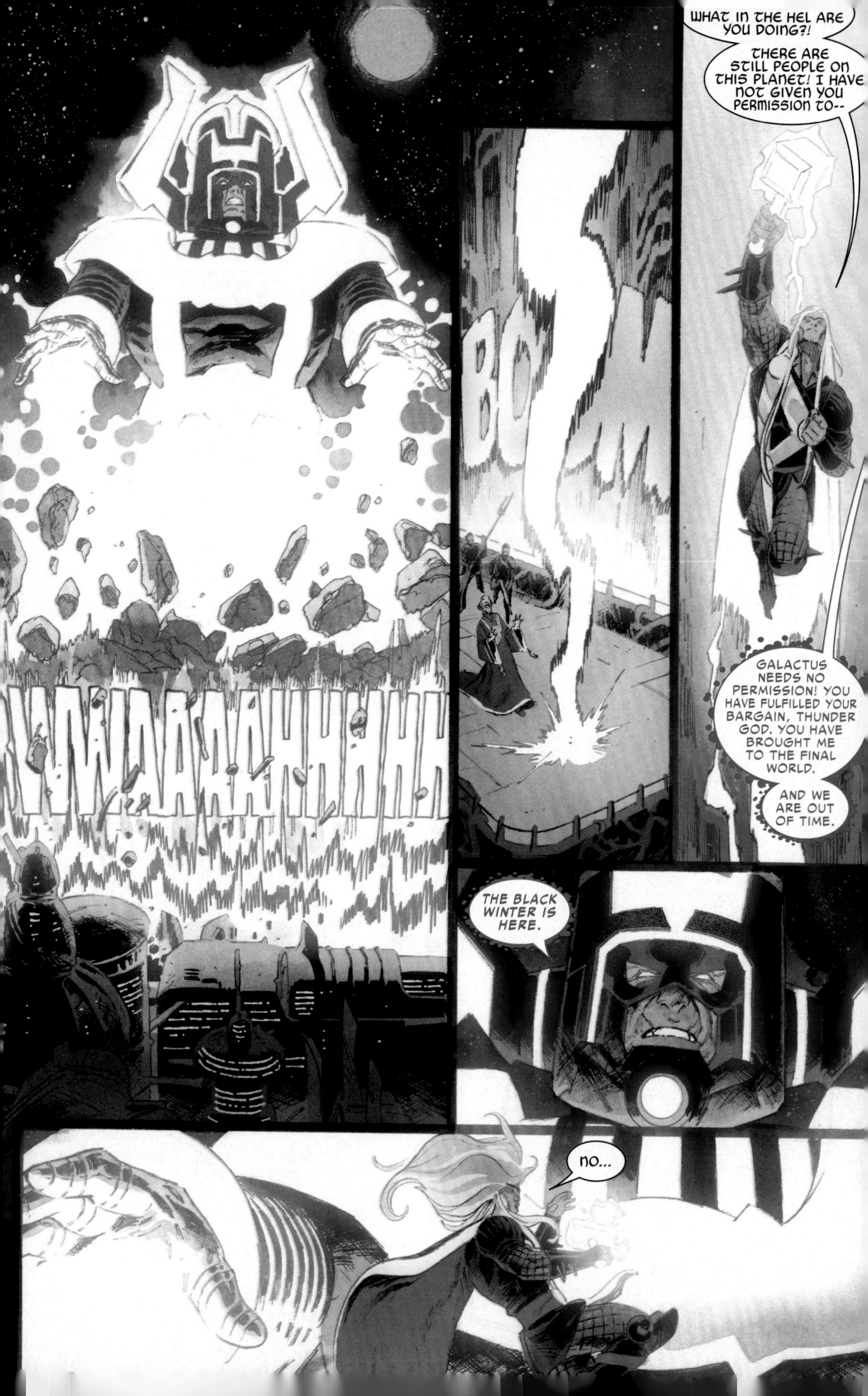
VWAAAHHHHH
WHAT IN THE HEL ARE YOU DOING?!
THERE ARE STILL PEOPLE ON THIS PLANET! I HAVE NOT GIVEN YOU PERMISSION TO--
GALACTUS NEEDS NO PERMISSION! YOU HAVE FULFILLED YOUR BARGAIN, THUNDER GOD. YOU HAVE BROUGHT ME TO THE FINAL WORLD.
AND WE ARE OUT OF TIME.
THE BLACK WINTER IS HERE.
no...

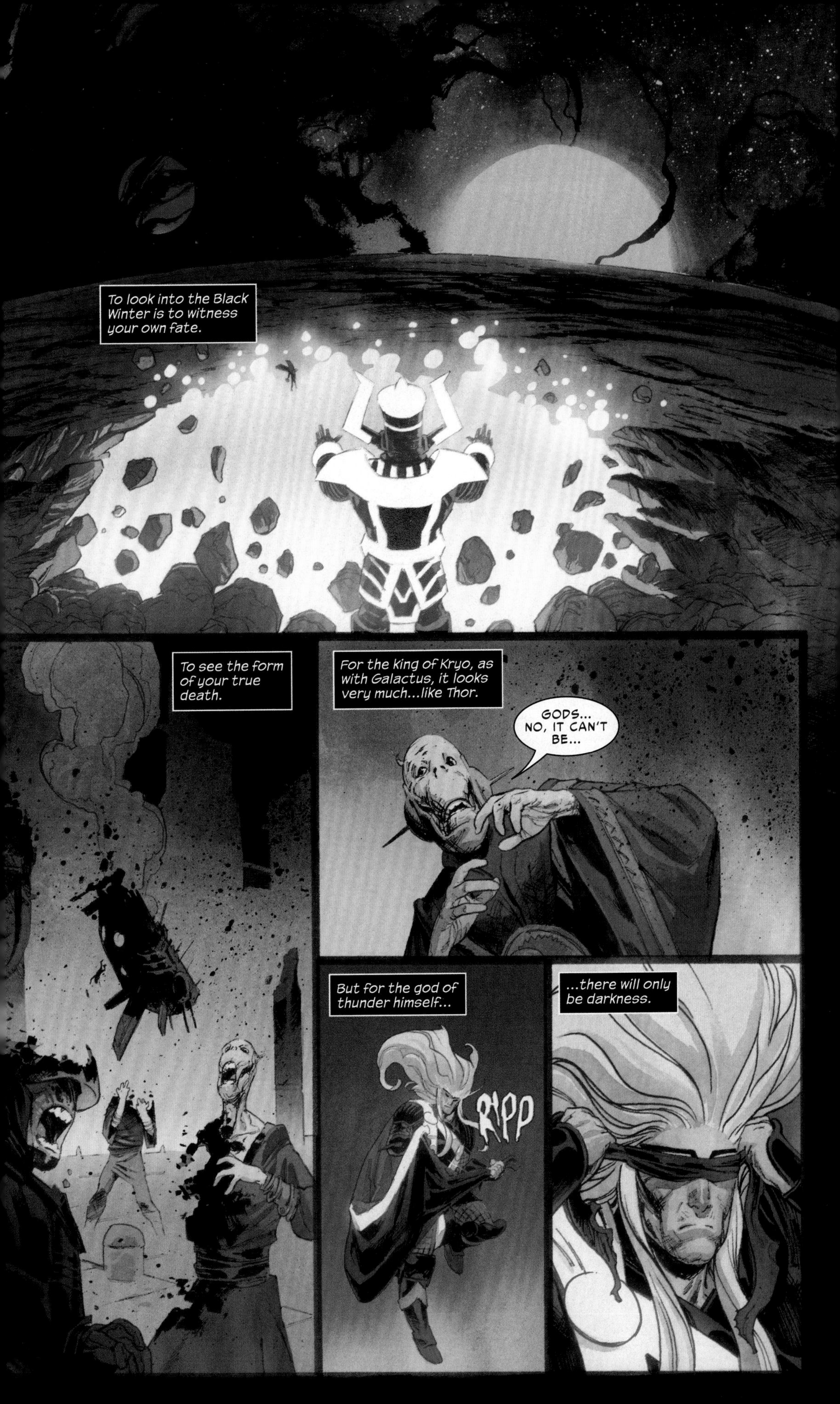

To look into the Black Winter is to witness your own fate.
To see the form of your true death.
For the king of Kryo, as with Galactus, it looks very much...like Thor.
GODS... NO, IT CAN'T BE...
But for the god of thunder himself...
RIPP
...there will only be darkness.

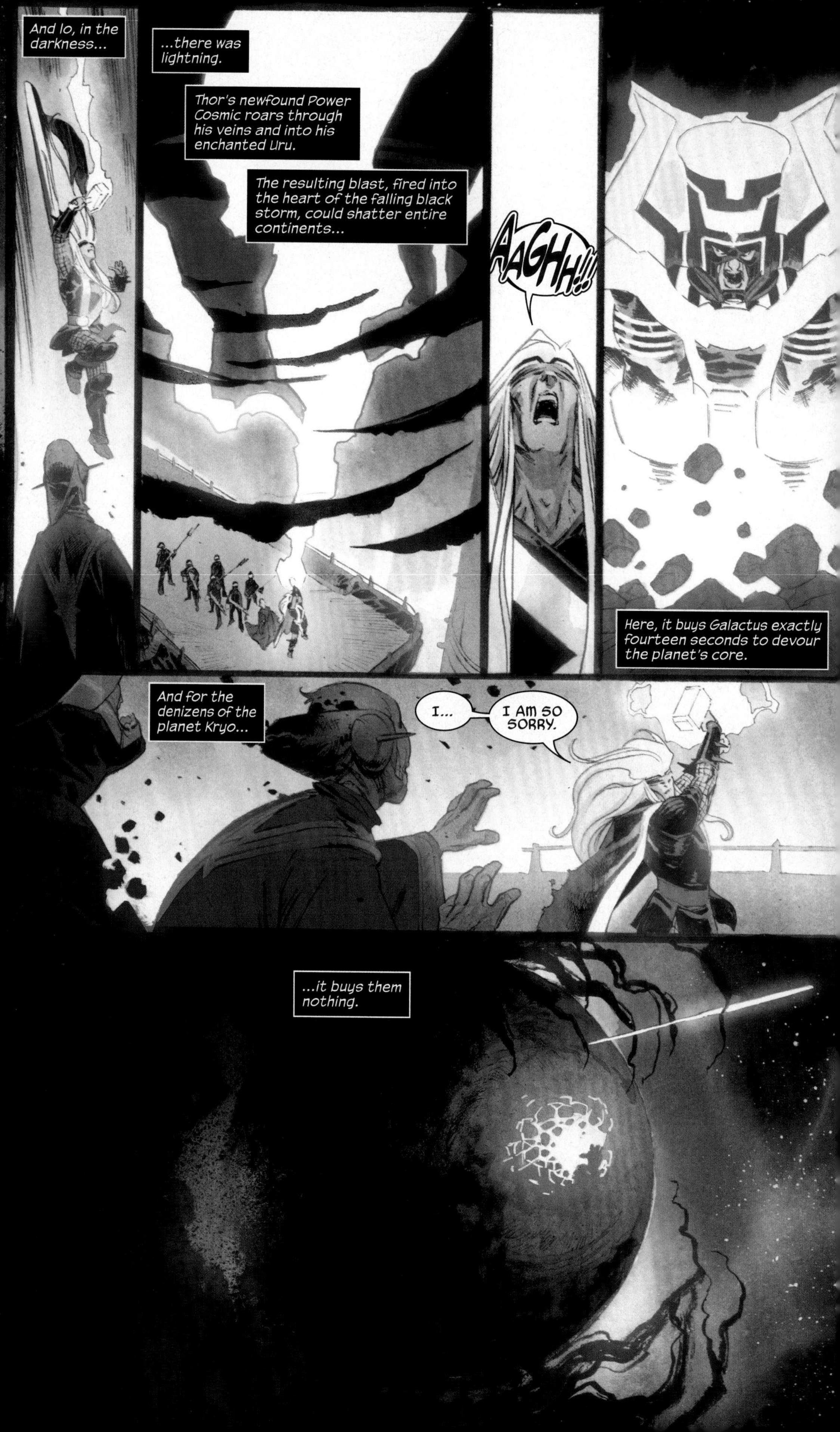

And lo, in the darkness...
...there was lightning.
Thor's newfound Power Cosmic roars through his veins and into his enchanted Uru.
The resulting blast, fired into the heart of the falling black storm, could shatter entire continents...
AAGHH!!!
Here, it buys Galactus exactly fourteen seconds to devour the planet's core.
And for the denizens of the planet Kryo...
I...
I AM SO SORRY.
...it buys them nothing.

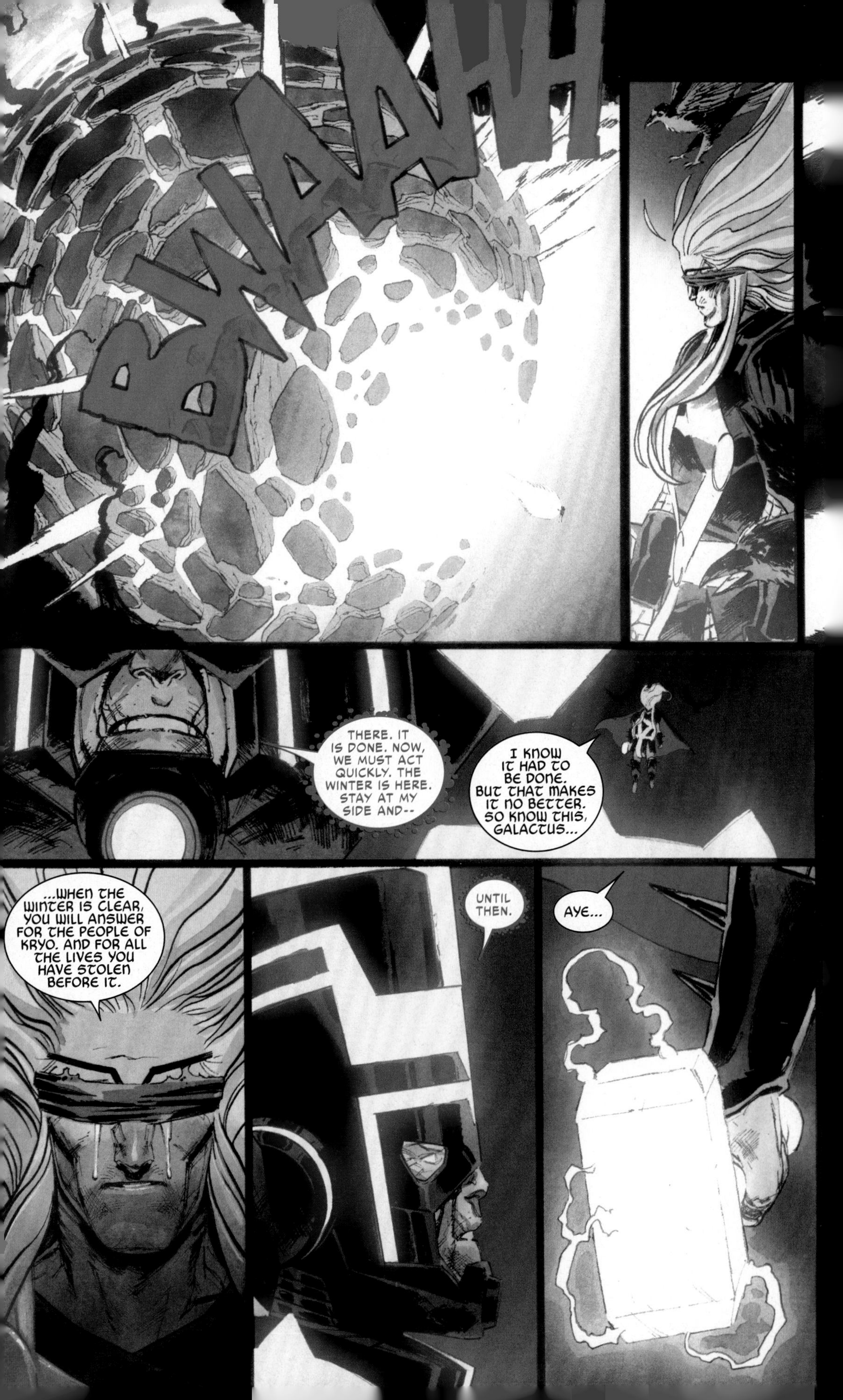
BKAAAH
THERE. IT IS DONE. NOW, WE MUST ACT QUICKLY. THE WINTER IS HERE. STAY AT MY SIDE AND--
I KNOW IT HAD TO BE DONE. BUT THAT MAKES IT NO BETTER. SO KNOW THIS, GALACTUS...
...WHEN THE WINTER IS CLEAR, YOU WILL ANSWER FOR THE PEOPLE OF KRYO. AND FOR ALL THE LIVES YOU HAVE STOLEN BEFORE IT.
UNTIL THEN.
AYE...

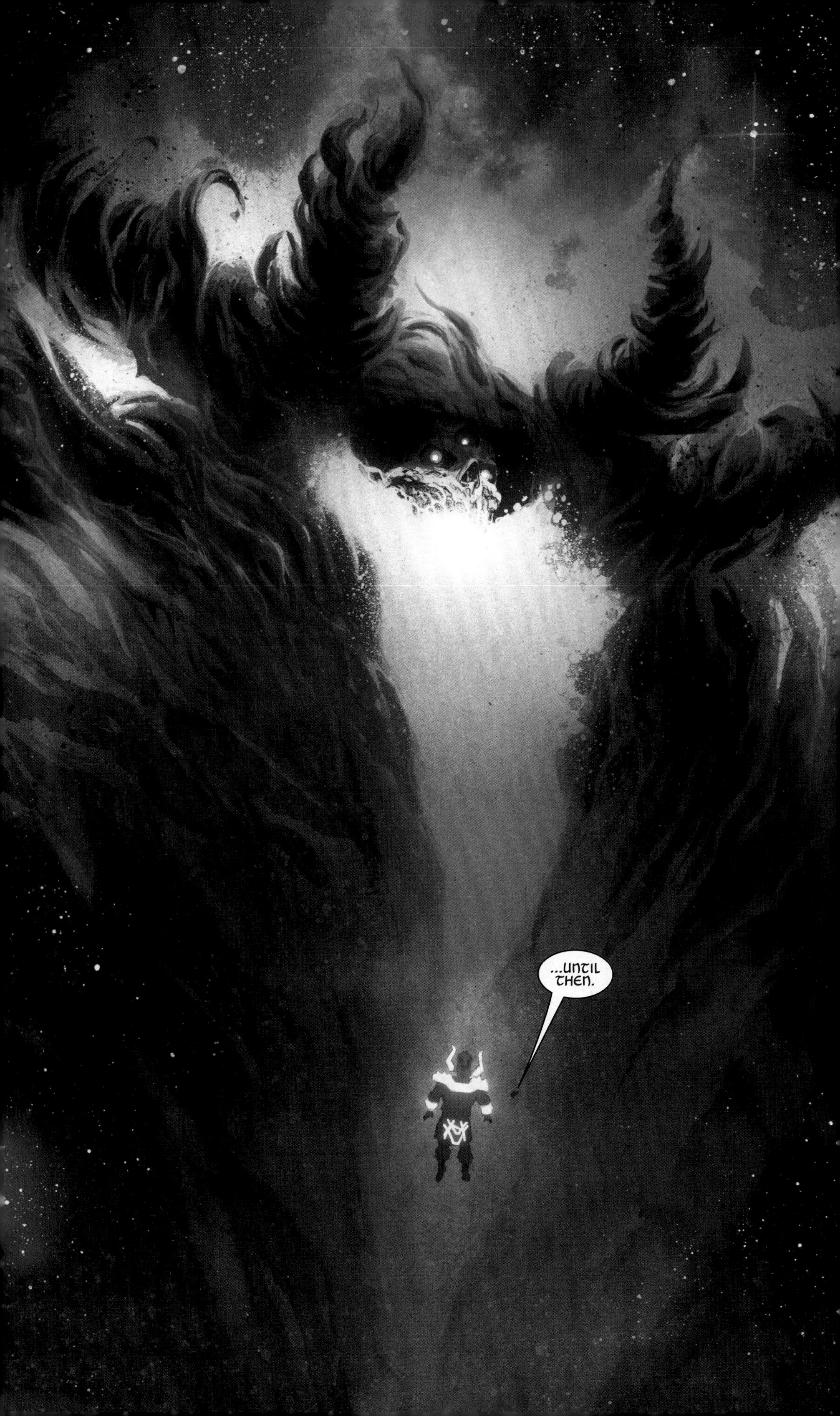
...UNTIL THEN.

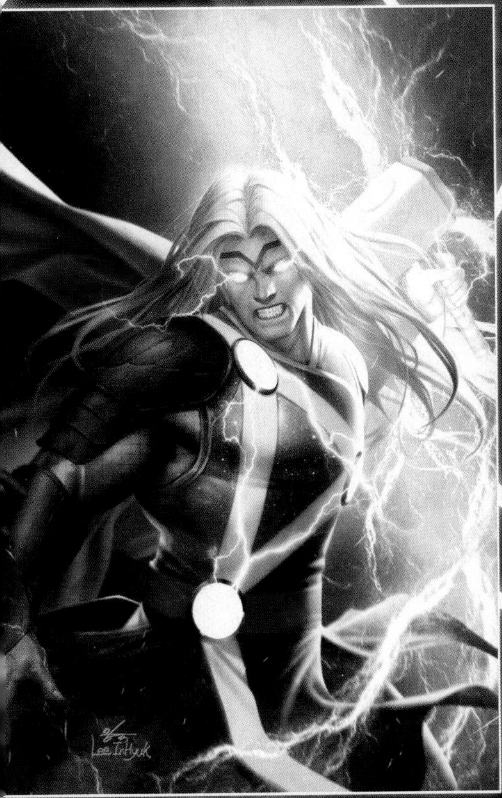
Lee InHyuk

THOR 2 VARIANT BY
InHyuk Lee

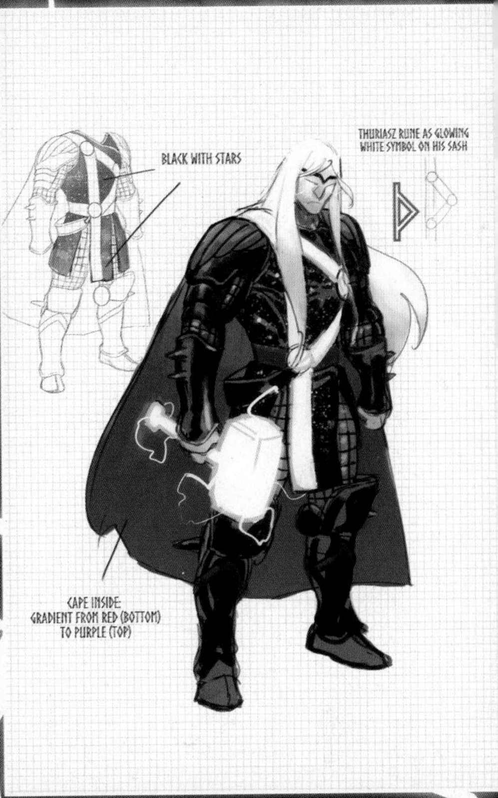
BLACK WITH STARS
THURIASZ RUNE AS GLOWING WHITE SYMBOL ON HIS SASH
CAPE INSIDE: GRADIENT FROM RED (BOTTOM) TO PURPLE (TOP)

THOR 2 DESIGN VARIANT BY
Nic Klein

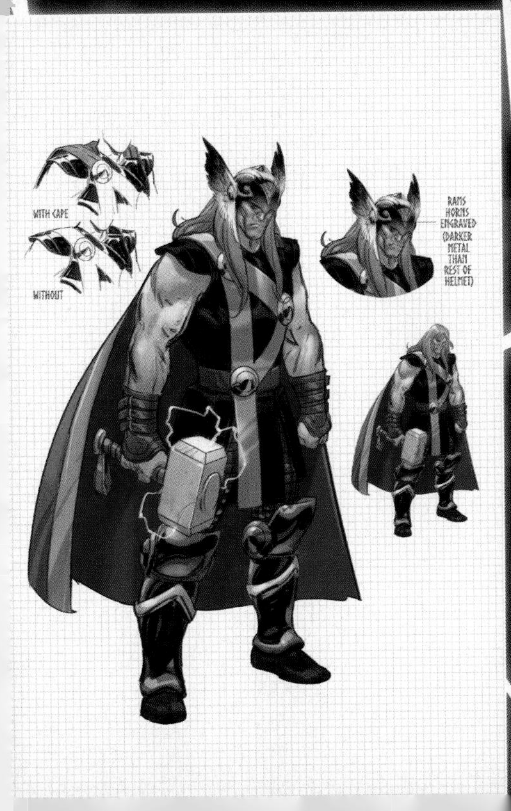
WITH CAPE
WITHOUT
RAMS HORNS ENGRAVED (DARKER METAL THAN REST OF HELMET)

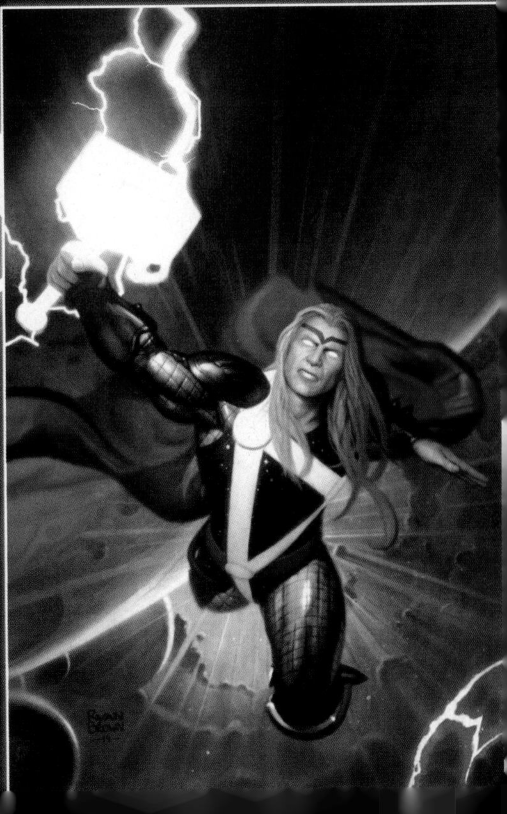

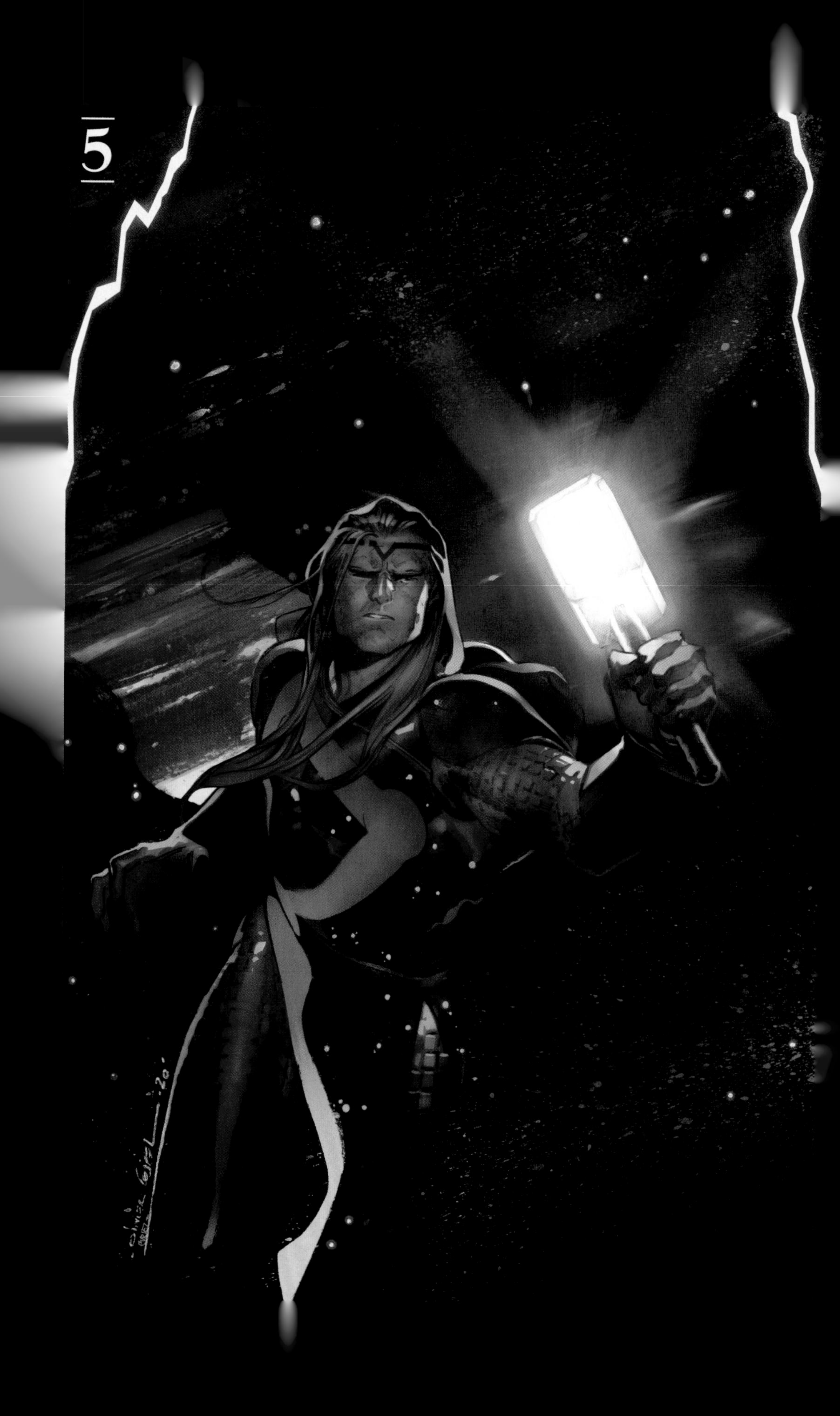
5

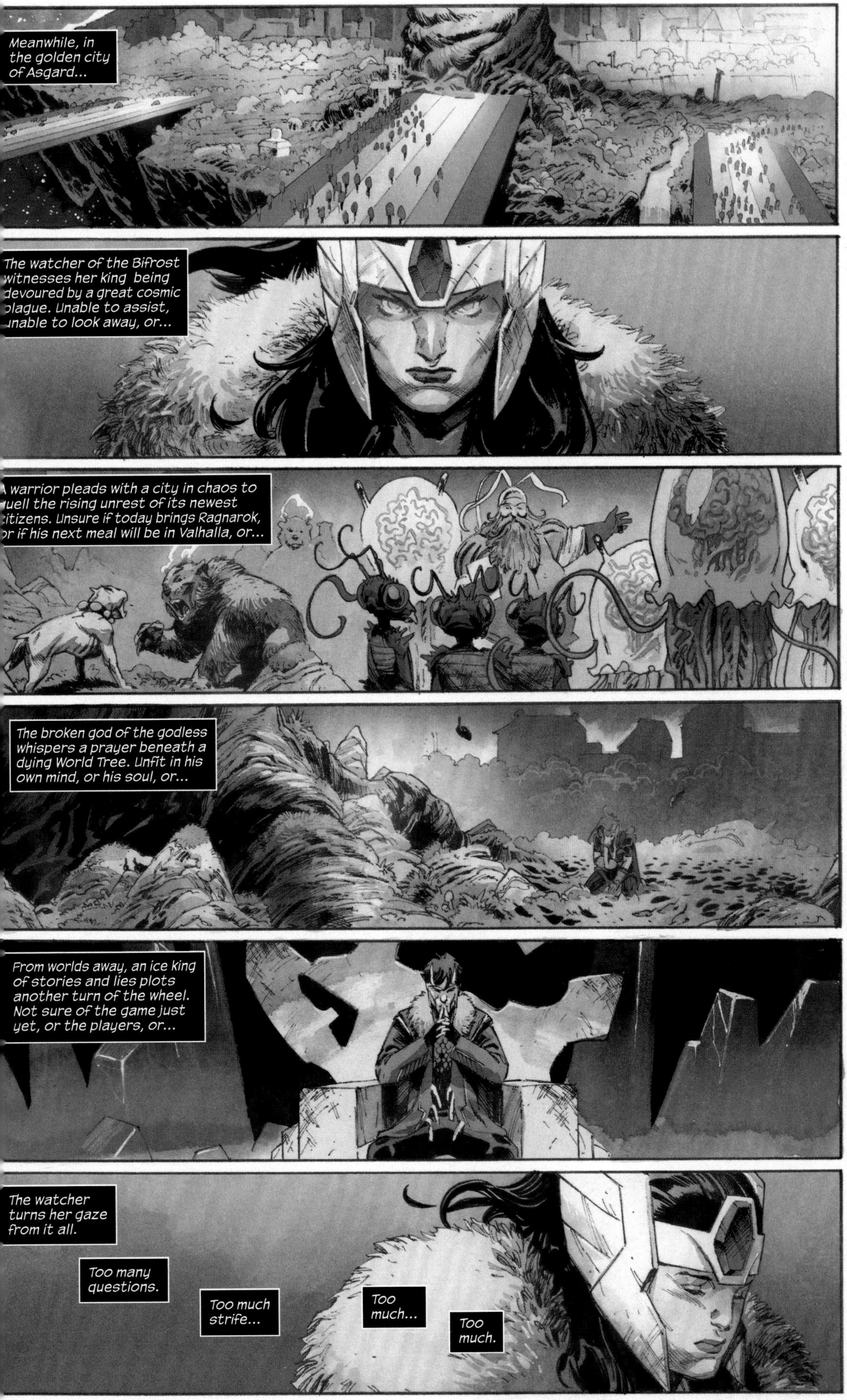
Meanwhile, in the golden city of Asgard...
The watcher of the Bifrost witnesses her king being devoured by a great cosmic plague. Unable to assist, unable to look away, or...
warrior pleads with a city in chaos to uell the rising unrest of its newest itizens. Unsure if today brings Ragnarok, r if his next meal will be in Valhalla, or...
The broken god of the godless whispers a prayer beneath a dying World Tree. Unfit in his own mind, or his soul, or...
From worlds away, an ice king of stories and lies plots another turn of the wheel. Not sure of the game just yet, or the players, or...
The watcher turns her gaze from it all.
Too many questions.
Too much strife...
Too much...
Too much.

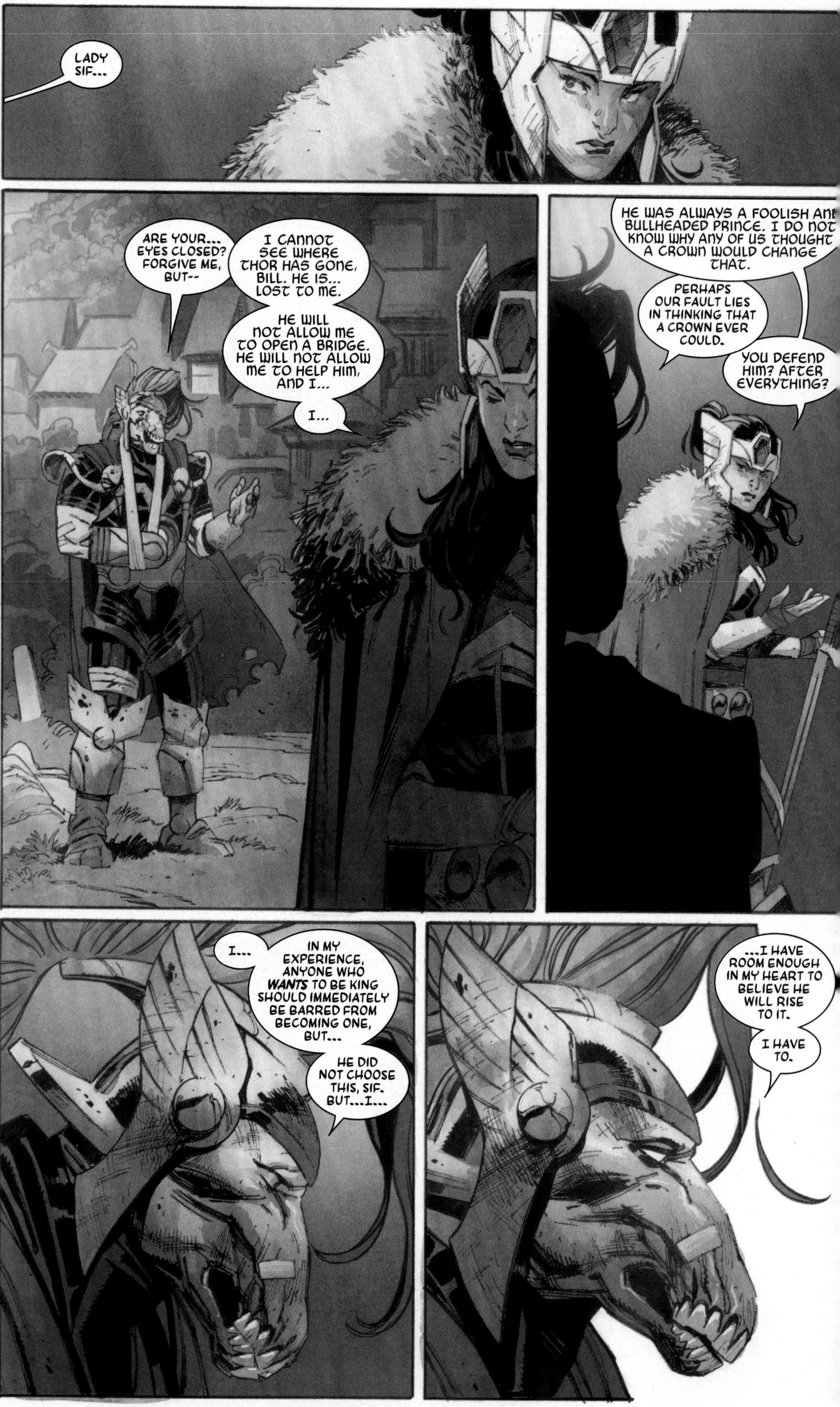

LADY SIF...
ARE YOUR... EYES CLOSED? FORGIVE ME, BUT--
I CANNOT SEE WHERE THOR HAS GONE, BILL. HE IS... LOST TO ME.
HE WILL NOT ALLOW ME TO OPEN A BRIDGE. HE WILL NOT ALLOW ME TO HELP HIM, AND I...
I...
HE WAS ALWAYS A FOOLISH AND BULLHEADED PRINCE. I DO NOT KNOW WHY ANY OF US THOUGHT A CROWN WOULD CHANGE THAT.
PERHAPS OUR FAULT LIES IN THINKING THAT A CROWN EVER COULD.
YOU DEFEND HIM? AFTER EVERYTHING?
I...
IN MY EXPERIENCE, ANYONE WHO *WANTS* TO BE KING SHOULD IMMEDIATELY BE BARRED FROM BECOMING ONE, BUT...
HE DID NOT CHOOSE THIS, SIF. BUT...I...
...I HAVE ROOM ENOUGH IN MY HEART TO BELIEVE HE WILL RISE TO IT.
I HAVE TO.

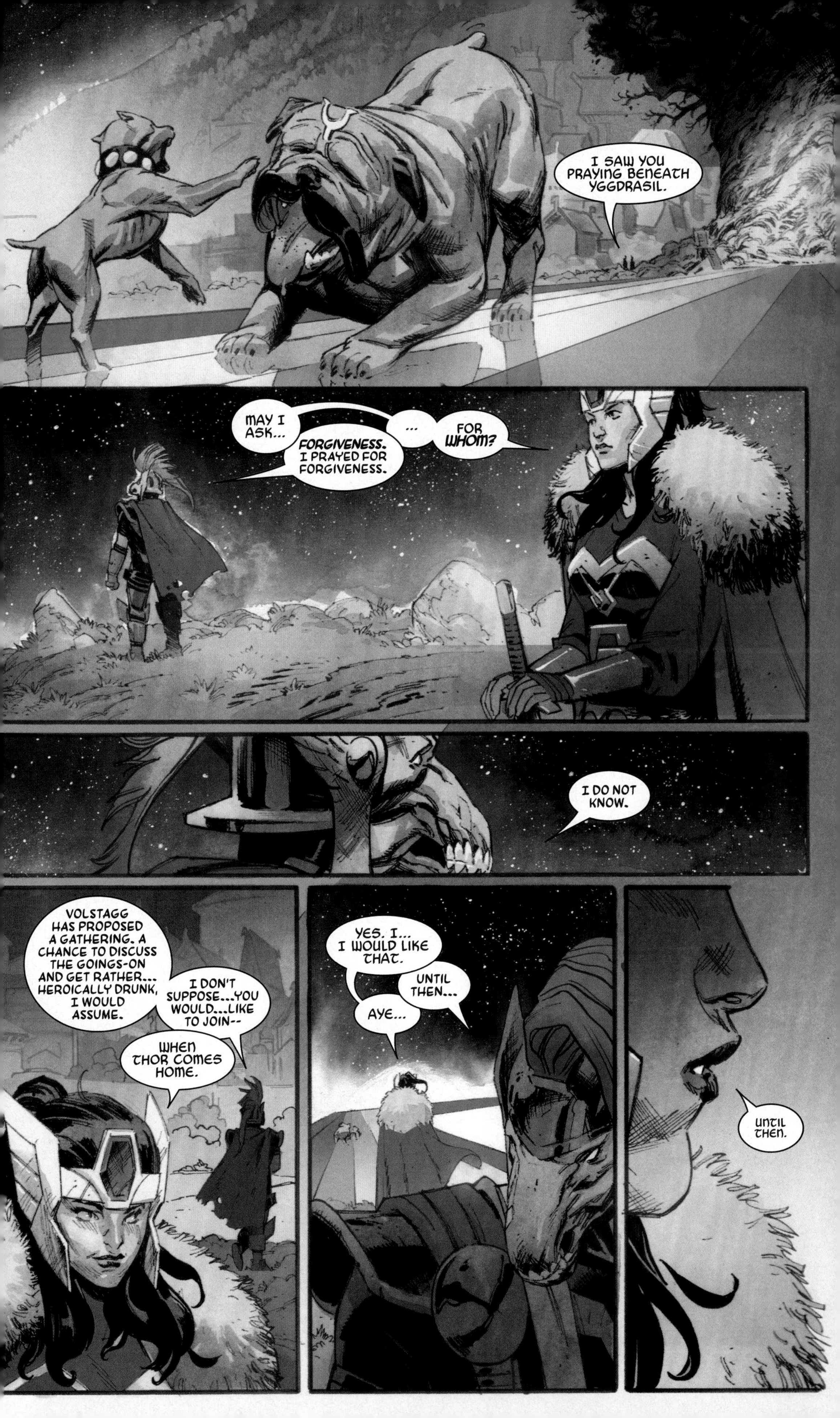
I SAW YOU PRAYING BENEATH YGGDRASIL.
MAY I ASK...
FORGIVENESS. I PRAYED FOR FORGIVENESS.
...
FOR WHOM?
I DO NOT KNOW.
VOLSTAGG HAS PROPOSED A GATHERING. A CHANCE TO DISCUSS THE GOINGS-ON AND GET RATHER... HEROICALLY DRUNK, I WOULD ASSUME.
I DON'T SUPPOSE...YOU WOULD...LIKE TO JOIN--
WHEN THOR COMES HOME.
YES. I... I WOULD LIKE THAT.
UNTIL THEN...
AYE...
UNTIL THEN.

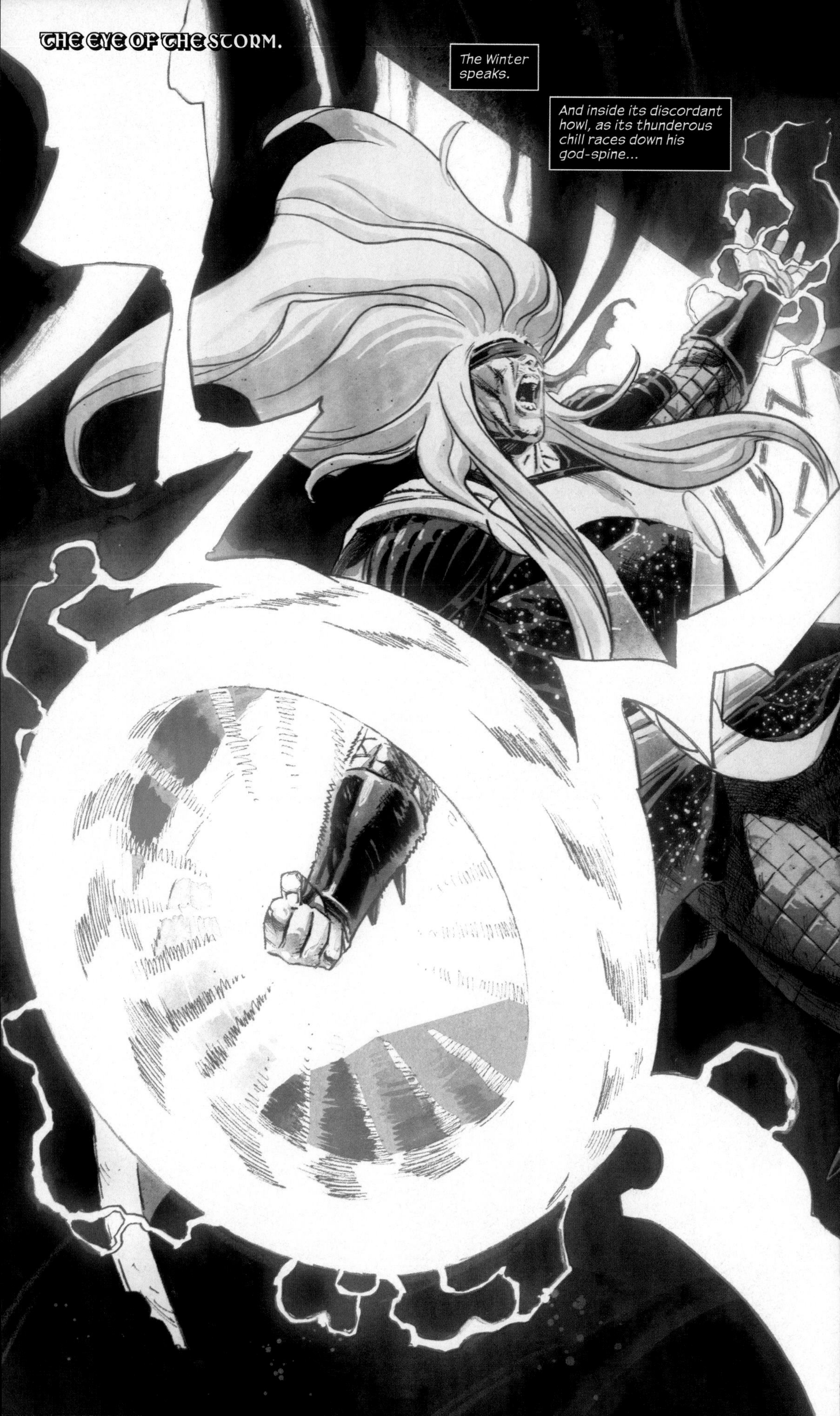
THE EYE OF THE STORM.
The Winter speaks.
And inside its discordant howl, as its thunderous chill races down his god-spine...

...Thor hears something he has never heard before... but recognizes at once:
AGHHH!!!
The sound of the end.
The last choking breath of the universe.

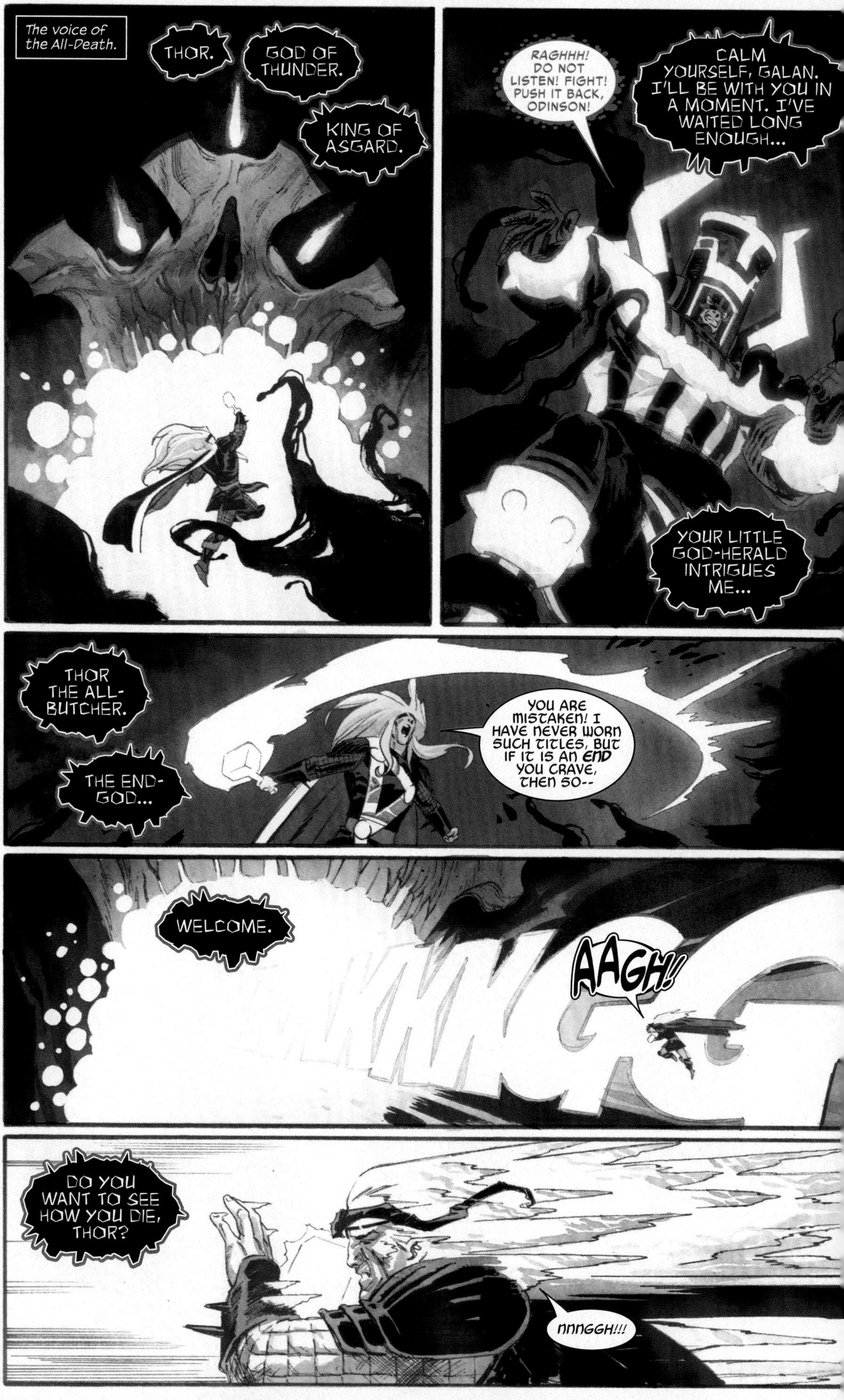

The voice of the All-Death.
THOR.
GOD OF THUNDER.
KING OF ASGARD.
RAGHHH! DO NOT LISTEN! FIGHT! PUSH IT BACK, ODINSON!
CALM YOURSELF, GALAN. I'LL BE WITH YOU IN A MOMENT. I'VE WAITED LONG ENOUGH...
YOUR LITTLE GOD-HERALD INTRIGUES ME...
THOR THE ALL-BUTCHER.
THE END-GOD...
YOU ARE MISTAKEN! I HAVE NEVER WORN SUCH TITLES, BUT IF IT IS AN END YOU CRAVE, THEN SO--
WELCOME.
AAGH!!
DO YOU WANT TO SEE HOW YOU DIE, THOR?
NNNGGH!!!

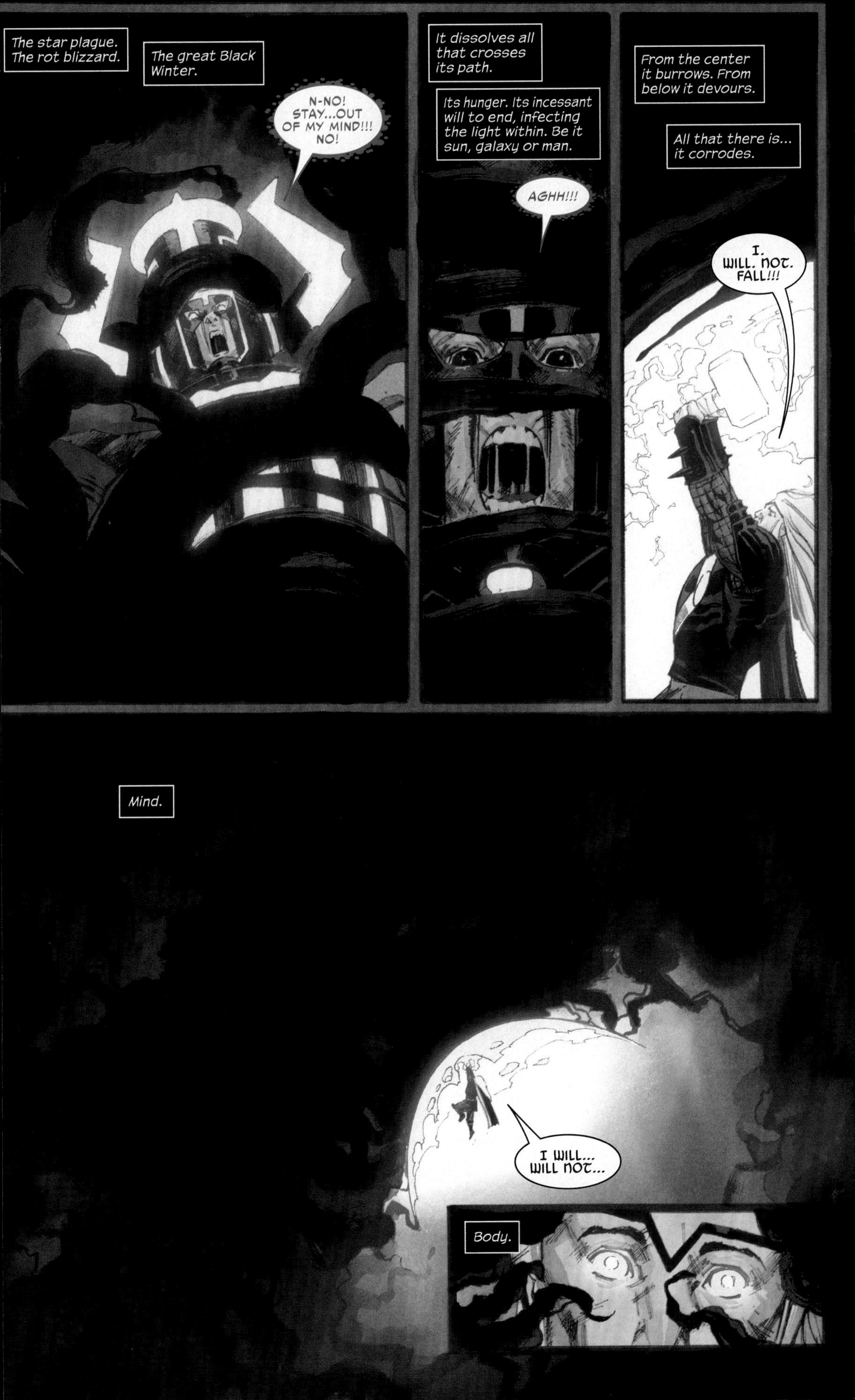

The star plague. The rot blizzard.
The great Black Winter.
N-NO! STAY...OUT OF MY MIND!!! NO!
It dissolves all that crosses its path.
Its hunger. Its incessant will to end, infecting the light within. Be it sun, galaxy or man.
AGHH!!!
From the center it burrows. From below it devours.
All that there is... it corrodes.
I. WILL. NOT. FALL!!!
Mind.
I WILL... WILL NOT...
Body.

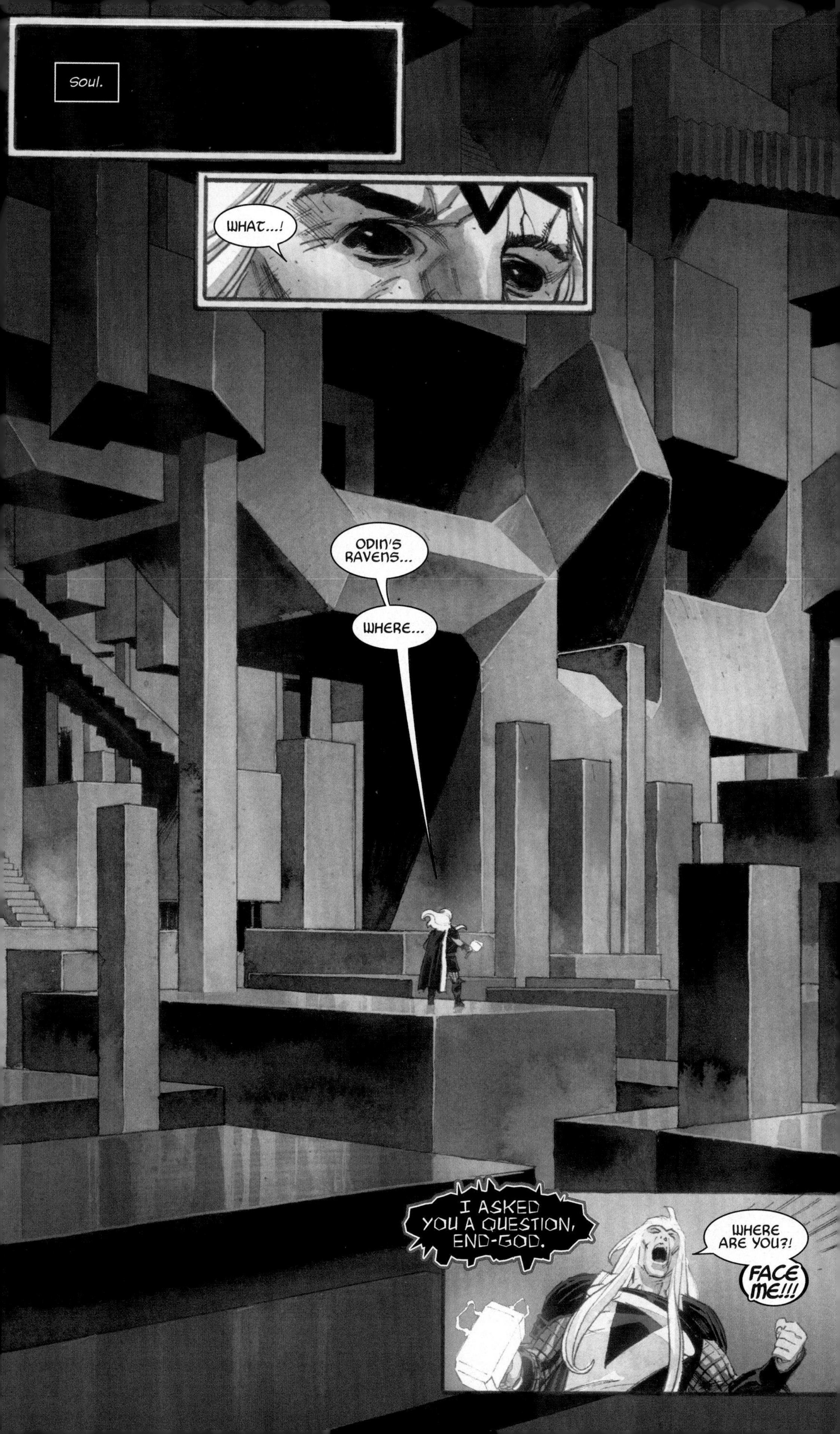

Soul.
WHAT...!
ODIN'S RAVENS...
WHERE...
I ASKED YOU A QUESTION, END-GOD.
WHERE ARE YOU?!
FACE ME!!!

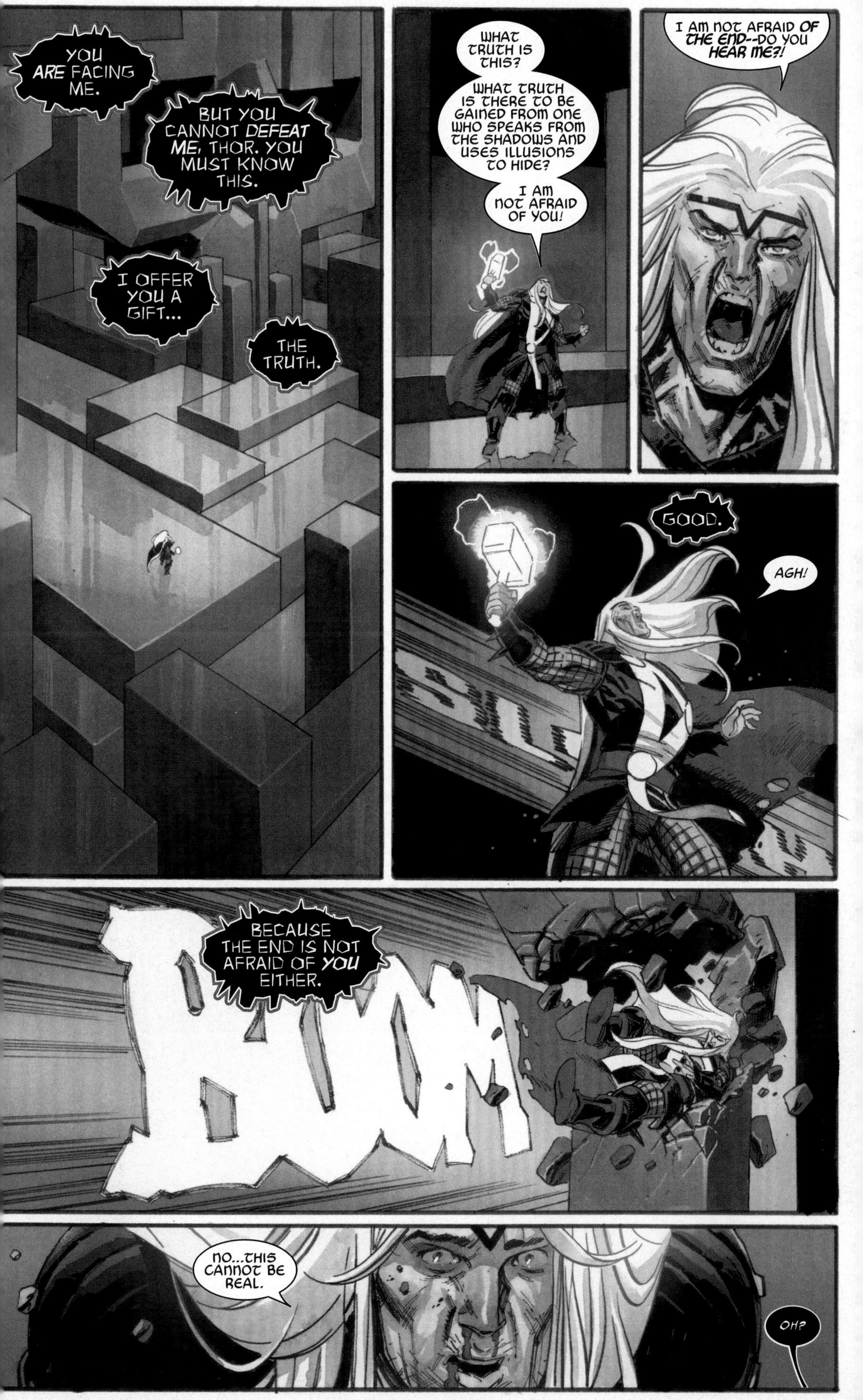

YOU ARE FACING ME.
BUT YOU CANNOT DEFEAT ME, THOR. YOU MUST KNOW THIS.
I OFFER YOU A GIFT...
THE TRUTH.
WHAT TRUTH IS THIS?
WHAT TRUTH IS THERE TO BE GAINED FROM ONE WHO SPEAKS FROM THE SHADOWS AND USES ILLUSIONS TO HIDE?
I AM NOT AFRAID OF YOU!
I AM NOT AFRAID OF THE END--DO YOU HEAR ME?!
GOOD.
AGH!
BECAUSE THE END IS NOT AFRAID OF YOU EITHER.
NO...THIS CANNOT BE REAL.
OH?

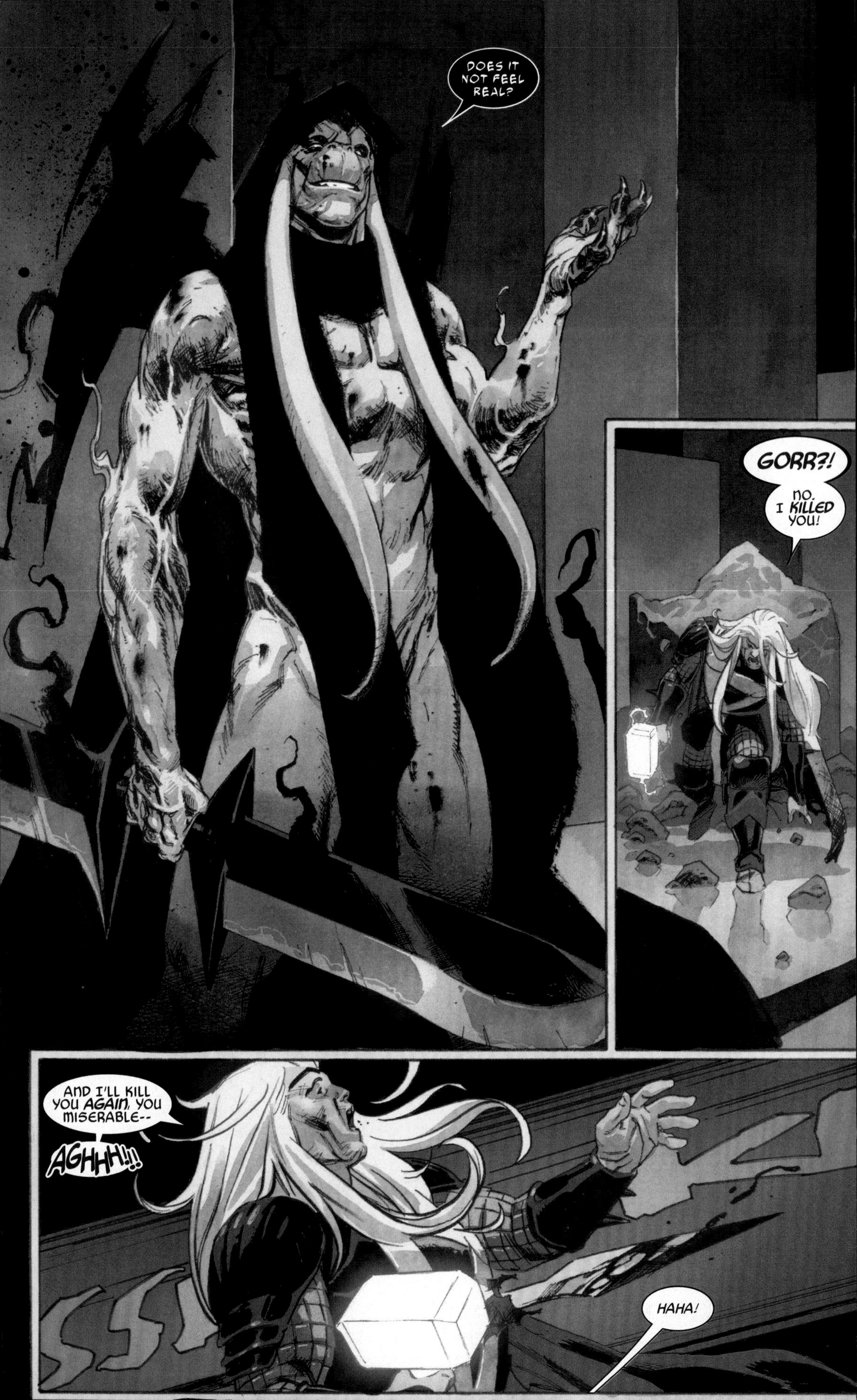
DOES IT NOT FEEL REAL?
GORR?!
NO. I KILLED YOU!
AND I'LL KILL YOU AGAIN, YOU MISERABLE--
AGHHH!!!
HAHA!

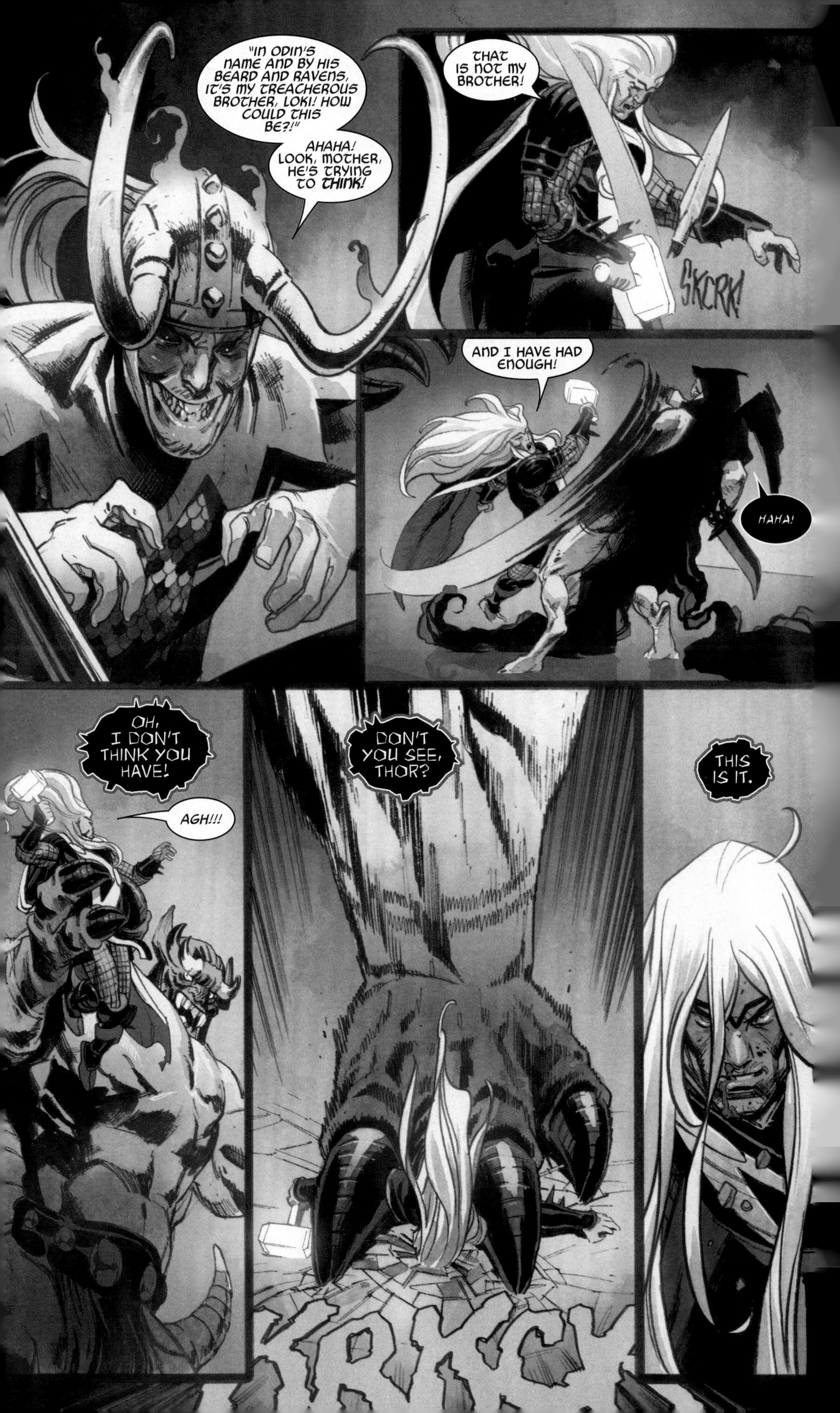
"IN ODIN'S NAME AND BY HIS BEARD AND RAVENS, IT'S MY TREACHEROUS BROTHER, LOKI! HOW COULD THIS BE?!"
AHAHA! LOOK, MOTHER, HE'S TRYING TO THINK!
THAT IS NOT MY BROTHER!
SKCRK!
AND I HAVE HAD ENOUGH!
HAHA!
OH, I DON'T THINK YOU HAVE!
AGH!!!
DON'T YOU SEE, THOR?
THIS IS IT.

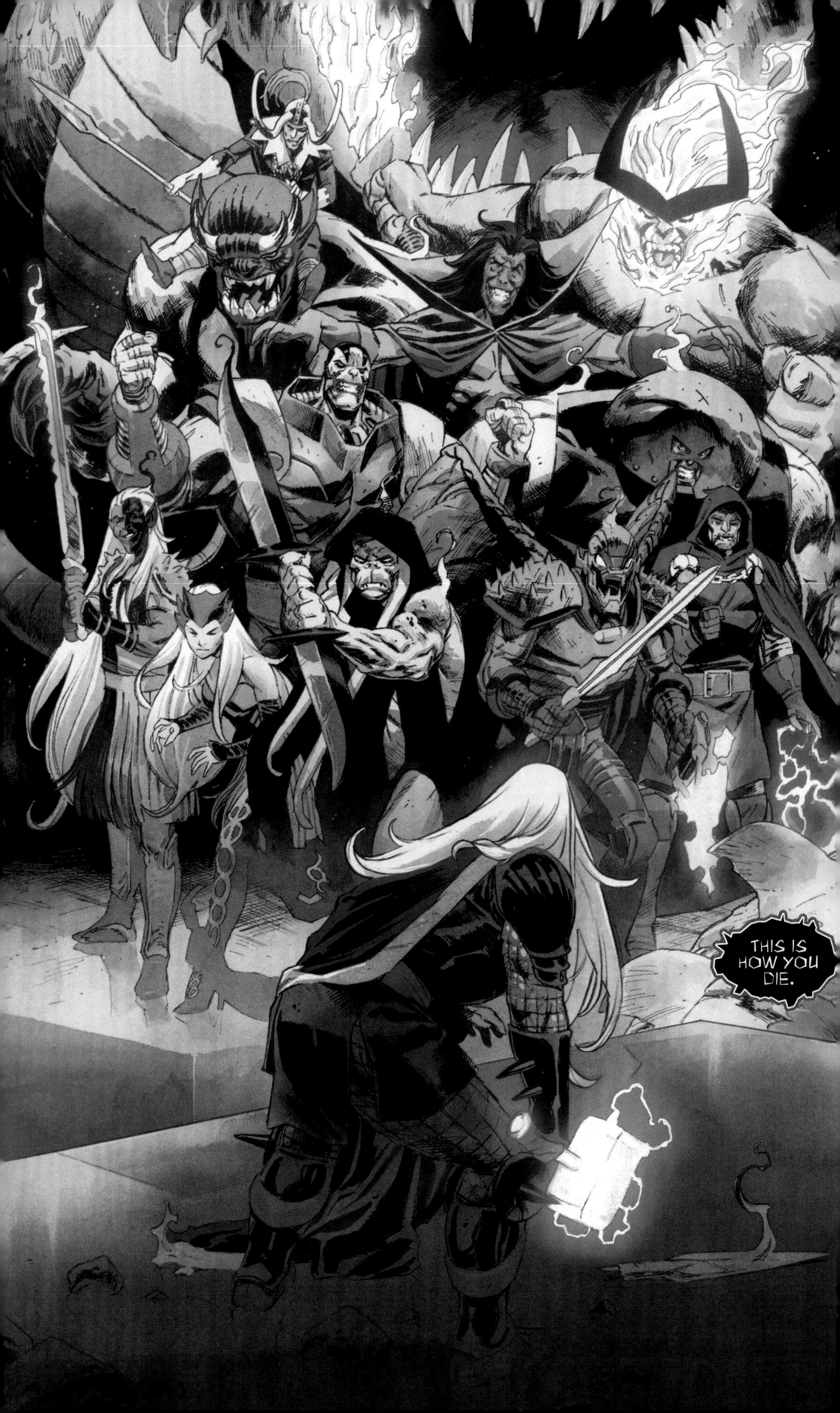
THIS IS HOW YOU DIE.

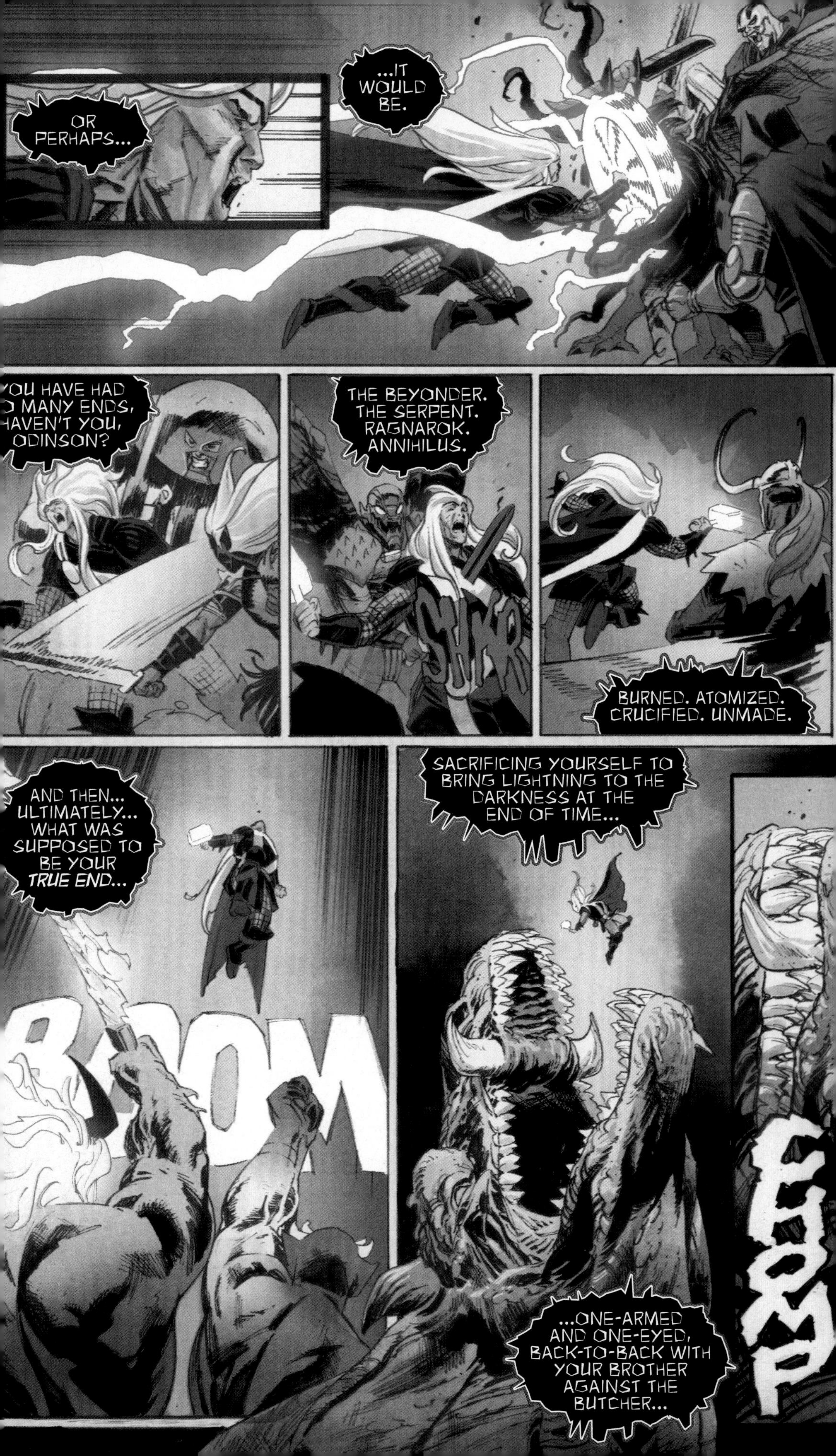
OR PERHAPS...
...IT WOULD BE.
YOU HAVE HAD SO MANY ENDS, HAVEN'T YOU, ODINSON?
THE BEYONDER. THE SERPENT. RAGNAROK. ANNIHILUS.
SHNK
BURNED. ATOMIZED. CRUCIFIED. UNMADE.
AND THEN... ULTIMATELY... WHAT WAS SUPPOSED TO BE YOUR *TRUE END*...
SACRIFICING YOURSELF TO BRING LIGHTNING TO THE DARKNESS AT THE END OF TIME...
...ONE-ARMED AND ONE-EYED, BACK-TO-BACK WITH YOUR BROTHER AGAINST THE BUTCHER...
CHOMP

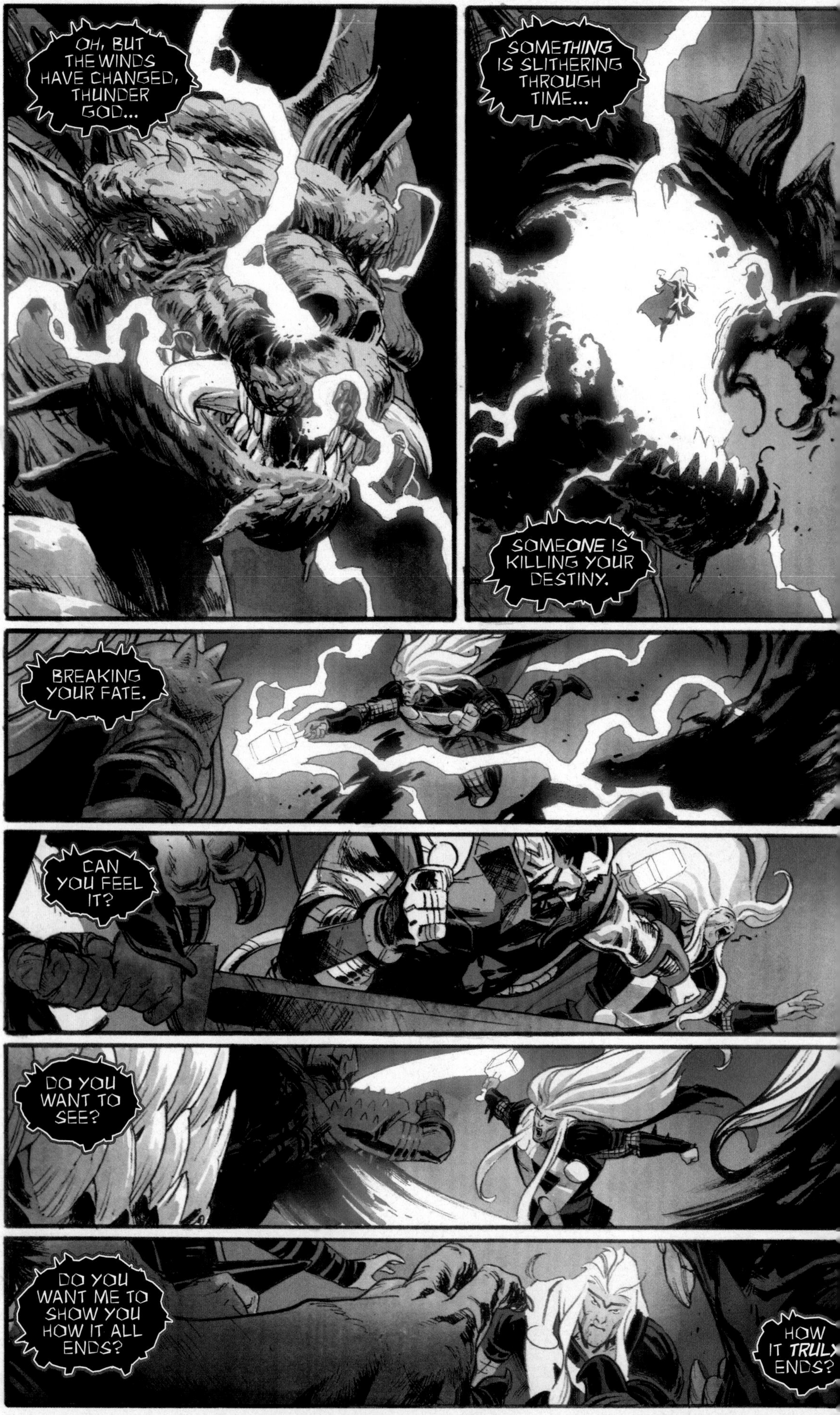

OH, BUT THE WINDS HAVE CHANGED, THUNDER GOD...
SOMETHING IS SLITHERING THROUGH TIME...
SOMEONE IS KILLING YOUR DESTINY.
BREAKING YOUR FATE.
CAN YOU FEEL IT?
DO YOU WANT TO SEE?
DO YOU WANT ME TO SHOW YOU HOW IT ALL ENDS?
HOW IT TRULY ENDS?

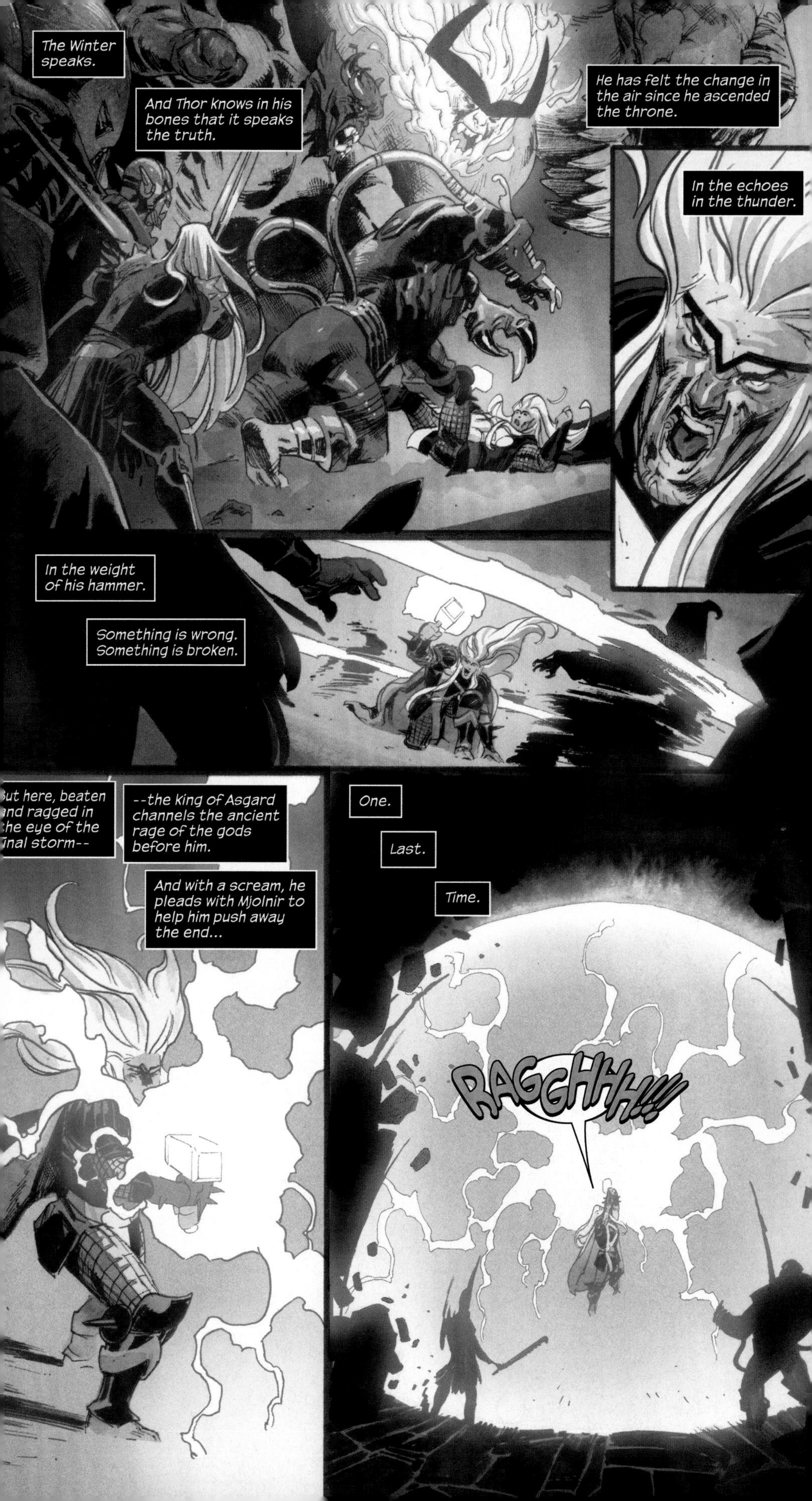
The Winter speaks.
And Thor knows in his bones that it speaks the truth.
He has felt the change in the air since he ascended the throne.
In the echoes in the thunder.
In the weight of his hammer.
Something is wrong. Something is broken.
ut here, beaten nd ragged in he eye of the nal storm--
--the king of Asgard channels the ancient rage of the gods before him.
And with a scream, he pleads with Mjolnir to help him push away the end...
One.
Last.
Time.
RAGGHHH!!!

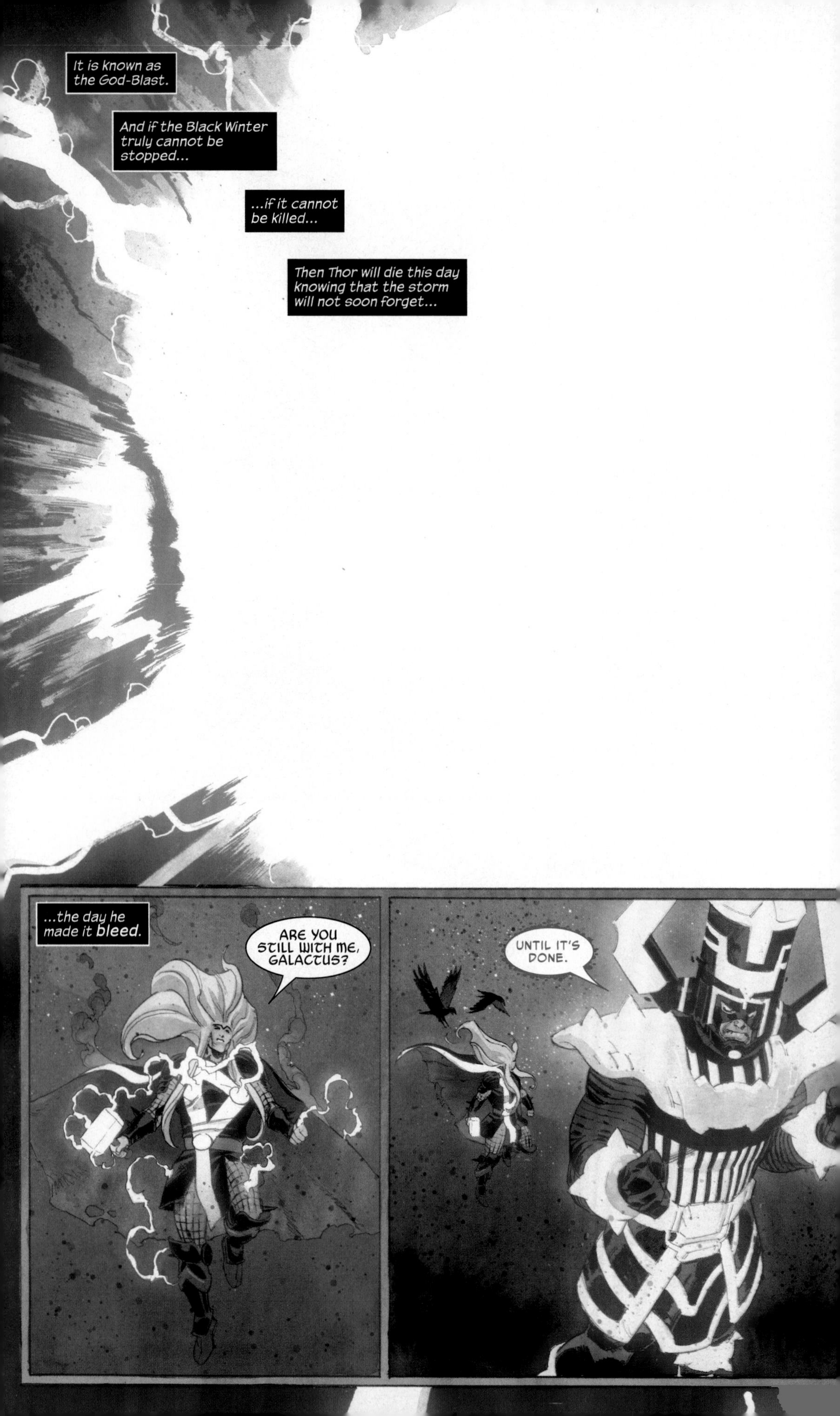
It is known as the God-Blast.
And if the Black Winter truly cannot be stopped...
...if it cannot be killed...
Then Thor will die this day knowing that the storm will not soon forget...
...the day he made it bleed.
ARE YOU STILL WITH ME, GALACTUS?
UNTIL IT'S DONE.

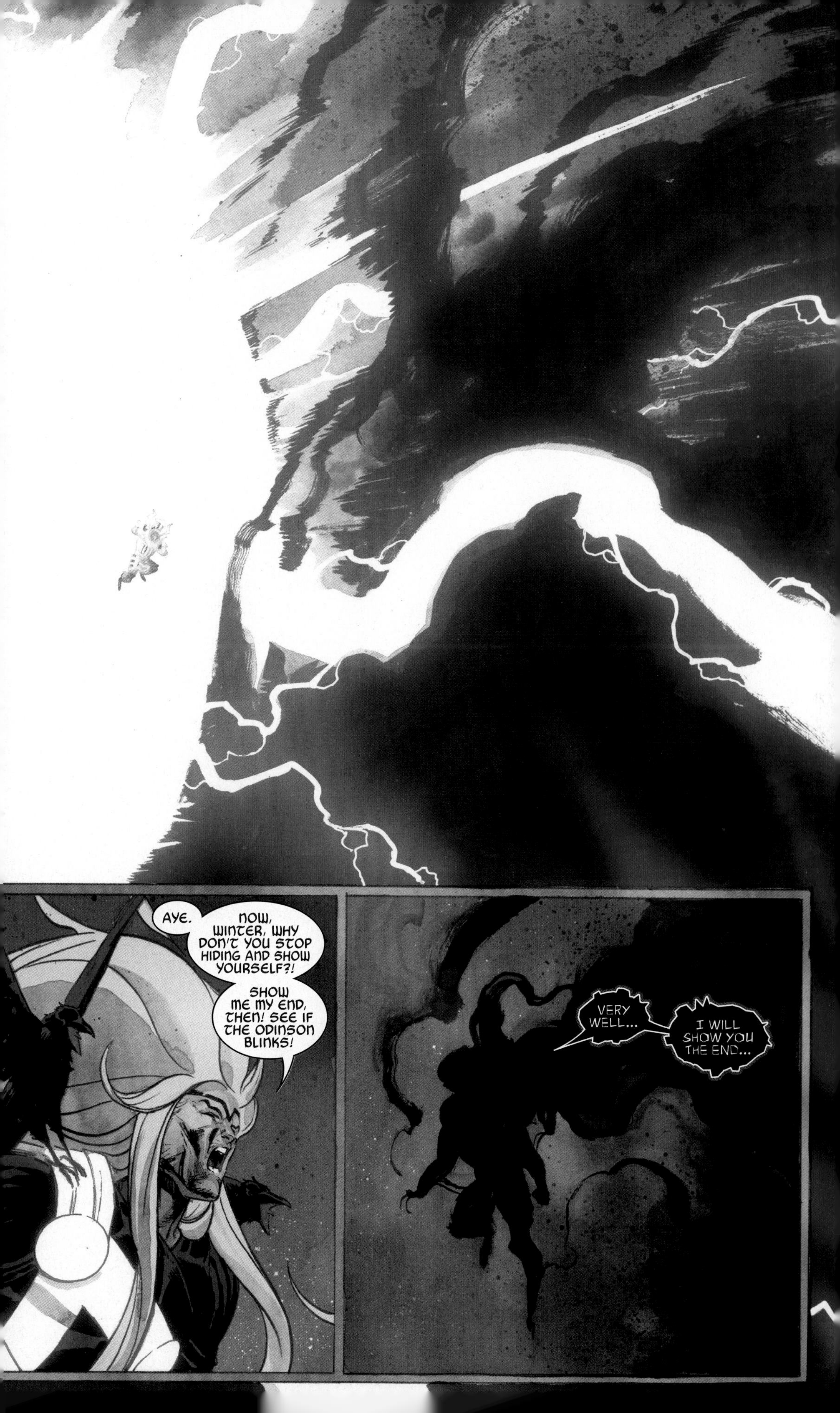
AYE.
NOW, WINTER, WHY DON'T YOU STOP HIDING AND SHOW YOURSELF?!
SHOW ME MY END, THEN! SEE IF THE ODINSON BLINKS!
VERY WELL...
I WILL SHOW YOU THE END...

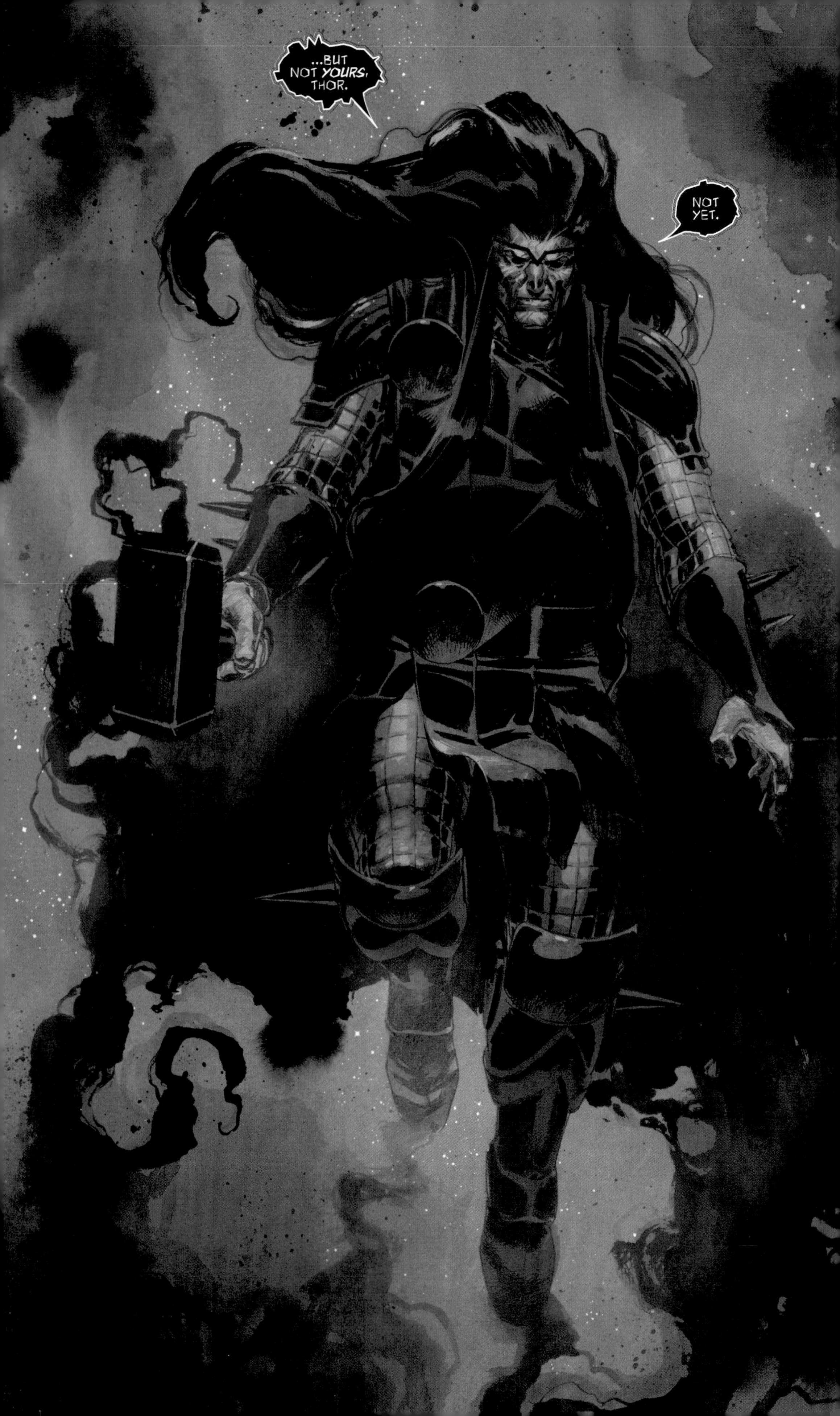
...BUT NOT YOURS, THOR.
NOT YET.

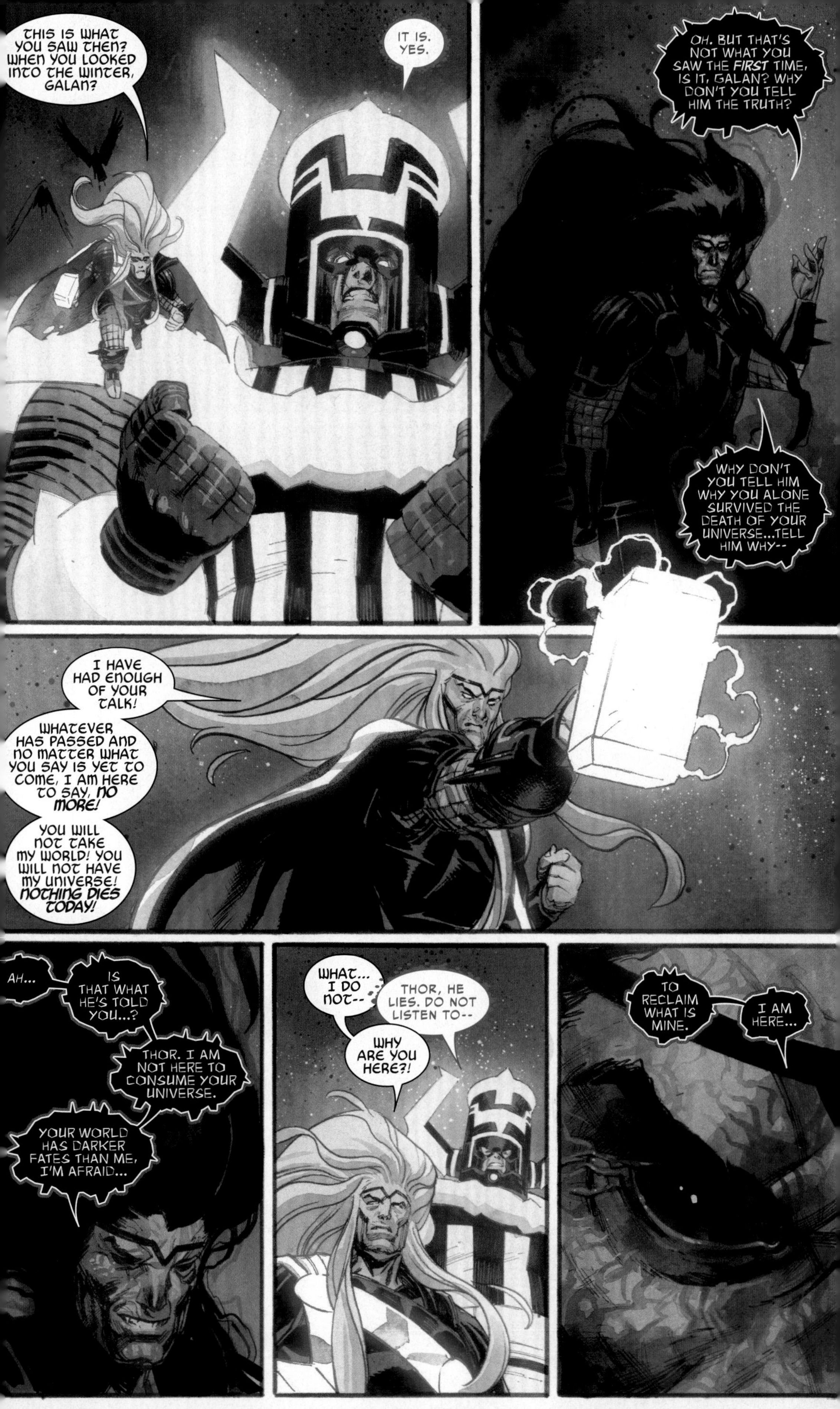
THIS IS WHAT YOU SAW THEN? WHEN YOU LOOKED INTO THE WINTER, GALAN?
IT IS. YES.
OH. BUT THAT'S NOT WHAT YOU SAW THE *FIRST* TIME, IS IT, GALAN? WHY DON'T YOU TELL HIM THE TRUTH?
WHY DON'T YOU TELL HIM WHY YOU ALONE SURVIVED THE DEATH OF YOUR UNIVERSE...TELL HIM WHY--
I HAVE HAD ENOUGH OF YOUR TALK!
WHATEVER HAS PASSED AND NO MATTER WHAT YOU SAY IS YET TO COME, I AM HERE TO SAY, *NO MORE!*
YOU WILL NOT TAKE MY WORLD! YOU WILL NOT HAVE MY UNIVERSE! *NOTHING DIES TODAY!*
AH...
IS THAT WHAT HE'S TOLD YOU...?
THOR. I AM NOT HERE TO CONSUME YOUR UNIVERSE.
YOUR WORLD HAS DARKER FATES THAN ME, I'M AFRAID...
WHAT... I DO NOT--
THOR, HE LIES. DO NOT LISTEN TO--
WHY ARE YOU HERE?!
I AM HERE...
TO RECLAIM WHAT IS MINE.

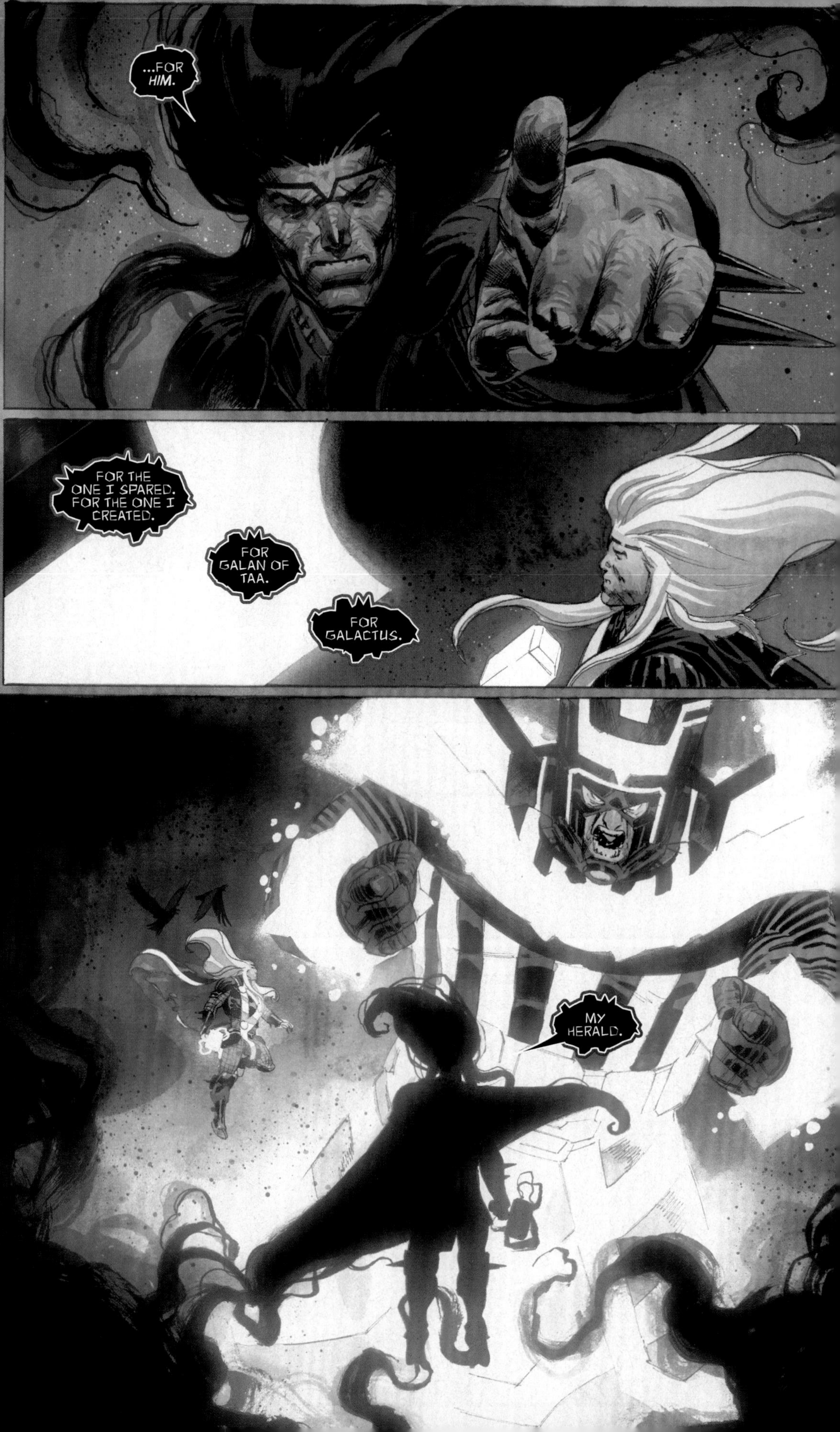
...FOR HIM.
FOR THE ONE I SPARED. FOR THE ONE I CREATED.
FOR GALAN OF TAA.
FOR GALACTUS.
MY HERALD.

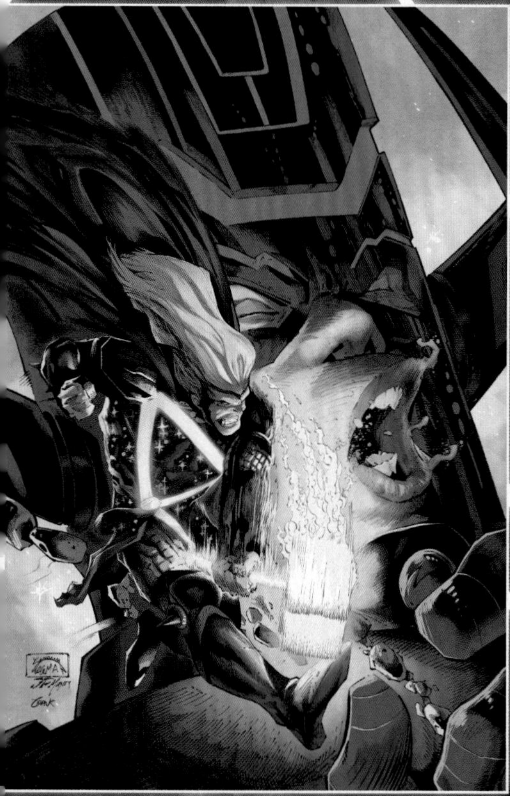

THOR 4 VARIANT BY
Ryan Stegman, JP Mayer & Frank Martin

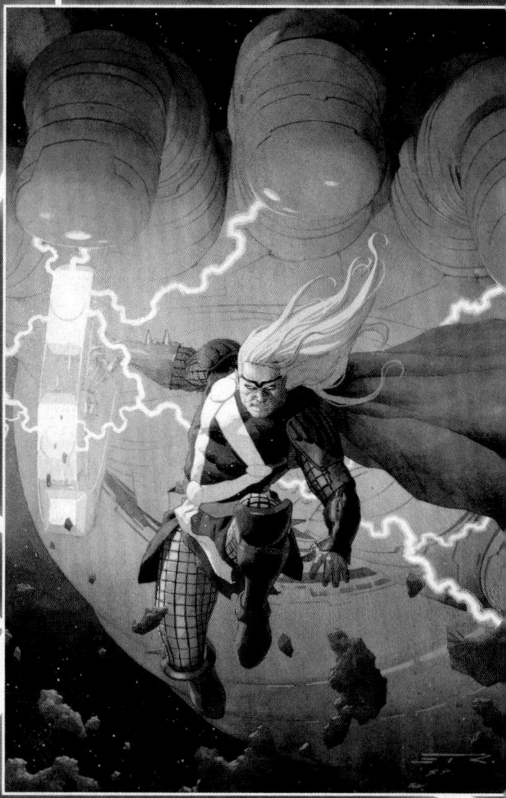

THOR 5 VARIANT BY
Esad Ribić

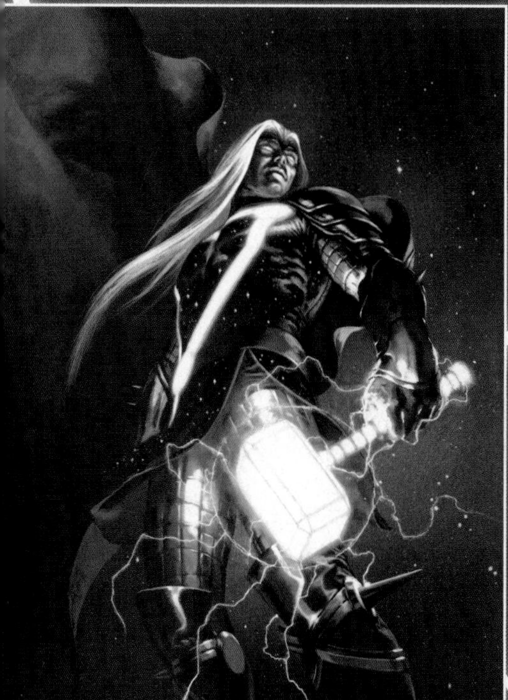

THOR 6 VARIANT BY
Gabriele Dell'Otto

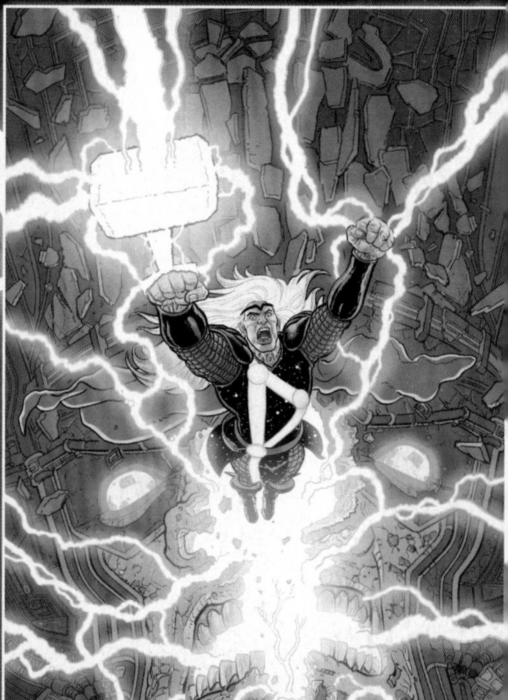

THOR 6 VARIANT BY
Steve Skroce & Dave Stewart

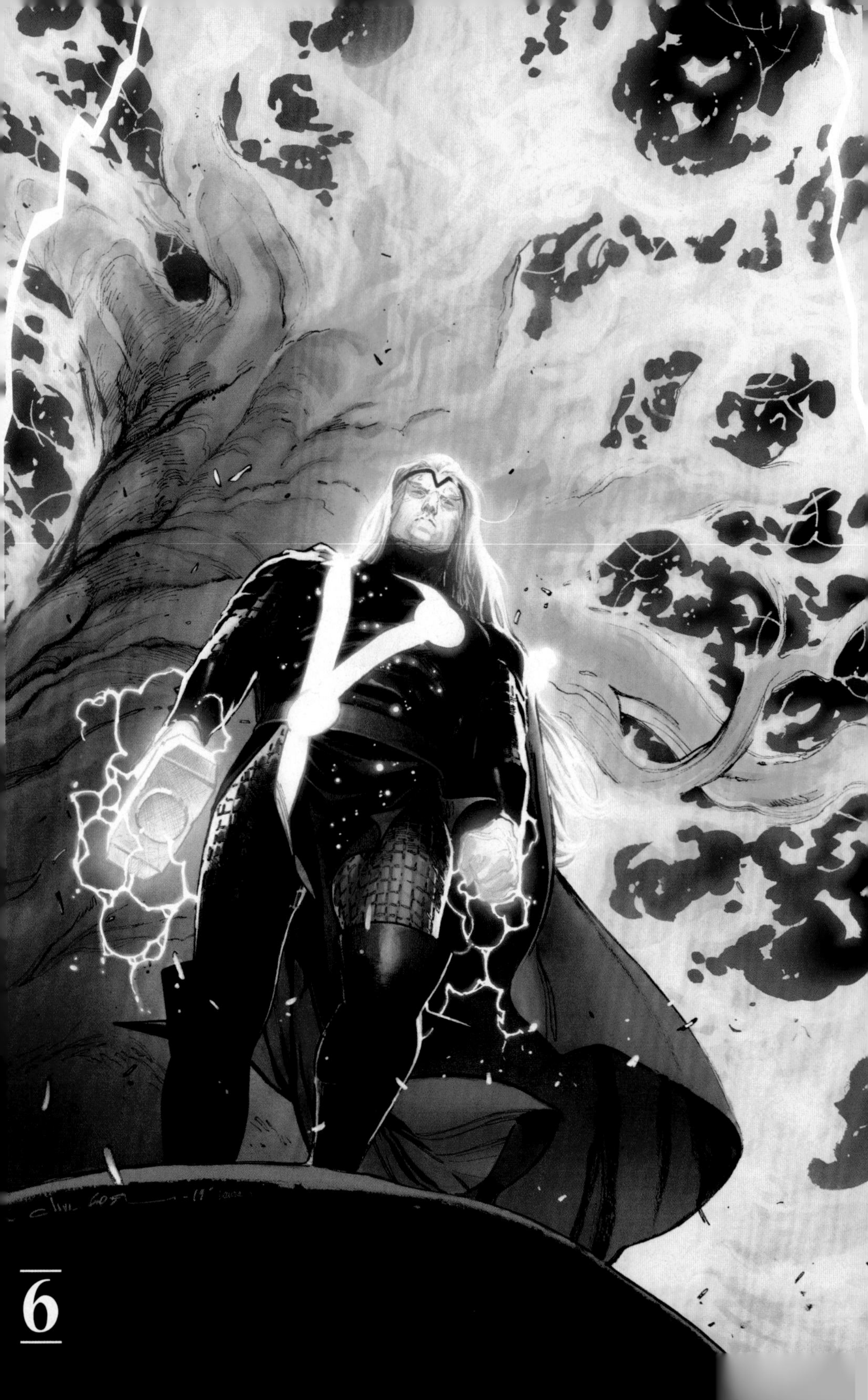

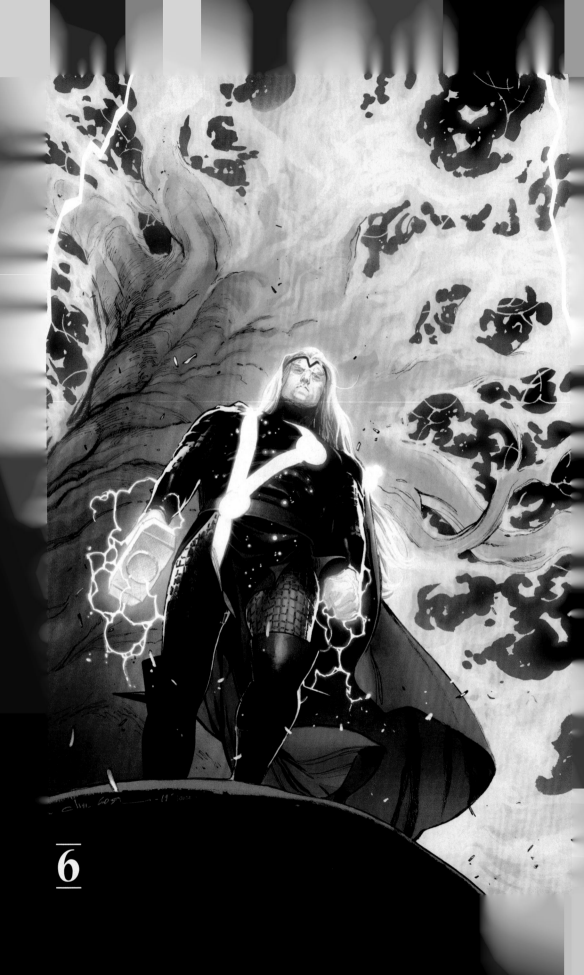

6

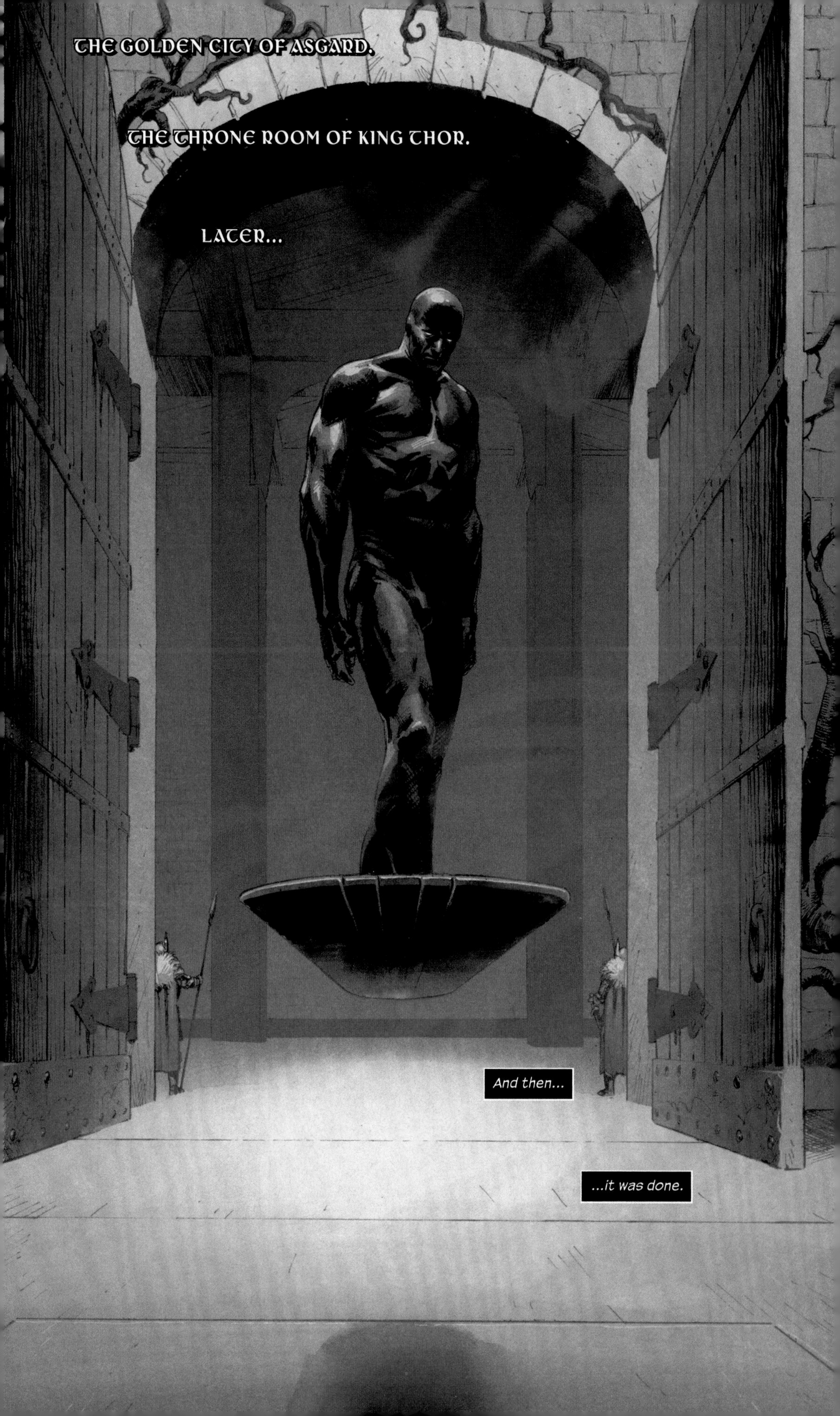
THE GOLDEN CITY OF ASGARD.
THE THRONE ROOM OF KING THOR.
LATER...
And then...
...it was done.

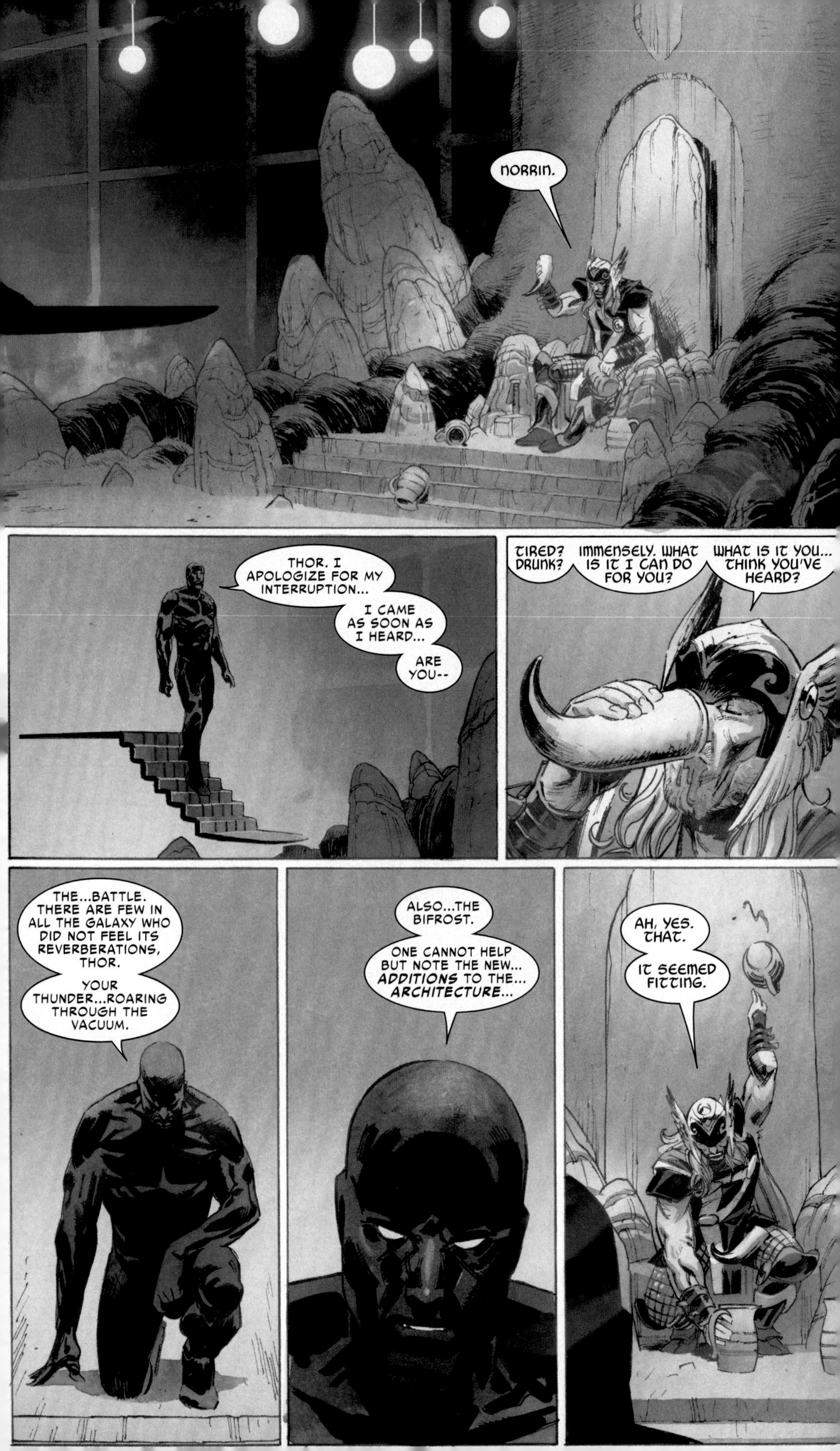
NORRIN.
THOR. I APOLOGIZE FOR MY INTERRUPTION...
I CAME AS SOON AS I HEARD...
ARE YOU--
TIRED? DRUNK?
IMMENSELY. WHAT IS IT I CAN DO FOR YOU?
WHAT IS IT YOU... THINK YOU'VE HEARD?
THE...BATTLE. THERE ARE FEW IN ALL THE GALAXY WHO DID NOT FEEL ITS REVERBERATIONS, THOR.
YOUR THUNDER...ROARING THROUGH THE VACUUM.
ALSO...THE BIFROST.
ONE CANNOT HELP BUT NOTE THE NEW... ADDITIONS TO THE... ARCHITECTURE...
AH, YES. THAT.
IT SEEMED FITTING.

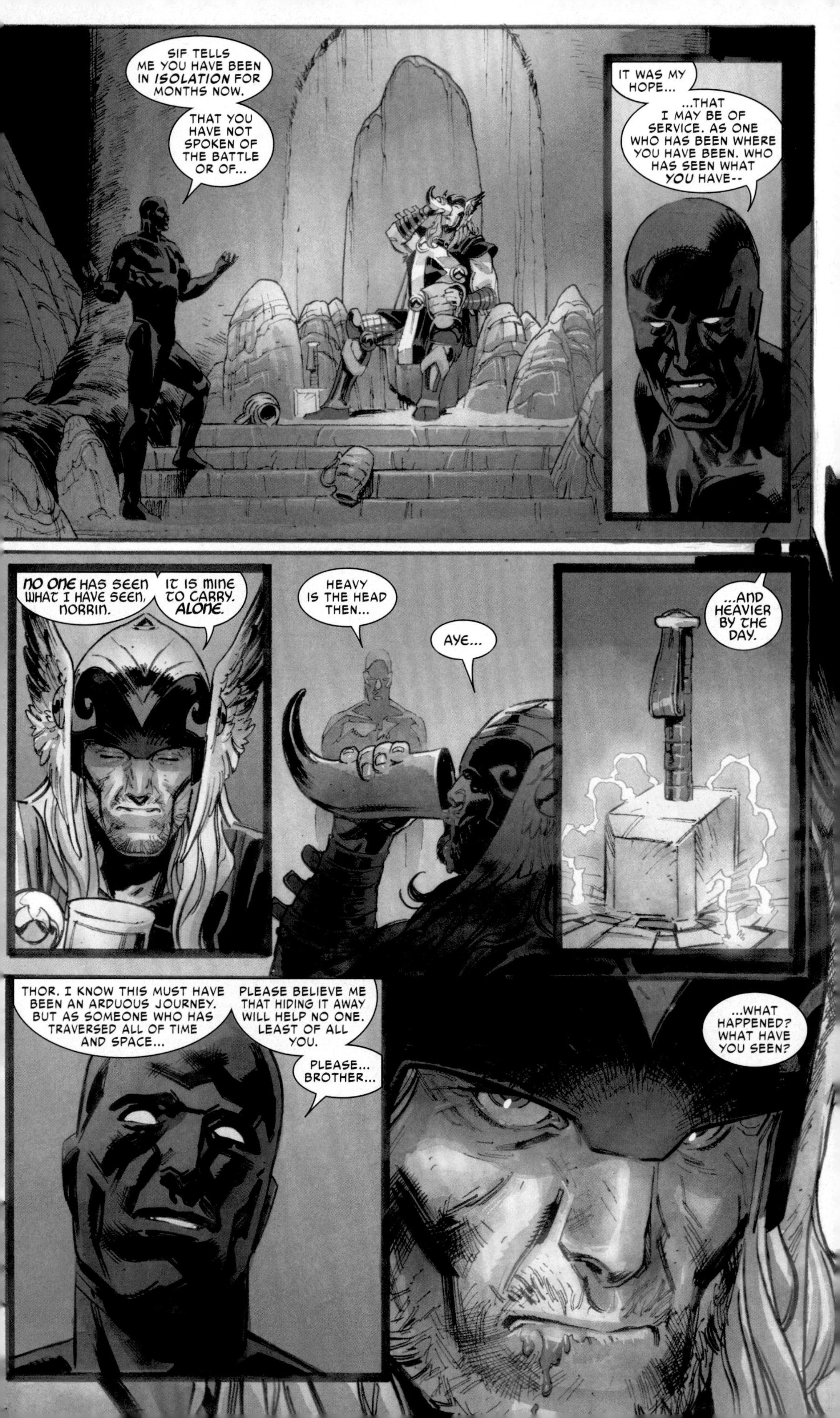
SIF TELLS ME YOU HAVE BEEN IN ISOLATION FOR MONTHS NOW.
THAT YOU HAVE NOT SPOKEN OF THE BATTLE OR OF...
IT WAS MY HOPE...
...THAT I MAY BE OF SERVICE. AS ONE WHO HAS BEEN WHERE YOU HAVE BEEN. WHO HAS SEEN WHAT YOU HAVE--
NO ONE HAS SEEN WHAT I HAVE SEEN, NORRIN.
IT IS MINE TO CARRY. ALONE.
HEAVY IS THE HEAD THEN...
AYE...
...AND HEAVIER BY THE DAY.
THOR. I KNOW THIS MUST HAVE BEEN AN ARDUOUS JOURNEY. BUT AS SOMEONE WHO HAS TRAVERSED ALL OF TIME AND SPACE...
PLEASE BELIEVE ME THAT HIDING IT AWAY WILL HELP NO ONE. LEAST OF ALL YOU.
PLEASE... BROTHER...
...WHAT HAPPENED? WHAT HAVE YOU SEEN?

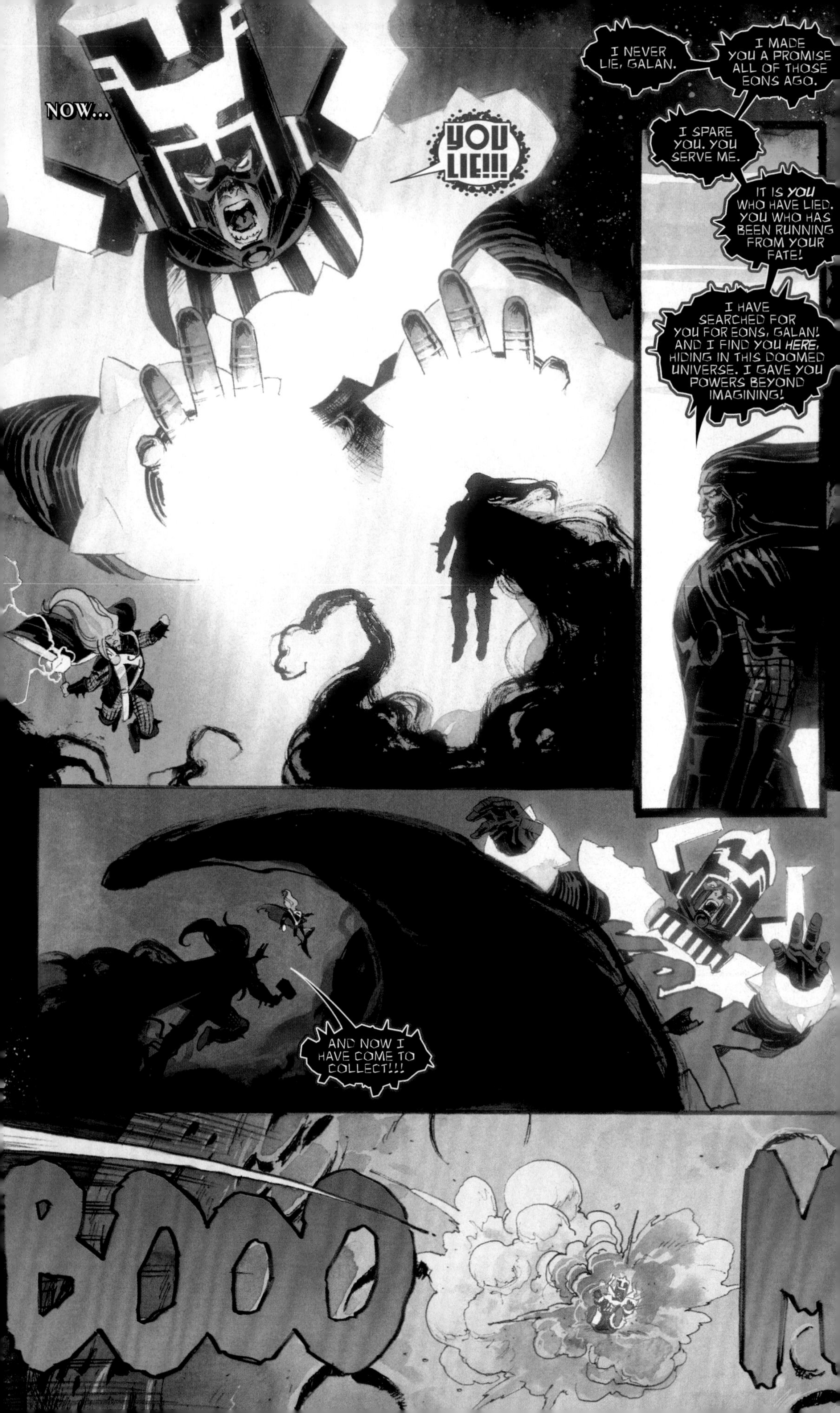
NOW...
YOU LIE!!!
I NEVER LIE, GALAN.
I MADE YOU A PROMISE ALL OF THOSE EONS AGO.
I SPARE YOU. YOU SERVE ME.
IT IS YOU WHO HAVE LIED. YOU WHO HAS BEEN RUNNING FROM YOUR FATE!
I HAVE SEARCHED FOR YOU FOR EONS, GALAN! AND I FIND YOU HERE, HIDING IN THIS DOOMED UNIVERSE. I GAVE YOU POWERS BEYOND IMAGINING!
AND NOW I HAVE COME TO COLLECT!!!
BOOOM

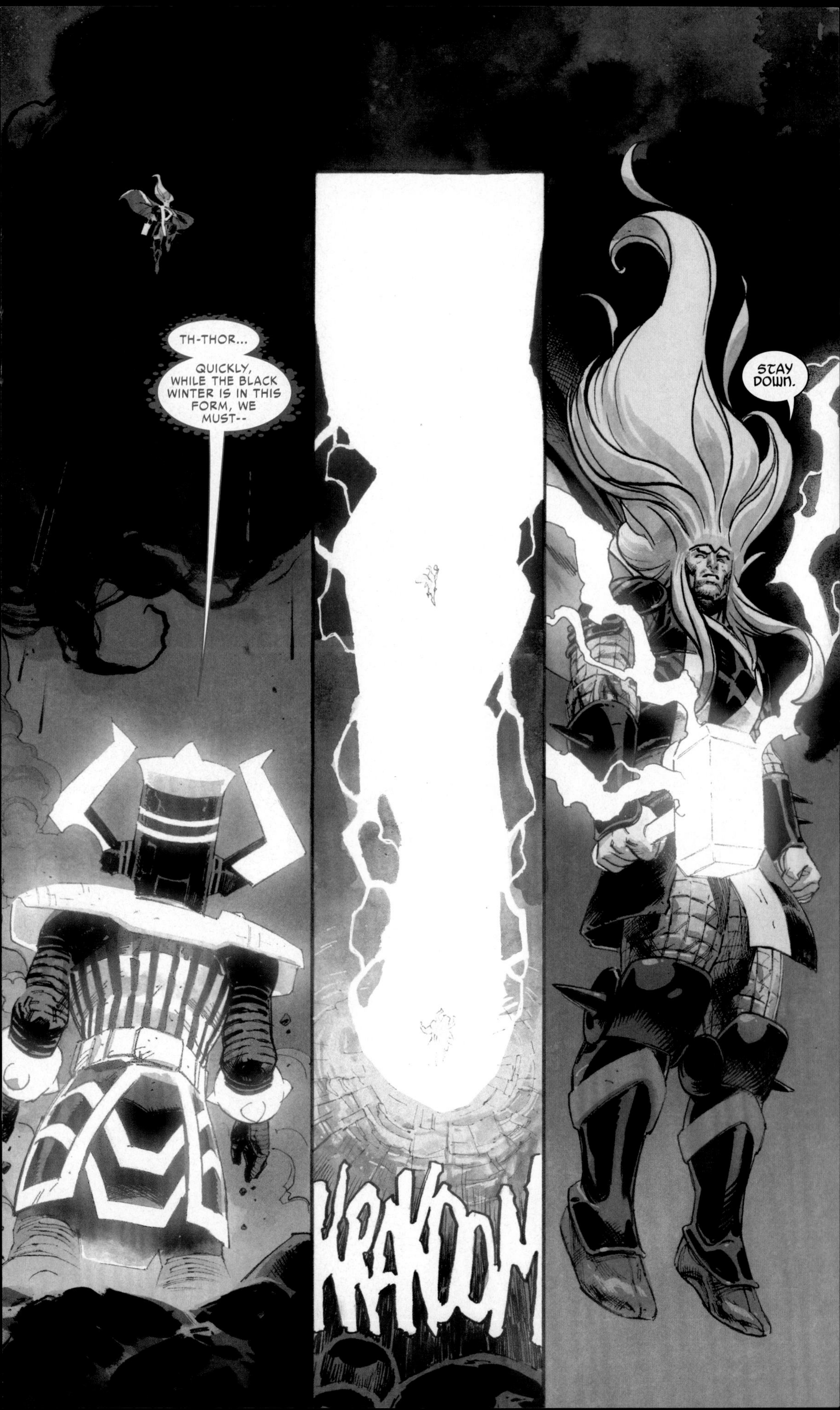
TH-THOR...
QUICKLY, WHILE THE BLACK WINTER IS IN THIS FORM, WE MUST--
KRAKOOM
STAY DOWN.

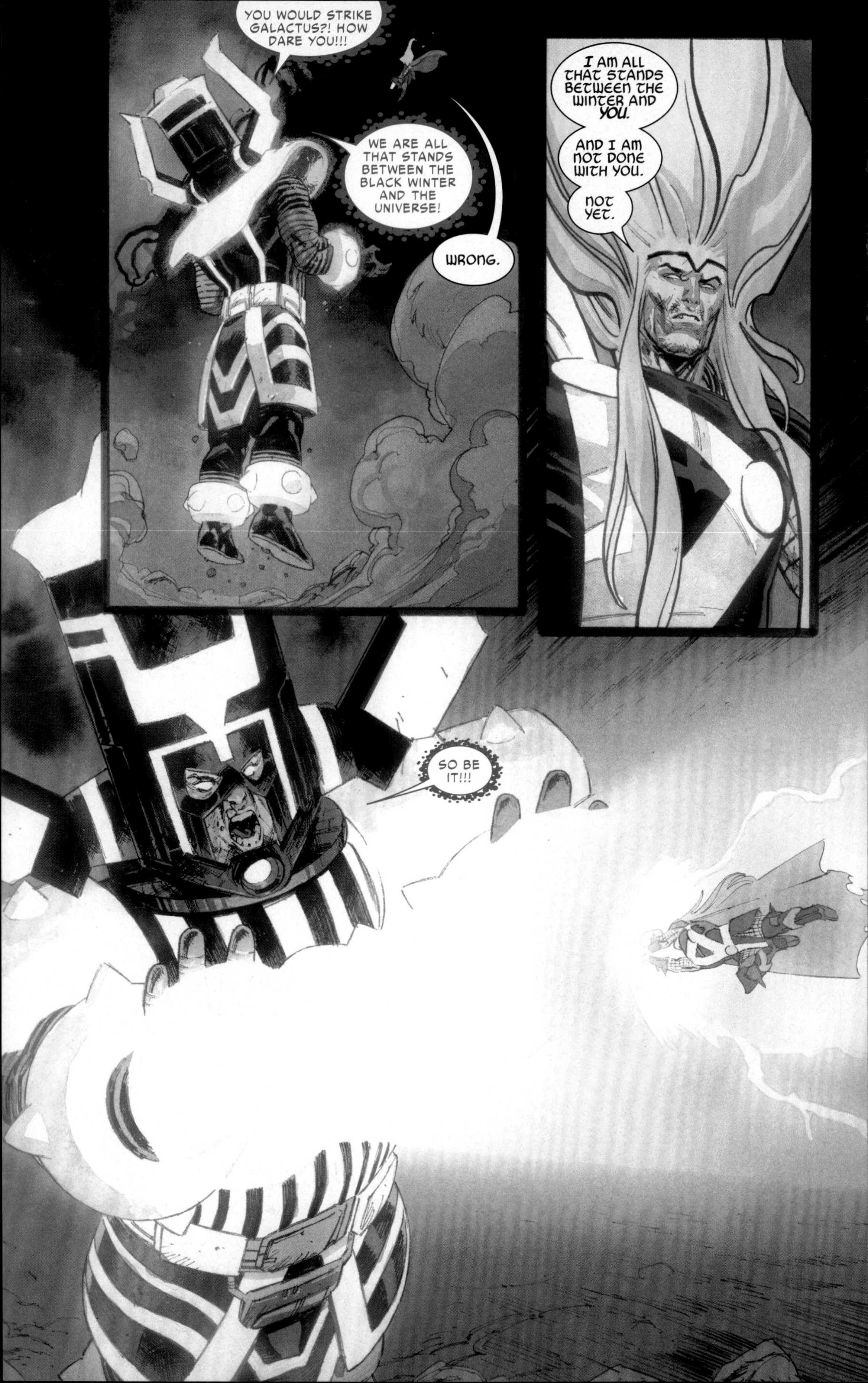
YOU WOULD STRIKE GALACTUS?! HOW DARE YOU!!!
WE ARE ALL THAT STANDS BETWEEN THE BLACK WINTER AND THE UNIVERSE!
WRONG.
I AM ALL THAT STANDS BETWEEN THE WINTER AND YOU.
AND I AM NOT DONE WITH YOU.
NOT YET.
SO BE IT!!!

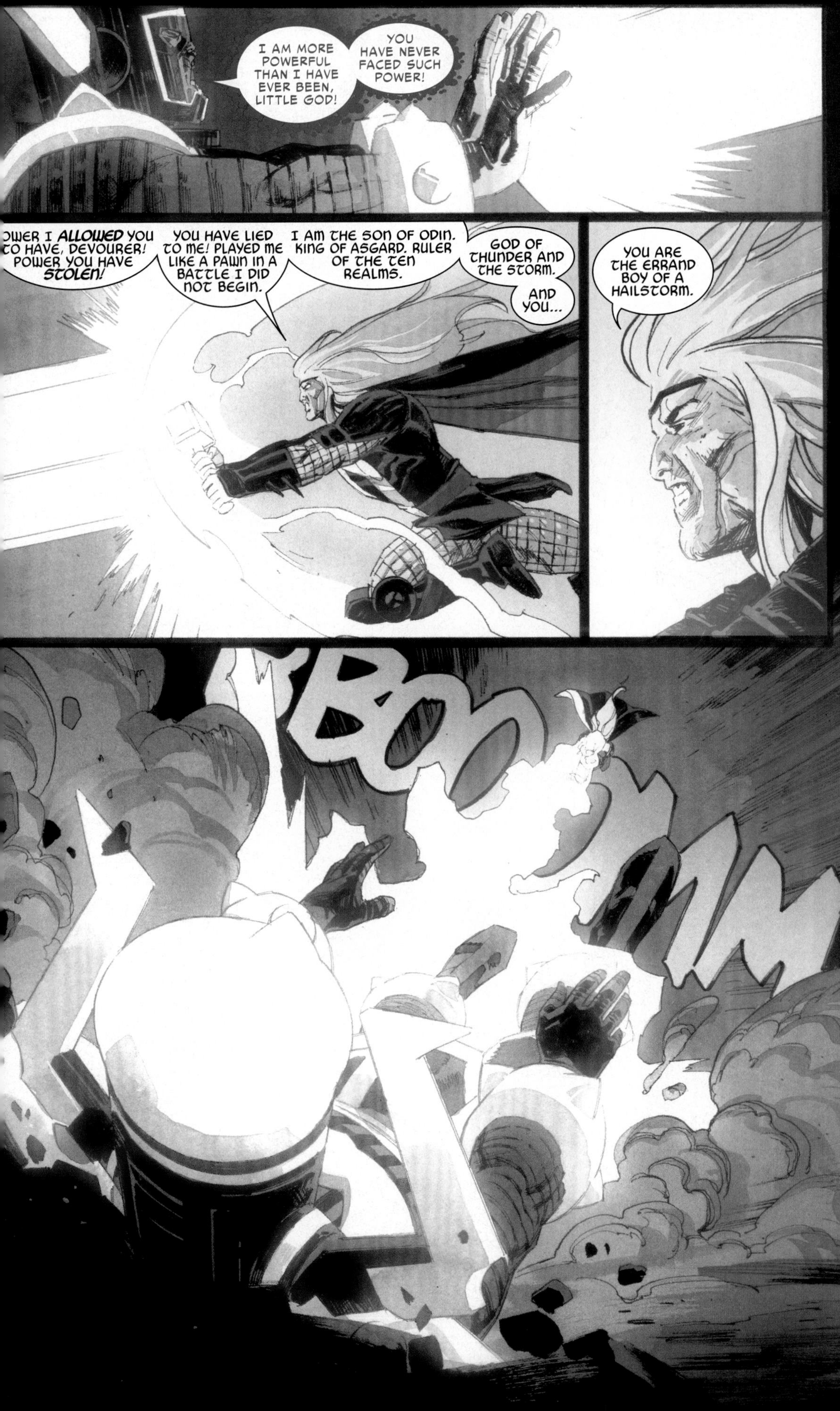
I AM MORE POWERFUL THAN I HAVE EVER BEEN, LITTLE GOD!
YOU HAVE NEVER FACED SUCH POWER!
OWER I ALLOWED YOU TO HAVE, DEVOURER! POWER YOU HAVE STOLEN!
YOU HAVE LIED TO ME! PLAYED ME LIKE A PAWN IN A BATTLE I DID NOT BEGIN.
I AM THE SON OF ODIN. KING OF ASGARD. RULER OF THE TEN REALMS.
GOD OF THUNDER AND THE STORM.
AND YOU...
YOU ARE THE ERRAND BOY OF A HAILSTORM.
BOOOM

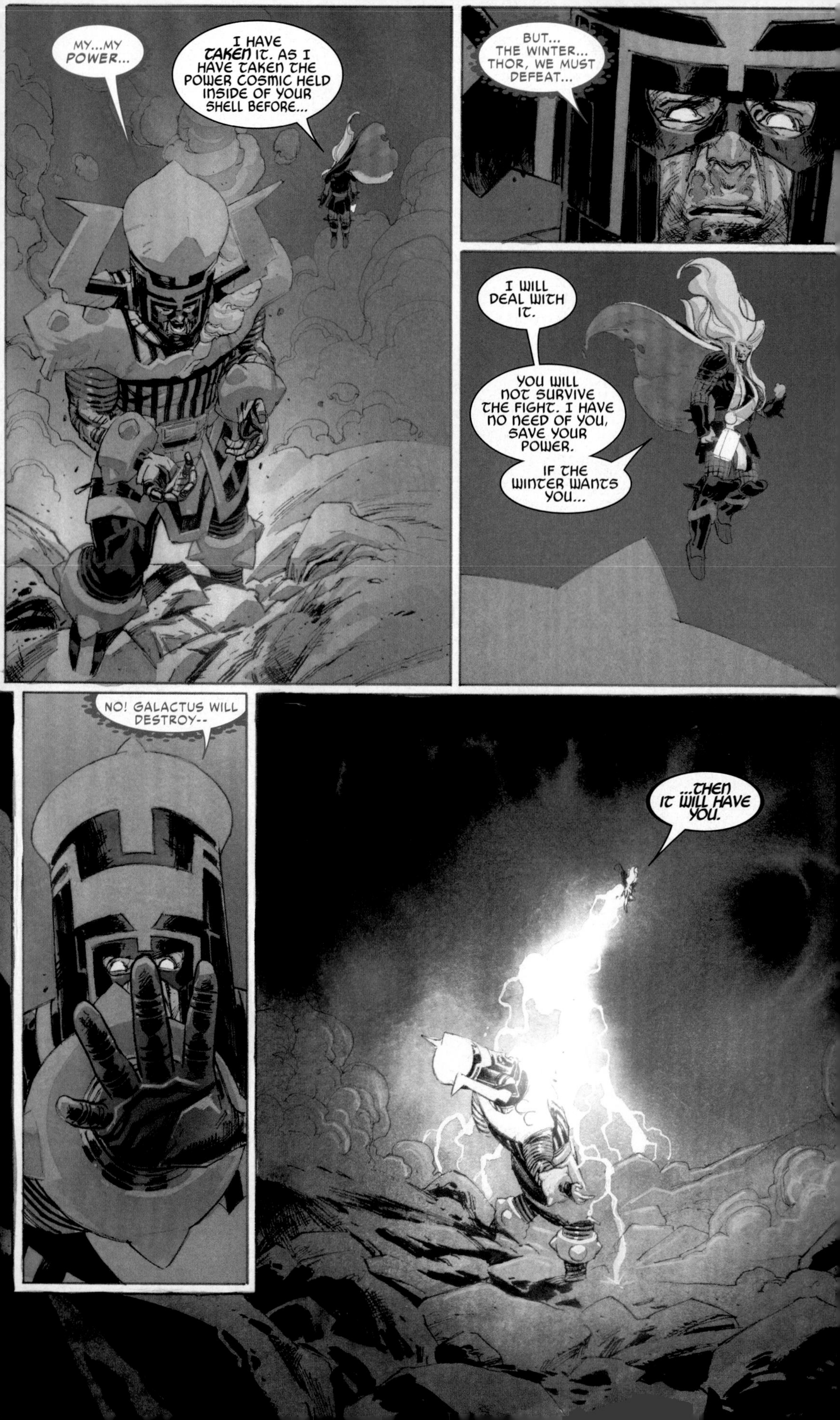
MY...MY POWER...
I HAVE TAKEN IT. AS I HAVE TAKEN THE POWER COSMIC HELD INSIDE OF YOUR SHELL BEFORE...
BUT... THE WINTER... THOR, WE MUST DEFEAT...
I WILL DEAL WITH IT.
YOU WILL NOT SURVIVE THE FIGHT. I HAVE NO NEED OF YOU, SAVE YOUR POWER.
IF THE WINTER WANTS YOU...
NO! GALACTUS WILL DESTROY--
...THEN IT WILL HAVE YOU.

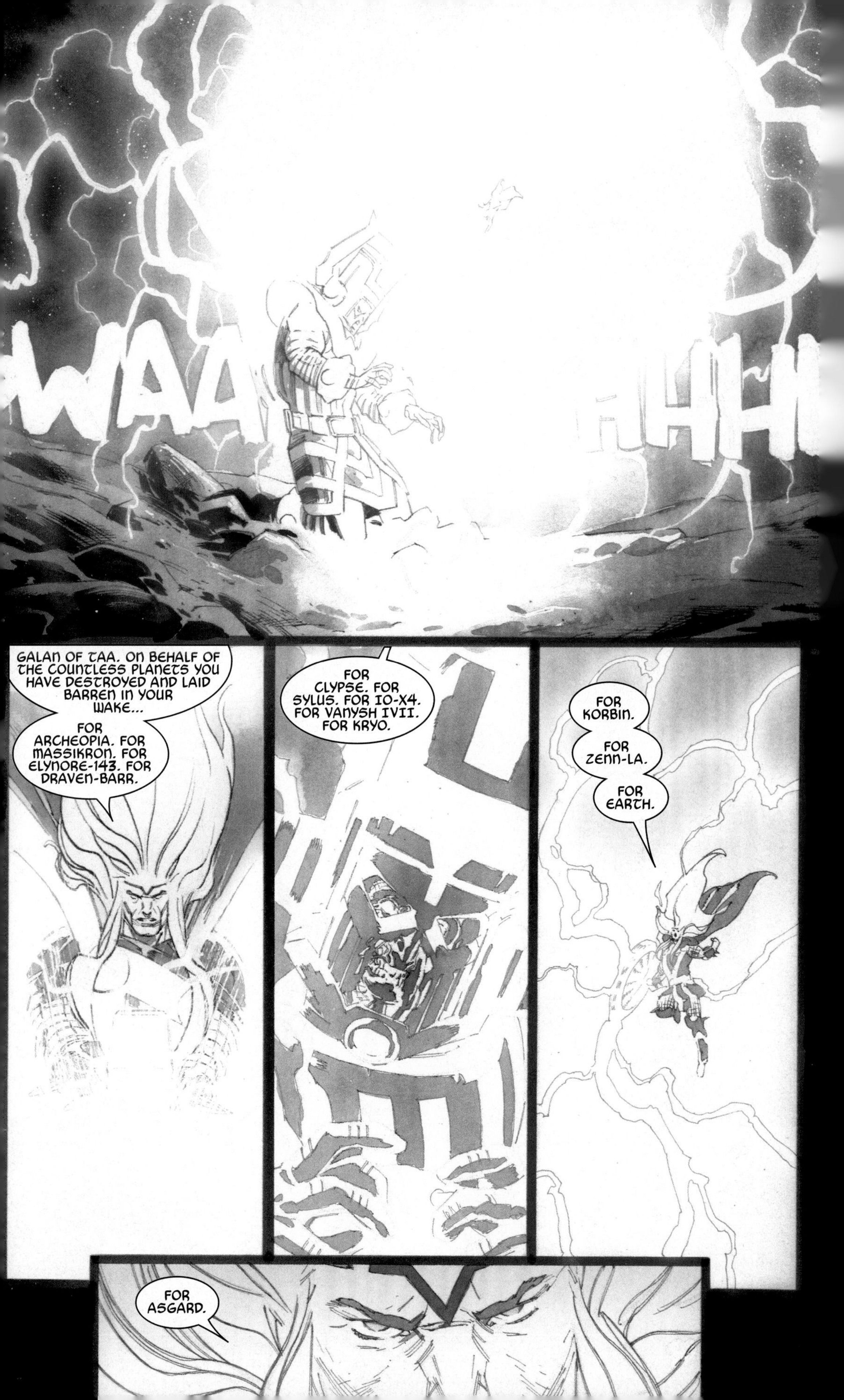
WAAAHHH
GALAN OF TAA. ON BEHALF OF THE COUNTLESS PLANETS YOU HAVE DESTROYED AND LAID BARREN IN YOUR WAKE...
FOR ARCHEOPIA. FOR MASSIKRON. FOR ELYNORE-143. FOR DRAVEN-BARR.
FOR CLYPSE. FOR SYLUS. FOR IO-X4. FOR VANYSH IVII. FOR KRYO.
FOR KORBIN.
FOR ZENN-LA.
FOR EARTH.
FOR ASGARD.

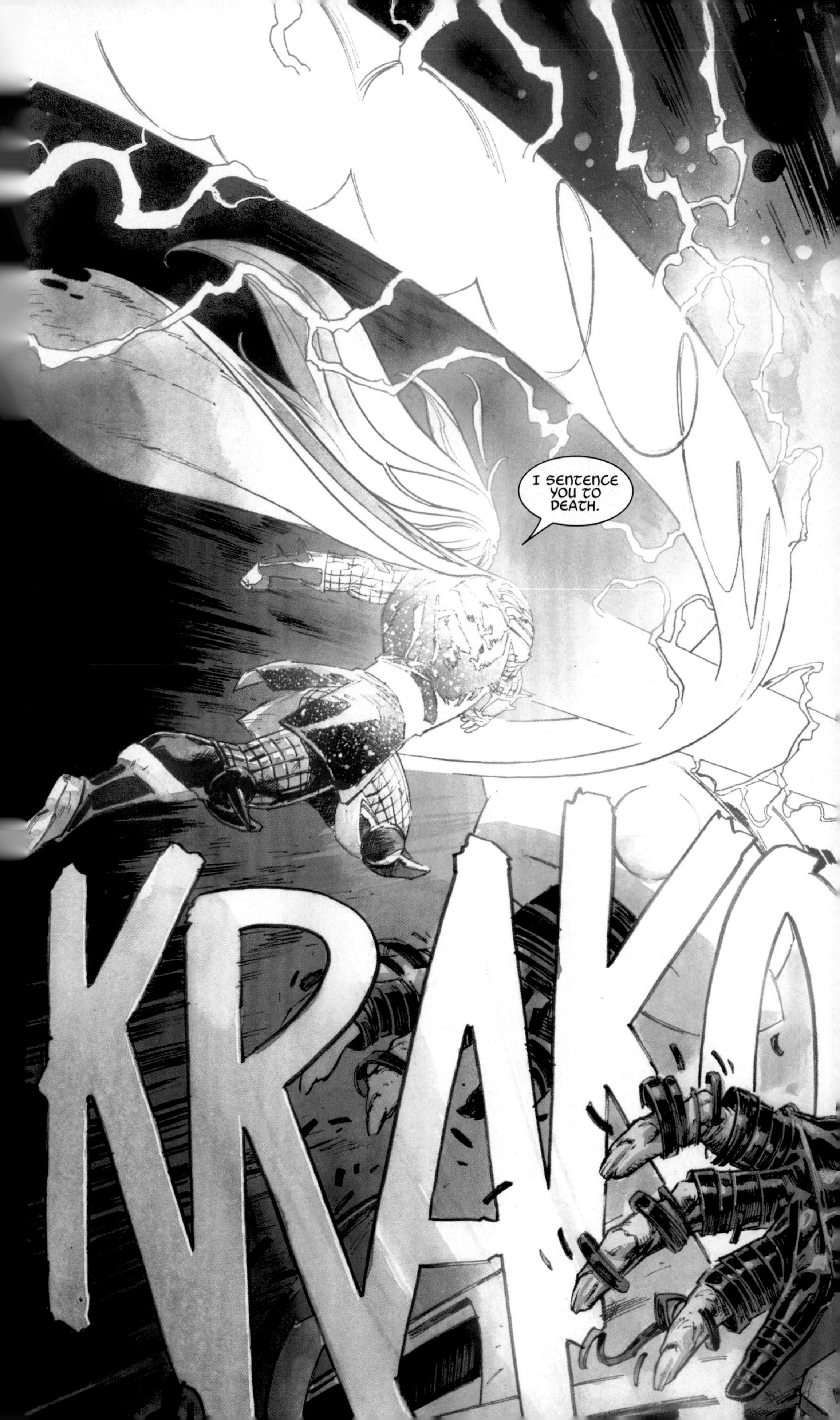
I SENTENCE YOU TO DEATH.
KRAK

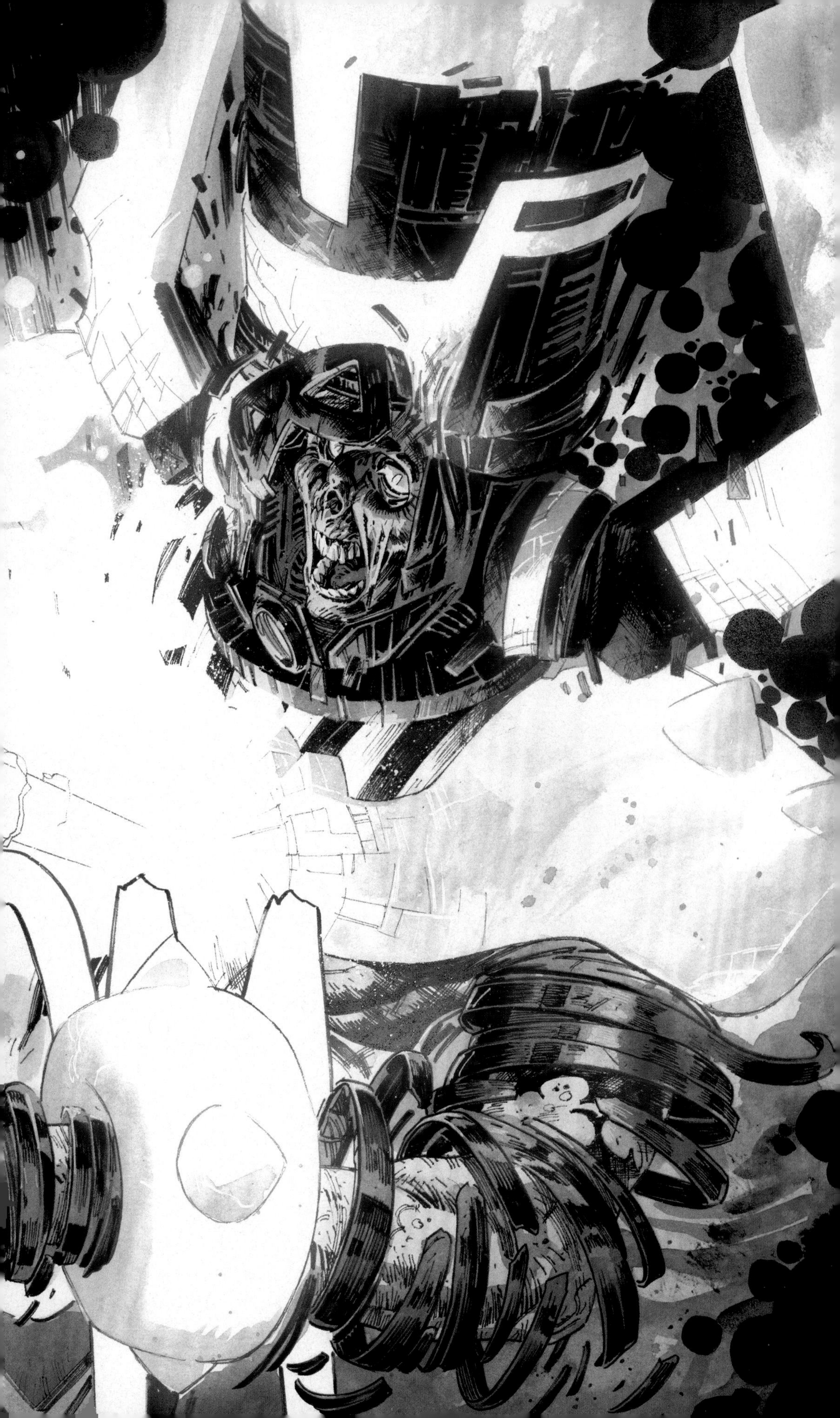

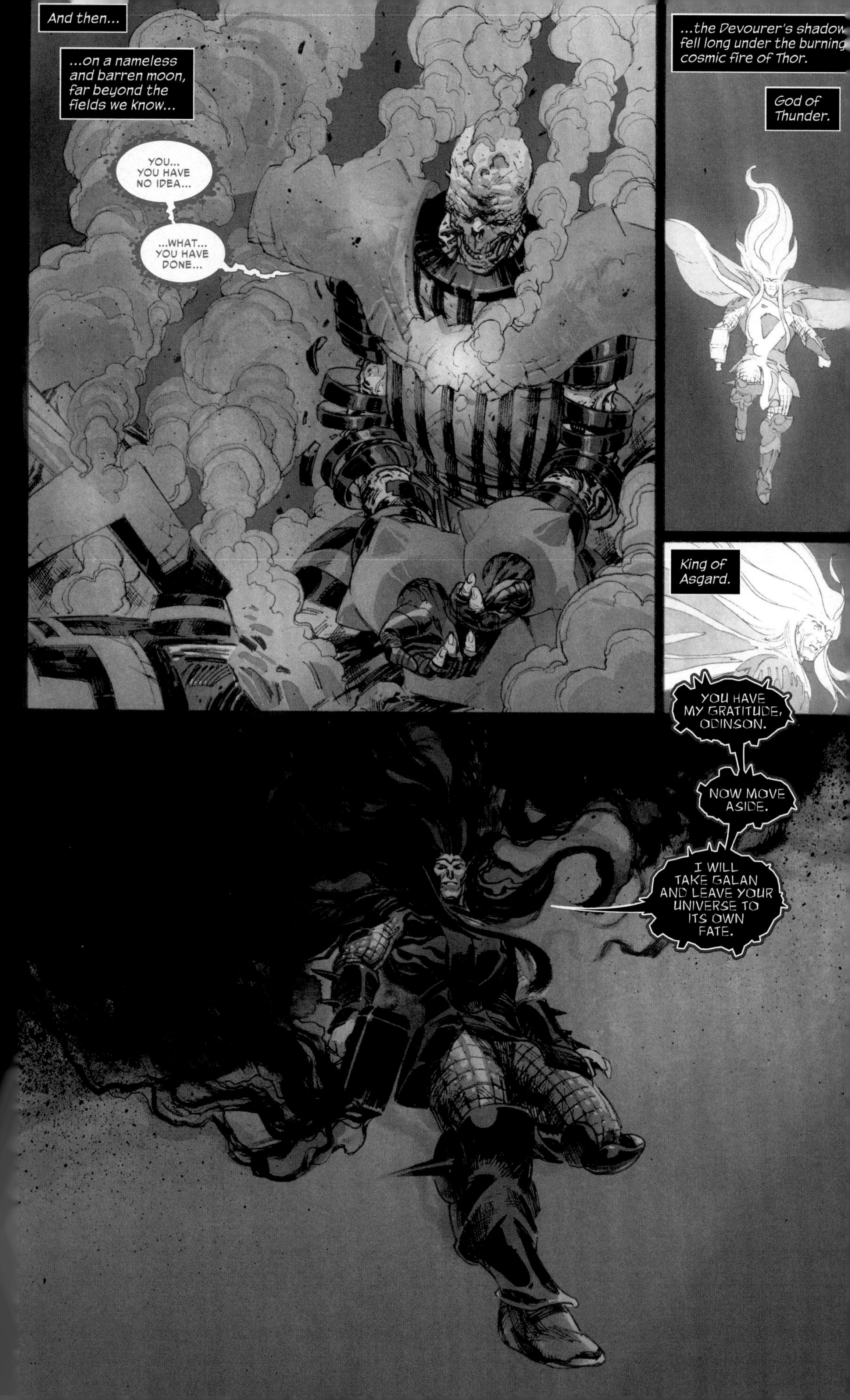

And then...
...on a nameless and barren moon, far beyond the fields we know...
YOU... YOU HAVE NO IDEA...
...WHAT... YOU HAVE DONE...
...the Devourer's shadow fell long under the burning cosmic fire of Thor.
God of Thunder.
King of Asgard.
YOU HAVE MY GRATITUDE, ODINSON.
NOW MOVE ASIDE.
I WILL TAKE GALAN AND LEAVE YOUR UNIVERSE TO ITS OWN FATE.

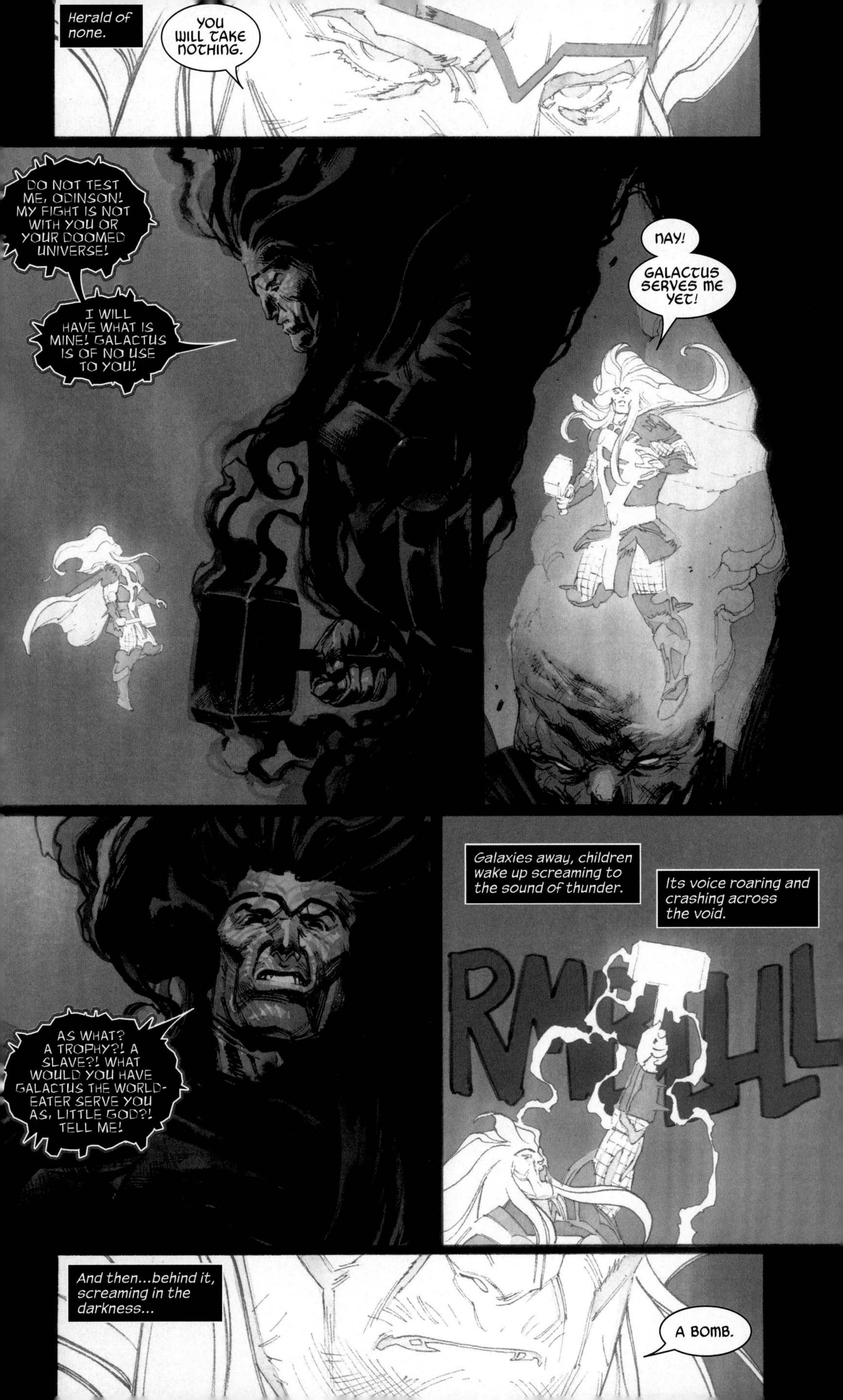

Herald of none.
YOU WILL TAKE NOTHING.
DO NOT TEST ME, ODINSON! MY FIGHT IS NOT WITH YOU OR YOUR DOOMED UNIVERSE!
I WILL HAVE WHAT IS MINE! GALACTUS IS OF NO USE TO YOU!
NAY!
GALACTUS SERVES ME YET!
AS WHAT? A TROPHY?! A SLAVE?! WHAT WOULD YOU HAVE GALACTUS THE WORLD-EATER SERVE YOU AS, LITTLE GOD?! TELL ME!
Galaxies away, children wake up screaming to the sound of thunder.
Its voice roaring and crashing across the void.
And then...behind it, screaming in the darkness...
A BOMB.

...there was lightning.

And burning inside of it, the full might of the immeasurable Power Cosmic...

...the bleeding life force of a universal constant...

...the energy of a hundred thousand devoured worlds.

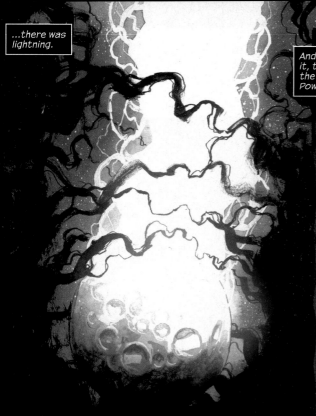

All of it...

...unleashed...

BBOOM

...by a god made king.

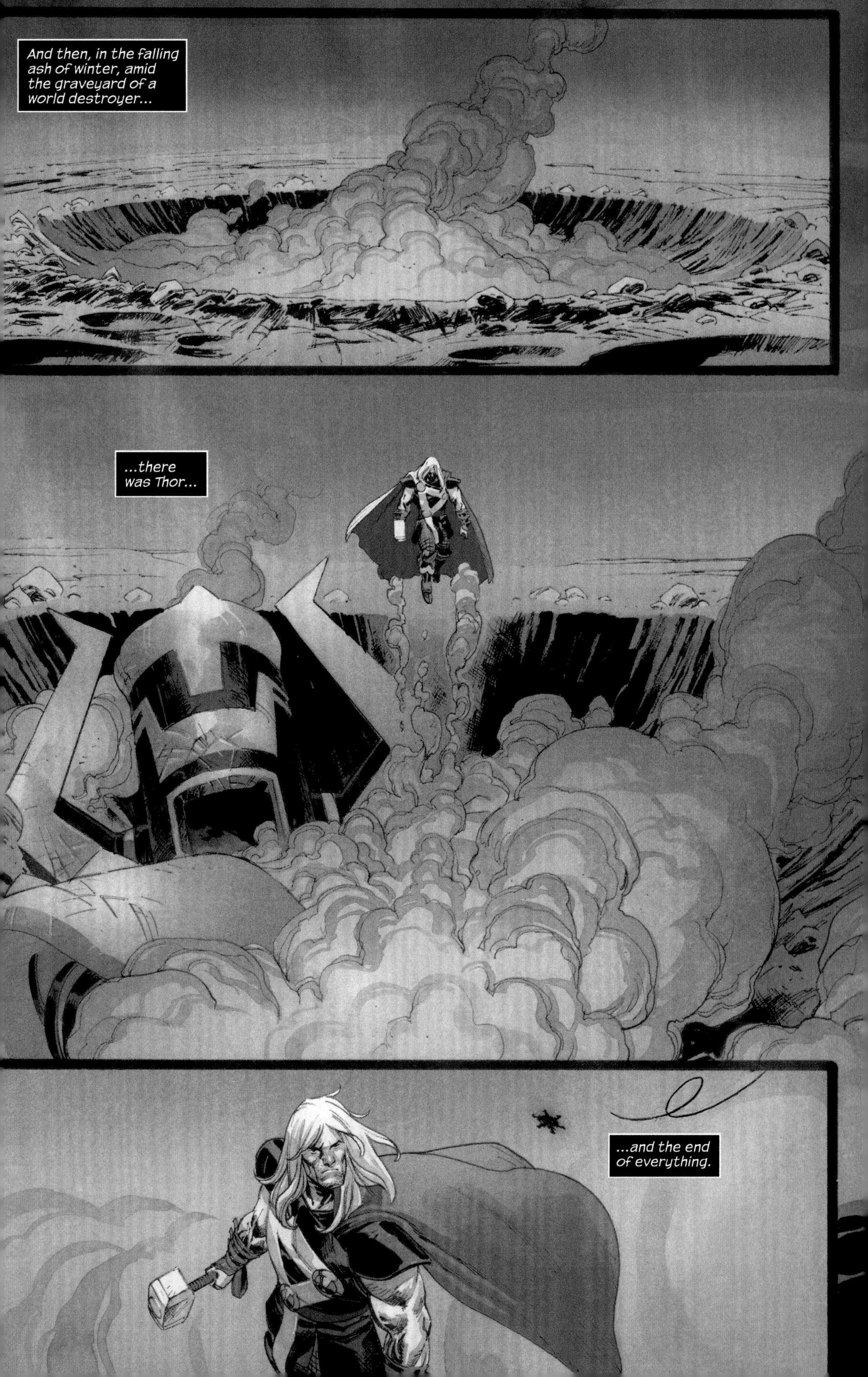
And then, in the falling ash of winter, amid the graveyard of a world destroyer...
...there was Thor...
...and the end of everything.

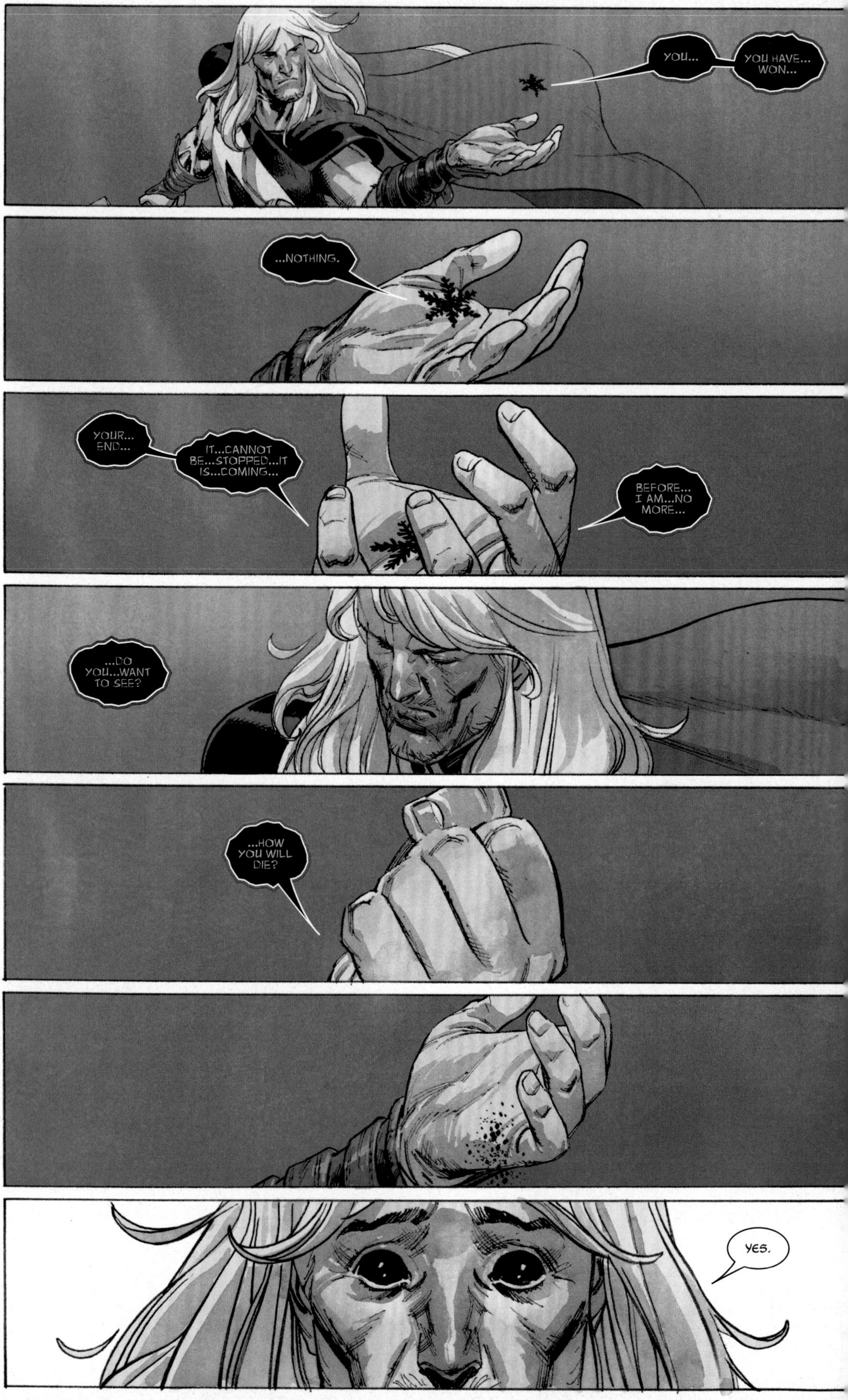
YOU...
YOU HAVE... WON...
...NOTHING.
YOUR... END...
IT...CANNOT BE...STOPPED...IT IS...COMING...
BEFORE... I AM...NO MORE...
...DO YOU...WANT TO SEE?
...HOW YOU WILL DIE?
YES.

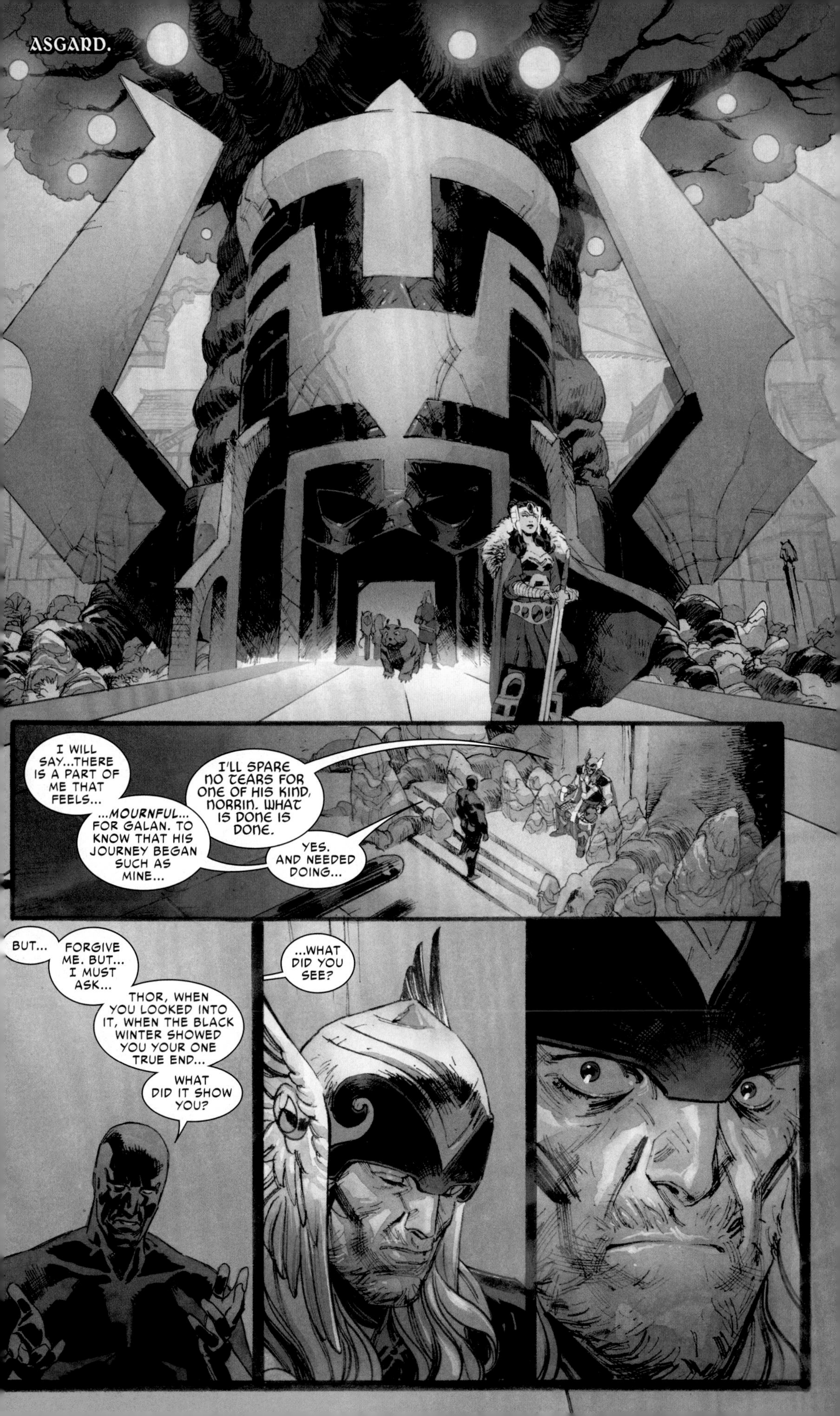
ASGARD.
I WILL SAY...THERE IS A PART OF ME THAT FEELS...
...MOURNFUL... FOR GALAN. TO KNOW THAT HIS JOURNEY BEGAN SUCH AS MINE...
I'LL SPARE NO TEARS FOR ONE OF HIS KIND, NORRIN. WHAT IS DONE IS DONE.
YES. AND NEEDED DOING...
BUT...
FORGIVE ME. BUT... I MUST ASK...
THOR, WHEN YOU LOOKED INTO IT, WHEN THE BLACK WINTER SHOWED YOU YOUR ONE TRUE END...
WHAT DID IT SHOW YOU?
...WHAT DID YOU SEE?

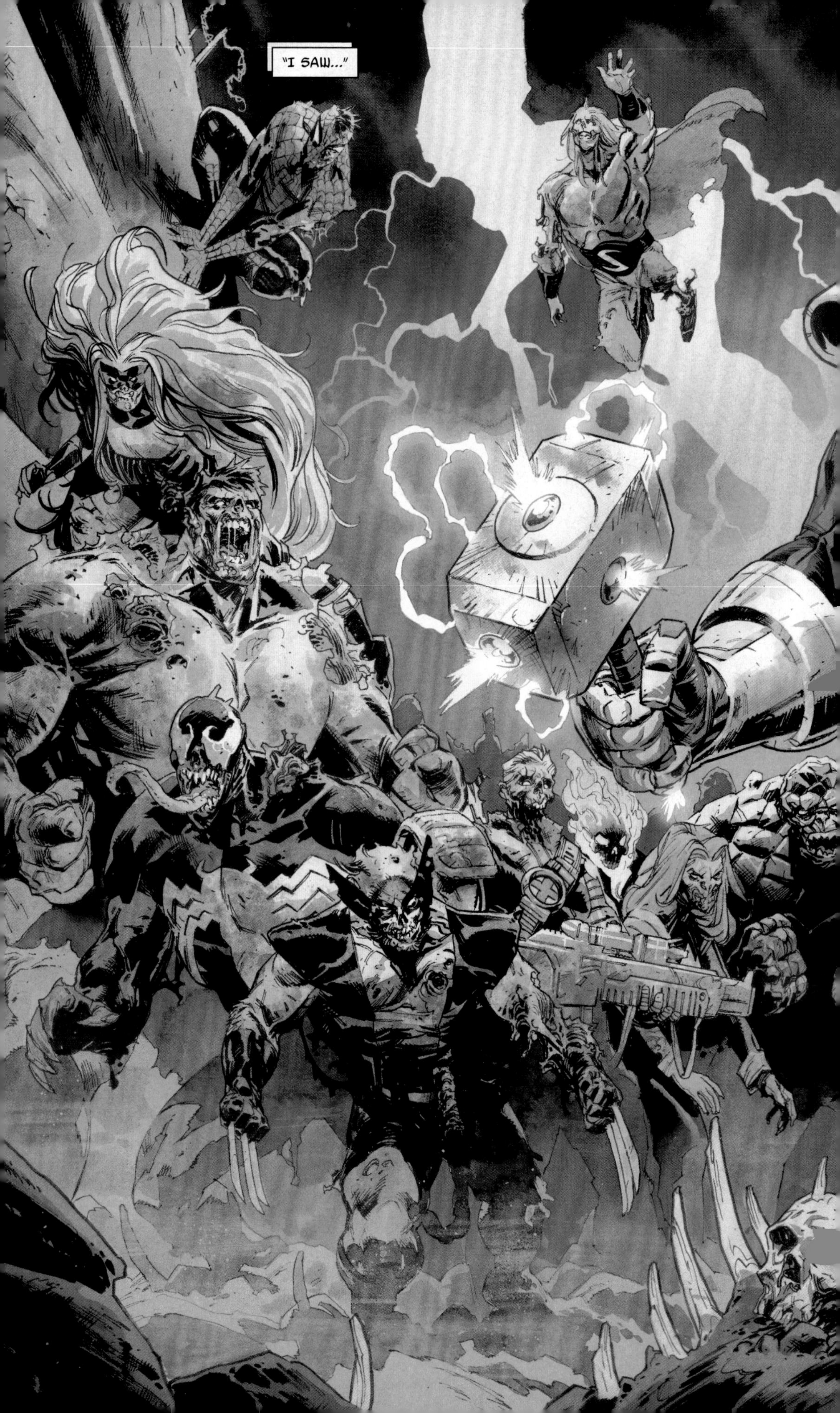
"I SAW..."

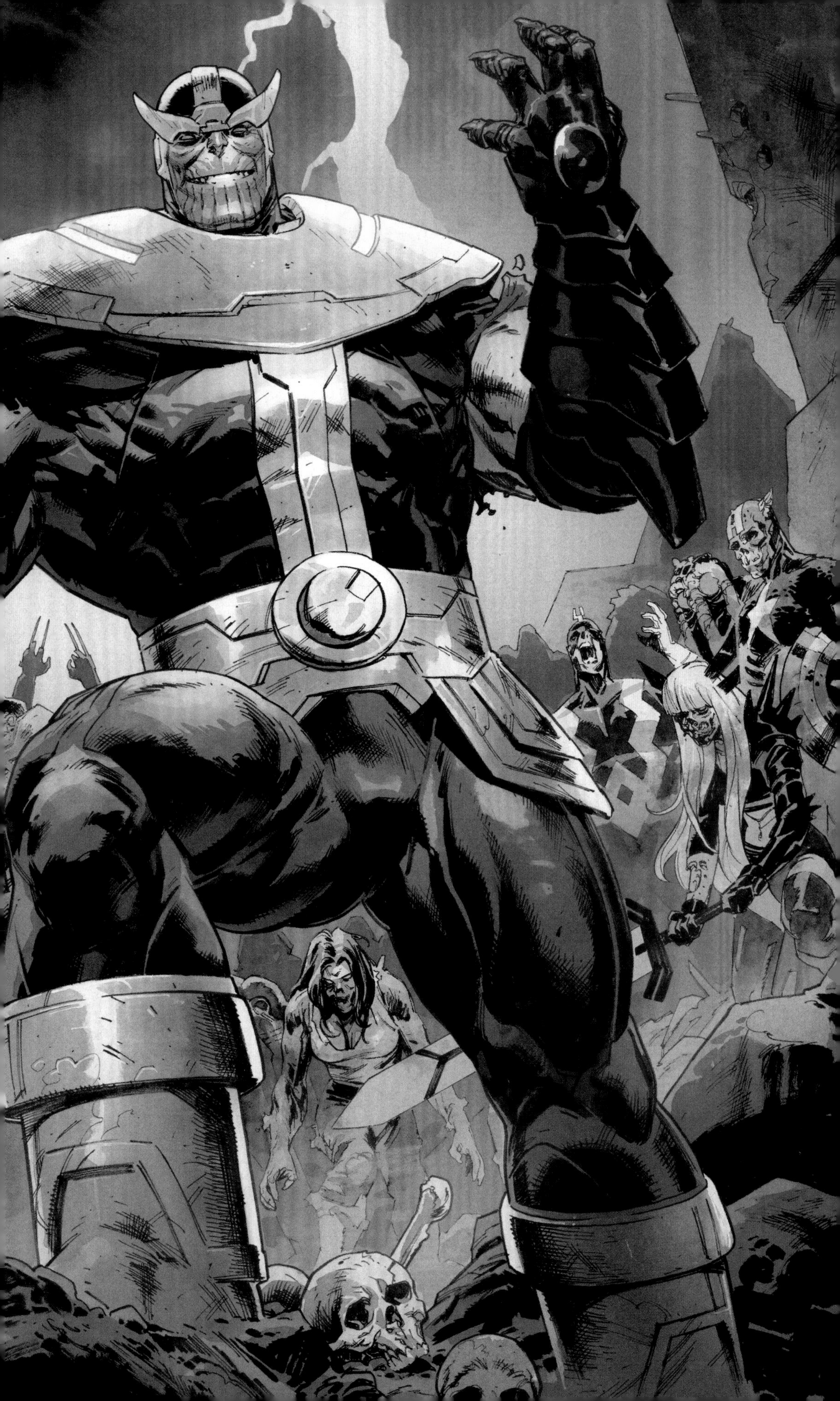

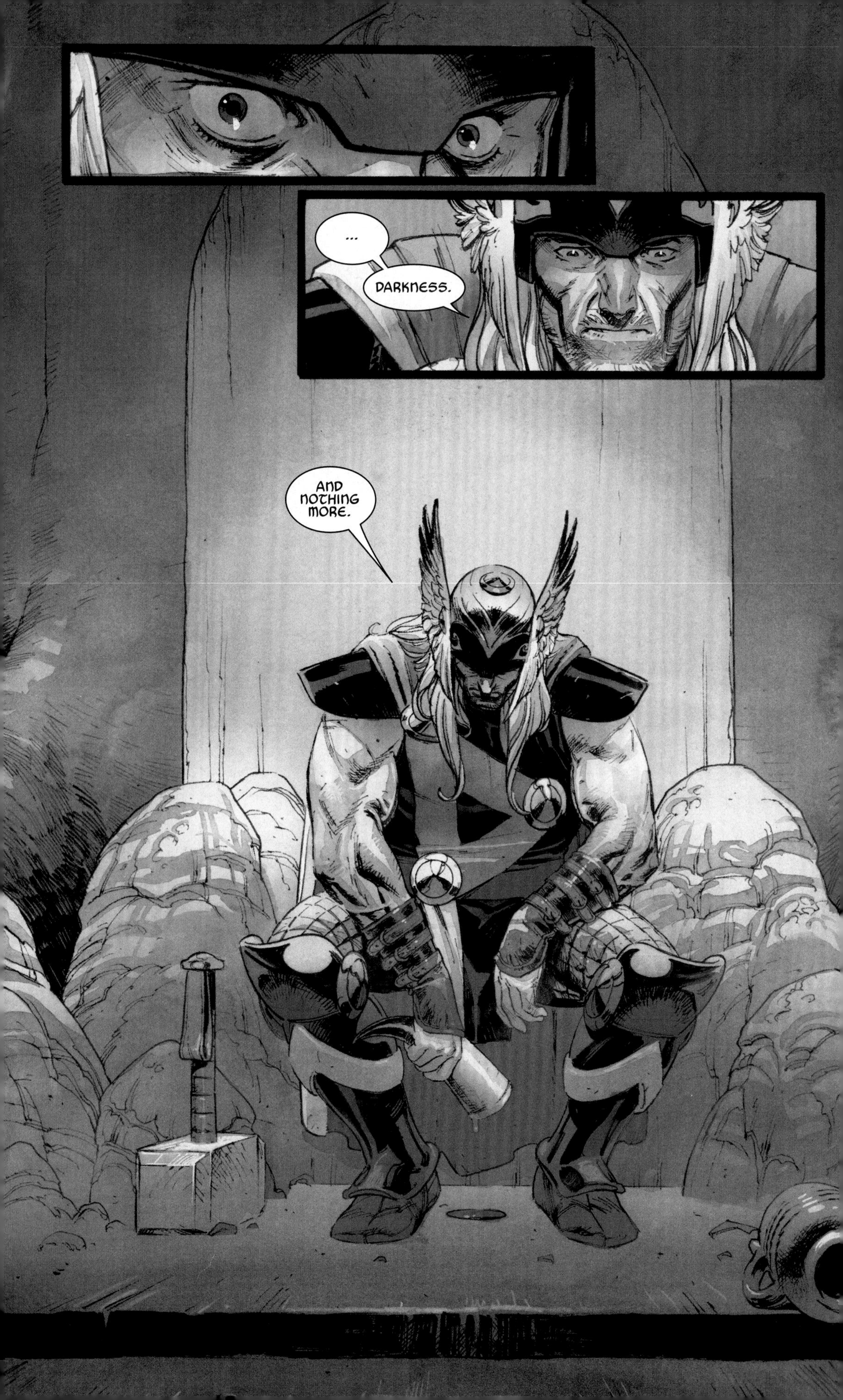
...
DARKNESS.
AND NOTHING MORE.